T0151263

THE GREATEST PRETENDER

"It is a story of redemption and repurpose—and I congratulate you for that."

—**Pat Boone,** Singer, composer, actor, writer, television
personality,motivational speaker, and spokesman

"Mark, I'm very happy to share the Pro Life stage with you. Your personal story of how abortion hurts men is hardly ever told but needs to be. A lot of people are going to be encouraged and healed by hearing your message."

—**The Late Norma McCorvey of Roe v. Wade,** Better known by
the legal pseudonym "Jane Roe," Norma was the plaintiff
in the landmark American lawsuit Roe v. Wade in 1973.

"Mark's journey is all too familiar, but rarely told. He courageously opens up his own life, filled with deep valleys as well as high mountain-top experiences. Mark bravely faces scrutiny and criticism, with the clear-eyed hope that more men (and women) will understand the power of redemption. Every man who reads this book will find themselves within its pages."

—**Jor-El Godsey,** President, Heartbeat International

"Mark Morrow's story is a picture of God's gift of grace and redemption played out in our world. Mark is funny and light-hearted while being transparent about the hurt that comes with abortion. His story is inspiring and uplifting and will leave you with a special reminder of God's grace and mercy in your life."

—**Lauren Nelson,** Miss America 2007

"Mark Morrow's book, The Greatest Pretender, is sadly all too familiar with many people who have fallen victim to abortion. Mark really laid himself out there for all to see, and just when the reader begins to consider him "a waste of skin," Jesus swoops in and does the unexpected. Coincidentally, that's about the same time we're reminded that we too have sinned and fallen short of the glory of God.

Many of us have struggled with similar demons, faced by Mark. If you or someone you know fits this description, read this book! Mark's unmistakable message is that God's full pardon and deliverance is available to all of us—regardless of our sins."

—**Bradley Mattes,** President, Life Issues Institute

THE GREATEST PRETENDER

1 Youth Leader, 4 Abortions, 18 Years of Secrecy

*One Man's Triumph
Over Hidden Shame*

MARK BRADLEY MORROW
with
BRAD RAHME

NASHVILLE

NEW YORK • LONDON • MELBOURNE • VANCOUVER

THE GREATEST PRETENDER

1 Youth Leader, 4 Abortions, 18 Years of Secrecy
One Man's Triumph Over Hidden Shame

© 2019 **MARK BRADLEY MORROW** with **BRAD RAHME**

Published in New York, New York, by Morgan James Publishing. Morgan James is a trademark of Morgan James, LLC. www.MorganJamesPublishing.com

Scriptures taken from the Holy Bible, New International Version®, NIV®. Copyright © 1973, 1978, 1984, 2011 by Biblica, Inc.™ Used by permission of Zondervan. All rights reserved worldwide. www.zondervan.com The "NIV" and "New International Version" are trademarks registered in the United States Patent and Trademark Office by Biblica, Inc.™

ISBN 978-1-64279-216-4 paperback
ISBN 978-1-64279-217-1 eBook
Library of Congress Control Number: 2018908761

Cover Design by:
Christopher Kirk
GFSstudio.com

Interior Design by:
Bonnie Bushman
The Whole Caboodle Graphic Design

MarkBradley**Morrow**
Author Speaker Counselor Comedian

In an effort to support local communities, raise awareness and funds, Morgan James Publishing donates a percentage of all book sales for the life of each book to Habitat for Humanity Peninsula and Greater Williamsburg.

Get involved today! Visit
www.MorganJamesBuilds.com

Dedication

I'm dedicating *The Greatest Pretender* to God the Father, Son and Holy Spirit. Thank you for turning my black-as-coal sins into radiant diamonds. I pray that You will do immeasurably more with this book then I could ever hope for, or imagine.

"⁷Blessed are they whose transgressions are forgiven, whose sins are covered. ⁸Blessed is the man whose sin the Lord will never count against him." *Romans 4:7-8 (NIV)*

Authors Note: I have tried to recreate events, locales and conversations as best as possible from my memories of them. In order to maintain their anonymity, in some instances I have changed the names of individuals and locations. I may have also changed some identifying characteristics and details such as physical properties, occupations and places of residence.

Table of Contents

Acknowledgements

To my wife Jeannie, this book could not have become a reality without your constant love, support and encouragement these past 25+ years. I'm blessed to have you as my friend, wife, mother of our children, and business partner.

Proverbs 12:4: "A wife of noble character is her husband's crown."

———

To my children Ricque, Faith and Ross: each one of you is a miracle and part of a phenomenal God-story. Throughout your lives, make me proud by making God proud. I love you with all of my heart and am honored to be called your "DAD."

Malachi 4:6: "He will turn the hearts of the fathers to their children,
and the hearts of the children to their fathers."

———

To Ron Raymond: From meeting in 1980 at Edinboro State College on W.F.S.E. 88.9 FM to doing *The Good Guys In The Morning* at W.C.T.L. 106.3 FM, God has blessed us with natural chemistry on and off the radio. Through all the concerts, sporting events, laughs and serious conversations we've shared, you're the brother I never had.

Proverbs 27:17: "As iron sharpens iron, so one man sharpens another."

———

To Brenda Bauer: You were the first person to hear about my story and invite me to speak at your crisis pregnancy center fundraiser and since that time we've become kindred spirits in Christ. I appreciate your friendship and faithfulness in praying for me and this book all these years. Your support and encouragement have meant a lot to me.

1 Thessalonians 5:11: "Therefore encourage one another
and build each other up, just as in fact you are doing."

———

To my unseen children and their mothers: I want the world to know that I take full responsibility for my past sinful behavior and poor choices thirty years ago. To the moms—our abortions are 100% my fault and no one else's. I'm truly sorry for how my words and actions affected you and pray that you will experience the healing and peace that I've found in Jesus.

Romans 8:28: "All things work together for good for those
who love the Lord and are called according to his purpose."

Foreword

I remember receiving a call at my office one afternoon, from a man who sounded emotionally exhausted. He informed me that in his younger years he had taken part in four abortions in a period of less than twenty months. He went on to say he had attempted to work through a couple of different abortion recovery study books and none had seemed to work for him, so he thought he'd give mine a try. His frustrated and pessimistic attitude let me know he wasn't expecting much.

We mailed him our Men's post-abortive Bible study as he had requested, and I assured him we were available to answer questions and help him in any way we could. His response was pretty much, "Well, I hope this helps me, but I kind of doubt it." I assumed I would never hear from him again. I was pleasantly surprised when, about three months later, this man called again, stated he was going to be in Nashville, and asked if he and his nineteen year-old daughter Ricque could treat my husband and me to breakfast. I agreed to meet, unsure of what I was going to hear.

On the day of our meeting I was cautiously intrigued, remembering the hurt and insecure man I had encountered over the phone. We ordered our pancakes and the four of us made small talk. The whole time I was wondering why he had his copy of "SaveOne—The Men's Study" sitting on the table next to his coffee.

Finally, as we waited for our food, he slid the book across the table and said, "I've worked through every page of your book and can honestly say I've finally been set free and healed from my past abortions." Tears filled my eyes and his, as he continued to tell me of his encounter with God. He had spent the last several weeks working through the pain of his past and I saw sitting in front of me, a new person. He was no longer broken, but a man filled with hope for the future.

I was reminded of how great God is, to take one of our worst mistakes and turn it around for good. Only a great Creator can do stuff like that. He told me that I could have his book and gave me permission to share any of his answers and journal entries to help others out. He then stated he felt called by God to take his new-found message of healing and hope to a much wider audience.

This pancake breakfast meeting was the start of my many years of friendship with Mark Bradley Morrow. I have seen him work relentlessly to take this important message of abortion's devastating effects on men to a hurting world. I have watched as he has been attacked needlessly and maliciously, lost friends and has even been greatly discouraged; all because he chose to obey God and travel down this very difficult—and at times—lonely road. The one thing I have always appreciated about Mark is that he has never given up; he has never backed down, knowing he has a story to tell that will help others.

The book that you hold in your hands was placed on Mark's heart around the time I first met him, but it wasn't until years later that he and Brad, his brother in Christ and professional writer actually began working on it. Within these pages is the honest and transparent story of a man who bought the lie society has told us for way too long—that abortion is the easy way out. You will read on the following pages a long--awaited story written from a man's perspective, allowing other post abortive father's to come forward and deal with their own pain.

Mark realizes the aftermath from abortion is not just a woman's issue, but also a man's issue and family and societal crisis. His bravery to come forward, tell his story and share his worst sins is going to blaze a path for other post-abortive fathers to share their stories and find the hope and healing that only Jesus Christ can bring.

My response to this book is BRAVO! It's way past time we recognize the hurt and devastation abortion is doing to our fathers all across America and around the world. My prayer is this book will be the catalyst for a revolution of men to, at long-last, have permission and courage to come forward and tell their stories as well.

It is my honor and privilege to write this foreword and to know that my organization *SaveOne,* played a unique and integral part in Mark's personal healing and this subsequent book. May all the glory and praise go to the Ultimate Healer, Jesus Christ.

ENJOY!

Sheila Harper Founder and President—SAVEONE

Nashville, Tennessee

Chapter 1

A Sunday Storm

S
ummer afternoons in Edinboro, Pennsylvania are often idyllically sunny and warm, without clouds, or rain or storms. On that particular Sunday in 1989, there were, as expected, no clouds nor rain, yet a storm was brewing that would someday tear violently through my soul, instantly thrusting my breaking point upon me.

On any such Sunday, I might have been leading the *Edinboro United Methodist Church's* youth group in a game of flag football, or perhaps chauffeuring a group of gangly tweens to a live Christian concert. Sometimes I would lead by example, gathering the group to help our elderly church members with household chores like raking leaves, and painting fences. On less energetic days, we'd just hang out or watch a movie.

I loved my kids and I truly believed they loved me. Most of them were between the ninth and twelfth grades, while I was twenty nine. I felt it was the perfect age to lead the group; I had enough wisdom to impart what tomorrow's spiritual leaders needed, and enough cultural relevance to relate. I also considered myself the original "cool youth group leader," often donning a black leather jacket and wearing purple-tinted "John Lennon" glasses. I'd cruise around in my shiny black Corvette Stingray, through which I demonstrated the virtue, "Hard work pays off." I taught my kids the virtues of selflessness, responsibility, and even sexual abstinence until marriage. I suppose you could say I was their spiritual *Fonzie*.

Although I was raised in a moral, upright home, I hadn't entirely given my life to God until I was nineteen. Nine years earlier, I'd met the Lord and was one-hundred-percent born again when, after months of loving encouragement from my best friend, I became serious about my eternal future. On February 3, 1980 I completely submitted my life to God, and experienced the unspeakable joy of having my sins forever washed away. From that day forward, I just knew Jesus Christ was my Savior, my Lord and example. And boy did I love Him. This wasn't difficult because I literally felt the change, and I simply knew His Spirit lived within me. God made my days brighter somehow, and by 1989, aside from a couple of nagging issues, I'd say my faith was extremely real to me. I'd often witness to others about Christ when given an opportunity.

In almost all areas, I did my utmost to live His example for the *Edinboro United Methodist* youth, and in some ways I really *had to*. Aside from leading the youth group, I worked full time for *Harborcreek Youth Services* as a Child Care Counselor, in their West 25th Street Intensive Treatment Unit. Although it could be difficult at times, I loved my job working with troubled teenage boys; I felt like I was making a real difference in their lives. I also made pretty good money.

My pastor, Dr. Ron Hollein, also paid me a little for leading the youth group, and in addition, I worked part time for *Hermitage House Youth Services* as their Independent Living counselor. This was such a great situation because *Hermitage House* provided me with a large apartment where I had my own office, bedroom, living room, and bathroom. On the other side of the apartment, the two boys in my immediate care had their bedrooms, bathroom, and living room. In the center we shared a washer and dryer space, and a kitchen-slash-dining room.

Each week I would teach these boys life skills such as managing their money, shopping for groceries, filling out job applications and more. It was quite the turnaround from my previous few years of living. For now we'll just say I learned these things through the school of hard knocks, which I hoped my boys didn't have to repeat. I thought of my situation as rather like having younger brothers stay with me, except we all mutually respected each other's privacy as much as possible, and I was available for them as necessary.

The upside of living and working at *Hermitage House* was it resulted in a truly outstanding financial situation. Since I lived rent-free, my only expenses were food and long distance calling, so not only did I have zero rent or utilities to pay, in addition to my salary I also received a weekly stipend for each boy. I was truly blessed, and I was able to save anywhere from $700 to $1,200 *a month*. That was a small fortune in those years, and to be honest, I was very proud of myself, considering the rocky start I'd had to adulthood. The money I saved at that time was how I paid cash for my 'Vette and student loans, and by the end of that summer I'd saved enough to pay for the Master's degree I was starting in the fall.

I was exceptional at juggling my three jobs and even made time for a pretty healthy social life. My typical start to each day would include getting ready for work and making sure the boys in my program were awake, showered, and had eaten a good breakfast. I'd then put them on the bus and head to my job at *Harborcreek*. I'd usually be home by five, hang out and talk with the boys, run a group counseling session, and then maybe head down to The Hotel Bar to shoot pool with my best friend, Joe Miller. On a good night we'd rule the billiard tables and pick up some cute co-eds. Life was busy but I was a natural at time management, and I strove to impart this to my kids.

One particular Sunday in August, I had arranged for a friend to lead the youth group as I had two personal engagements to attend to. My girlfriend, Amy, and I were driving back from spending the weekend at my sister's house. Much to Amy's annoyance, we were leaving a little earlier because I had agreed to meet with an ex-girlfriend, Lisa, to discuss something she deemed important enough to drive all the way up to Edinboro. I hadn't seen Lisa in about three months, and had started dating Amy in the meantime. The last time I had seen Lisa was quite the special event. She had already moved away to pursue a business degree near her hometown of Slippery Rock, which was about seventy miles away from Edinboro, but that weekend three months ago, she came up specifically to celebrate my grandparents' fiftieth anniversary with me. In a wonderful ceremony, they were renewing their vows and had asked me to officiate as pastor over the proceedings. That was on May 21, 1989.

As Amy and I cruised up highway I-79 North in my clean, black Vette, to my surprise we actually passed Lisa in her bright yellow Volkswagen Beetle I'd helped her purchase only a year earlier. As Lisa looked over in astonishment at me, and then Amy, I experienced a very anxious, uncomfortable feeling. I floored it as Amy whirled around to look back, sensing something strange. I kept on heading to Edinboro but I suddenly had a slight uneasiness about what Lisa wanted to discuss. Initially, I'd kind of looked forward to it. It was always good to see Lisa, even though I was dating someone else.

It was safe to say Lisa had always been pretty crazy about me, and I'd helped her through a lot of personal issues, so it was flattering to hang out with the girl even though we'd broken up. Amy, of course, picked up on this, and despite my protests that Lisa and I were completely done, she was pretty angry by the time I dropped her off. She got out of the car, slammed the door and stalked off without looking back. I just pulled off and grinned to myself, thinking, *Girls! You can't live with 'em and you can't shake 'em.*

I'd arranged with Lisa to meet at a little park in town. It was a stunningly beautiful day, and under any other circumstances I would have swung by the house and packed a picnic lunch. I wondered for the hundredth time if she wanted to discuss getting back together. Perhaps she'd changed her mind about business school and wanted to move back to Edinboro? Lisa always had a little flair for the dramatic, so it could just be she wanted to hang out again, and didn't like me dating anyone else. She was already sitting elegantly on the grass when I rolled up, and waved me over to the shady spot. She wore the prettiest floral sun-dress, and cutely sipped on a bottle of Coke. I had to admit, she looked absolutely gorgeous. I waved back and smiled as I strutted over.

"Hey pretty girl!"

"Hi Mark." Her tone was flat.

Uh-oh, I thought.

"Was that you driving up I-79?"

"Yeah, it sure was. I was coming back from my sister's. Thought I saw your little Bug."

"Was that your new girl with you in the car?"

Oh, that's why she's mad, I figured. "Uh, yeah, that's Amy," I replied awkwardly. "She's pretty cool." Lisa rolled her eyes, telling me she didn't need to hear that, and I changed the subject rapidly. "So how have you been? How's business school?"

"Fine, Mark. Listen I have something very important to tell you, but you probably need to sit down."

Whoa. Why do I need to sit down? I wondered. "Oookay... what's up?" I asked, plonking down on the grass next to her while managing to grin and frown at the same time.

"Mark, I'm pregnant again."

Time ground to a halt. At first all I could do was blink stupidly as I stared at Lisa. Her eyes locked onto mine, and I could tell she was absolutely serious.

"Whaaat?" She looked into my soul and sighed, "You heard me, Mark."

An invisible giant swung a sledgehammer square into my gut, and my head spun crazily. *Oh God, not again!*

"How... are you sure? How long?"

"I just found out this week. Yes, I'm sure Mark. Three pregnancy tests. Just like the last time... And no, unlike you, I haven't been seeing anyone else."

I swallowed violently, as my stomach threatened to expel my lunch. "Ooh God..." I dropped my head into my hands.

"Yes, I'm fine, thanks Mark... don't worry about me."

"Lisa—I'm sorry. It's just... you sprung this on me, you know?" *Why was this happening to me again?* my mind screamed. *Why me?*

I looked up "Are you okay? Do your folks know?" I asked, seeing her scowl for the first time.

"No, I haven't told them yet. I wanted to talk to you first."

"So when... so you have to be like..." I counted back to my grandparents' anniversary. "...what, three months along?"

"Yes. We knew the condom broke."

"Oh my g..." I trailed off, remembering. A giant, unseen anvil crushed down on my chest. I wanted to jump up and run but I knew I could not escape.

I sighed heavily and stared at the grass for a long time. Suddenly the happy, airy Sunday afternoon became a desperate nightmare filled with despair. I found myself envying the carefree laughter of the kids playing nearby.

I'm lonely but no one can tell...

"What are you going to do?" I asked bluntly. She knew what I meant.

"I don't know yet, Mark," Lisa murmured, looking up at me with forlorn eyes. Those eyes that said *We have so much history together, why can't we just make it work?* "We're not even together, Mark."

"Lisa… I'm really sorry…" I interjected abruptly, "…but you know where I stand on this."

"Oh, you'll marry me but you don't want kids, right? Where have I heard this before?" she said bitterly, anger flashing like lightning in her eyes.

"No Lisa. I can't marry you now," I corrected. "I'm seeing someone else. *But if you want to have this baby, I'll provide for it financially. Or you can give it up for adoption, and I'll help you pay for the costs of the pregnancy; doctor visits and all that. I just cannot be a father to this child. You know my past. I just can't do it."

Lisa's mouth tightened and a lone tear formed in the corner of her left eye. My heart suddenly sank. Lisa put her head down and sniffed loudly, then started to quietly weep. In a moment, the lowest scumbag on the planet felt like a Mother Teresa compared to me.

"Aw Lisa… honey… c'mon, please don't cry. I'm sorry. I didn't mean to be… rough with you." I moved closer, put my arm around her and looked up to the sky. She tucked her head into my shoulder, and sobbed harder.

"Hey… hey listen, we'll be ok. We'll figure it out. We always do." She continued to weep, and I wished I could die.

I let Lisa cry for a few minutes, until she finally ran out of tears and sat up, wiping her eyes.

"It's a boy," she said, staring at the grass.

"Huh?" I asked in surprise. "You've been to the doctor?"

"No, but I just know. It's a little boy. I've named him…" I sat there silently. This was textbook Lisa. As if it wasn't stressful enough without getting overly attached by naming the baby before we'd even made a decision? I didn't say a word. She looked at me, and her finger traced the circles of my glasses. "Lennon James," she whispered.

"Huh?"

"Lennon—because you love *The Beatles* so much. And James—after your grandfather. That's his name. Lennon James."

Holy Lord in Heaven! I sighed as I looked away. It was my turn to wipe away a tear. And I resented shedding it.

We sat in silence for several minutes, neither of us knowing what else to say. I hoped no one I knew would come to the park, as I sat there comforting my ex-girlfriend. Finally I had to do something.

"Say, do you want to get up and walk around a bit? Maybe stretching our legs will do us some good?" I had a desperate need to escape, or at the very least, provide myself with a distraction. Lisa nodded and I took my arm from her shoulders, then helped her up. She gave me a look that melted my heart again. A single glance that encapsulated the volumes of what we'd been through together. How I'd never let go of her hand as she walked through some truly dark valleys, and how she'd lifted my head, helping me believe I was worth something as a human being. It all connected us in a supremely powerful way, yet it somehow still wasn't enough for me to face raising a child with her. So I looked away. I could feel her heart breaking all over again, but I took a step toward the street. She straightened up, took a deep breath and wiped her eyes again, then followed me.

My body was entirely numb, but as we walked around the 'Boro, looking at closed stores, pretending to window shop, anxiety began to churn in my stomach. I also worried about Amy; if Lisa decided to have the baby, it would definitely wreck us. I dreaded that conversation with Amy. I knew Amy wouldn't want to deal with it, but *That really wouldn't be the end of the world*, I told myself. I was approaching the three month mark with her, anyway… right around the time I would start losing interest in a girl; so I figured, *Whatever.*

We absently window shopped a little longer, trying to talk about options, and what the various scenarios looked like. Eventually we made our way over to the *Village Cinema*, Edinboro's little two-screen movie theater. I looked up at the sign and saw one of the movies playing was called, *Parenthood.*

What are the odds? I thought to myself. I looked over at Lisa, who read my mind and shrugged, *Why not?* I suppose somewhere deep down within both of us, we were searching for a reason not to abort. I bought two tickets, and we found our seats. It struck me that I knew nothing about this movie. I also realized that sitting down again might not have been the best idea. My head started spinning and I began to feel claustrophobic. As it turned out, *Parenthood* was undoubtedly the worst possible choice of movies to see on that given day. Lisa and I watched in uncomfortable silence as Steve Martin led the Buckman family on, what would normally be hilarious escapades, all revolving around pregnancies, babies, and untimely marriage. I felt Lisa flinch when one of the characters brought up the "A-word" as a solution to the protagonist's problems. I wanted to melt into my chair.

After an excruciating hour and a half, we left the cinema, and I found myself desperate for any distraction from reality.

"I have to get back to Slippery Rock, Mark."

"Yeah… I guess I should be going too."

"So…what now?"

"I don't know, Lisa. Well… maybe—you know my aunt, Toni? It occurred to me during the movie, she was never able to have any kids of her own. If you want to think about it, she may want to adopt the baby if you want to go through with it."

Lisa bit her lip, and stared at the sidewalk absently. Then she looked up and said, "I'll think about it. I have to get going. Will you walk me back to my car?"

"Of course…"

We walked back to the park, Lisa got into her little yellow Volkswagen, and gave me one last, forlorn gaze. I looked away again. She started the engine, and pulled away. I drove home and walked into my apartment in a total daze, and ignored the three messages I knew Amy had left on my machine. I flopped onto my bed, and stared at the ceiling. I just hated moments like this. I knew what I was doing was wrong, and every situation like this was a reckoning. I just couldn't stop. I loved being the great guy at church, the successful dude with the Corvette, making money but still doing good by helping kids out. *Except, this was a lie, wasn't it? How badly would it shatter these kids' ideals if they knew about your sexual habits.* The still, small voice in my heart stung my conscience. *It's getting worse, Mark. These are young souls you're influencing. You have to turn from your sin, and stop. Stop now Mark, and come clean before it ruins you.*

I began to hyperventilate, the claustrophobia smothering me again. I jumped up, ran outside, plunged into my car and peeled out. Then I just drove. I turned the stereo up until the speakers distorted, and I drove and drove and drove.

———

It had been almost a week since my meeting with Lisa, and one evening, as I lay on my bed deep in thought, the phone rang, making me jump.

"Hello?"

"Mark?"

"Hey, Lisa… how's it going?"

"Fine… well, not really but I'm ok." That didn't sound good. I prayed she hadn't told her parents yet.

"What's going on?"

"I took care of the pregnancy, Mark."

"What?"

"I went to a clinic in Pittsburgh, and had the pregnancy terminated."

"What? Lisa! When? Why didn't you say anything?" I felt a sickening conflict of anguish and relief, and hated myself for it. The spinning suddenly returned, so I pulled out a chair and sat down.

"What was there to say, Mark? You don't want any part of me or the pregnancy you were a part of…" Her voice cracked. "So I took care of it. No problem, right?" Her words faltered into a whimper, and the crying began softly. A hot rush of moisture filled my eyes too, and suddenly a horrifying, familiar darkness crept through the air, wrapping its long, wispy tentacles around me.

"Aw Lisa. I wish you'd have spoken to me first. Look I'll help you with whatever it cost. Are you ok?" I wasn't sure if I was trying to be strong for her, or because I was terrified of facing my own feelings.

"I don't need your money, Mark. I just called to tell you it's taken care of. Okay?"

"Listen… Lisa, are you sure you're ok? I mean physically… the last time—"

"I have to go Mark," Lisa said, her voice faltering again. "I'll be fine. Bye."

She hung up.

My heart pounded. I furiously wiped away the burning tears and tried to gauge how close I was to puking.

Why does this keep happening to me?

After a minute of mentally stepping through the situation, I calmed myself a little.

What's done is done. It's for the best. You couldn't have stopped her. You didn't know. Besides, it's her choice.

I nodded, but I knew I was lying to myself. Again, I felt that schizophrenic surge of relief and simultaneous self-loathing.

Mark, you have to stop living in sin. It is destroying you. You're a spiritual leader, Mark. You're called to greater things. The quiet, gentle voice chastised me, which strangely produced a flicker of hope.

Dude, you know you cannot just marry every girl you meet, and you also know very well you can't escape these masculine desires. You've tried! It's impossible and seriously man, it's not that bad. Heck, remember some of these girls threw themselves at you. You're only human, so don't sweat it. Just be more careful from now on. This sounded like my voice, but a sinister edge lay beneath.

Mark, this is your fourth child that has been killed. What are you doing? I love you son, but you have to take responsibility...

I jumped up and ran out to my Vette. I cranked the engine, slammed it into gear and floored it, roaring out into the night. I desperately wished the two hundred-forty horses under the hood could outrun my conscience.

Chapter 2

When the Status Quo Just Doesn't Cut It

Despite only living the first eight years of my life in Mogadore, Ohio, the place still holds some of my most vivid and fond memories. It was a time of pure, uncontaminated happiness, a time I was proud of my family, when we were together, as a unit. It was a blissful ignorance really, having not one, but two parents as high school English teachers. My dad and mom had all the family's foundational bases covered, and I had no idea what life was like for those kids who only had one parent. I knew friends who were without their dad, or mom, but I had never really stepped into their shoes, thinking about what that might mean for them. How it impacted their life forever. Instead, I happily rolled along with my prim and proper mom, and my dad... well I was a lot like my dad. In fact, I couldn't have idolized him more..

One of dad's fortes was also coaching the high school's golf team, and I'll never forget the year they went 25-0, making it to the state championships. I'd never been so proud to be the son of the man leading the team the town had nicknamed

"Morrow's Marauders." After their final match, most of the town was waiting to welcome them home and celebrate, as Ross Lee Morrow was handed nothing less than a key to the city. I couldn't have been prouder.

Dad was truly loved by everyone. He was always the life of the party and was a fixture at the local *Lions Club* (of which he even served as president in 1978.) Dad was a man's man, drinking either Rolling Rocks or whiskey sours, and smoking two packs of Pall Mall a day. He always drove either an old Rambler or an old station wagon, and didn't really care what either looked like, inside or out. This was surprising because dad was a stickler for excellence. He always wore a collared shirt and suit jacket to work, despite not being required to. He hated seeing other teachers dressing "casually." Dad expected excellence from his students and his children as well, but maybe he just followed through with his students. Dad was tough and demanded a lot, but it was always in a caring, respectful way. His students feared him, but also idolized and loved him.

I don't remember having any meaningful conversations with my dad. It was more like a life of sound bites between us:

"Pass the pepper."

"Mow the lawn tomorrow."

"Let's get you a new winter coat on Saturday."

"I need your help splitting firewood on Friday."

But I know my dad loved me. I just don't remember him telling me. He was my hero though, and I knew I had big shoes to fill.

If dad was the carefree life of the party, mom was the model citizen. Judith Carol Armstrong was voted the Titusville Rockets' Class President for three years in a row. She was also the homecoming queen, prom queen, dated the star football player, and to boot, was the valedictorian. And it didn't end in high school. Mom did just as well in college, earning her bachelor's and master's degrees while being a full time mom and housewife. My mother is honestly one of the hardest workers you'll ever meet. Although she taught English earlier in life, she later entered the corporate arena, and became an influential member of the *American Women's Business Association* for many years. My mom believed it was extremely important for women to be represented equally in the corporate world. She, like my dad, always dressed professionally, and always carried herself with an air of neatness and refinement.

Mom is a perfectionist, and expected the same of me. I am my dad's son, however, and depending on how important the achievement is to me, I can often settle for a lot less than gold. In fact, I can become rather stubborn in the face of pressure, and I may have even gone out of my way at times, to upset the proverbial apple cart. On occasion I'd bring home some Ds and occasionally an F, simply because I didn't care that I was an underachiever. Of course, bad grades would upset my school-teacher parents terribly. Ironically, however, it was in those times I caught a glimpse of my mom's underlying motivations. Her dad was an alcoholic, as was his dad and his three brothers. I'm sure his alcoholism, and my mom carrying the responsibility of being the eldest of three children, played a huge part in her determinations. But we were just so different, my understanding of her drives and ambitions only went so far. After all, I was just a kid.

If I am my dad's son, my sister, Beth, is my mom's daughter. Born in 1964, Beth is four years younger than me, and is a model student, citizen, and daughter. Beth always achieved straight As, won the Louis Armstrong music award in her senior year (saxophone and piano,) and was even the Faculty Choice to speak at graduation. I think it's safe to say Beth and I love each other, but we've never been close. In fact, to this day, we barely even talk.

Our home life was the picture of a very typical middle class, hard-working family where everyone knew what they had to do, and just did it. We never overtly fought much. I'd hear my dad yell at my mom here and there, but who doesn't experience that? I'm grateful there was never any type of abuse in our house, and never any outbursts. But I never really saw my parents being affectionate to one another either. They never held hands, had no hugs around the waist, no random kisses, or walking and laughing through the park. My dad's parents were also not affectionate, so I guess that model started with him, and just continued. To be honest, there was very little real communication in our house. It seemed we were four individuals, sharing DNA, and living under the same roof but all with our own personal agendas and schedules.

That's my family. As awesome and dysfunctional as any in our fine nation. I can't really complain though; I had a happy, if somewhat emotionally empty childhood, but that didn't stop me from having fun. My best friend in Mogadore was a skinny but hilarious kid named Ted Evans, and back in those days, we could ride our bikes a couple of miles away from home and our parents wouldn't worry in the least. My memories in Mogadore are mostly of playing wiffle ball in my back yard, games of tag, football (of course) and just generally being rough-and-tumble young boys. It was awesome! If you've ever seen the television show, *The Wonder Years*, that was kind of my life.

Then in the fourth grade my dad was transferred into a new teaching position at General McLane High School in Edinboro for one year, while the brand new middle school was being built. So we moved, and my life in Edinboro began.

Spiritually, our family was again, pretty typically mid-western for the time. My parents considered themselves good people, who work hard, and know the difference between right and wrong. Our family believed we knew what morals were, and we went to church with my mom on Sundays because that was the right thing to do. But I would never say I was raised in a Christian family, or even a religious family. We never read a family Bible, and rarely talked about God.

Dad went to church on major holidays and sporadically in between. Sometimes he would attend adult Sunday school, where instead of really studying the Bible, the group would talk more about the latest news and high school sports scores in Edinboro. Sure we were raised with Christian beliefs as our foundation, but I can't say we were ever serious about our faith. It was more of a set of guidelines for us to live by, with the social aspect of church to maintain.

My mom grew up Baptist, and I think she had a genuine encounter with God as a little girl. I think she "got it." You know, the whole born again thing? My dad was born in Erie though, was raised a Methodist, and I think his religion was more social than heartfelt. Ironically, my mom took us to the *Edinboro United Methodist* Church, which was directly behind our house.

My foundation was solid enough though, and our family had a sound, moral core. That was enough to get me achieving when I wanted to. At least for things I was interested in. In sixth grade I played trombone in the school band, and sang in the choir. I've always loved music, and our school was planning a talent show for St. Patrick's Day, so I decided to start a band and work on a couple of songs for the show. I rounded up my four best friends for the lineup: Scott Nanns on drums, Dave Rocca on guitar, Dave Panhorst and Mark Farabaugh on backup vocals and tambourine, and of course, yours truly on lead vocals. I dubbed us *The Shamrock 5* (kind of like the Jackson 5.)

We rocked that talent show, not winning but doing well enough to keep us playing through the seventh and eighth grades. Later I let my best friend, Mark Terwilliger, and my girlfriend at the time, Melody Groves, join the band too. Mark was a great guitar player, and while the name didn't make sense any longer, I figured, *Whatever! We're just having fun.* We covered songs played by a range of artists: The Osmonds; The Archies; Peter, Paul and Mary; The Cowsills; The Monkees; and more. It was pure seventies awesomeness! We rocked school assemblies, church events, and one time, even a mother and son banquet. When the *Edinboro Independent* wrote an article on us, and featured our band picture, we thought we were the next *Beatles*. Well, I had the haircut for it anyways.

The band exemplified my attraction to the spotlight. Not only that, it demonstrated my drive toward leadership—if in my own, somewhat anarchic way. I craved fame and limelight more than I craved wealth, or any stereotypical success.

Chapter 3

A Calculated Path
to Salvation

After high school, not having a clue what I wanted to do with my life, I joined the Air Force very briefly. True to my nature, if I didn't like something, nothing could keep me doing it. As it turned out, I just wasn't cut out to be an Air Force Dental Lab Technician, learning to craft dentures. I was released early with an honorable discharge, and returned home late in 1978. I found a job working at a local machine shop called Ogden Tubular Manufacturing, or OTM, where I ran a drill press and did some stock supply stuff and any other odd jobs they asked of me. It wasn't exactly a highway to the top, but for an eighteen year old kid, it was, at least, a stable job. For the next year, I just worked, hung out with friends and tried to figure out what I wanted out of life.

During this time, my long time buddy, Mark Terwilliger, began drawing me into deeper conversations about God. Being the son of two teachers, and coming from a home that considered ourselves Christian, I thought I was doing pretty well spiritually. I figured I was a regular, decent, all-American kid. To me what that meant was, I didn't smoke, never touched drugs, and was even still a virgin. Heck, I'd never even touched a drink. I'd always been involved in sports and music, and was the kind of guy who had always been able to get along with everyone. Jocks, potheads, brainiacs… I didn't judge anyone. In fact, I possessed a pretty rare trait, which was the ability to easily navigate the boundaries these various cliques defined for themselves. I thought I was okay, but Mark's words about a real, personal relationship with Jesus resonated within a void deep in my heart.

Mark was very compassionate, yet also very frank with me. He began talking to me about the deeper aspects of "living" my claimed Christianity. When he explained the concept of being born again, I was intrigued. He told me that my spirit had died because of sin, even seemingly harmless ones, and without making Christ my Lord and accepting His Father's adoption, I would be eternally lost. Only God could revive my spirit, resurrecting it by His own Holy Spirit, thereby washing away my life's sins. I was intrigued, and listened intently, but I had many questions; I knew this was serious stuff and I wasn't the type of person to jump into anything.

I remember protesting, "Hey now, I'm a good person. I try to do right by people, and I've never done anything crazy like murder or even fight anyone!" But Mark answered my questions patiently, and was never too pushy. Instead he remained persistent, claiming we are all sinners, no matter how small our infraction. "The point is…" he explained, "all sin separates us from God, and that is deadly." What touched me most of all, however, was Mark lived his faith to the point I had to admit, he had something I didn't.

Mark had also always been an incredible musician. He could play a long list of different instruments, but he was most phenomenal at guitar, and classical guitar to be specific. In 1979, Mark was earning his bachelor's degree in music at Edinboro State, and knowing I was also an enthusiast, that fall he asked me to pledge to the College's chapter of Phi Mu Alpha Sinfonia—the national men's music fraternity. Figuring it was a great way to get back into music, I agreed. So there I was, not a college student, working in a machine shop, but pledging to a college fraternity. Yet I wore the pledge pin, collected the brothers' signatures in a notebook, and went through the process of "rushing." Rushing is a fraternity or sorority ritual in which American college kids get to know each other. This is through a series of specific social events. Well, I ended up getting voted in, and that was the start of my college journey. To be honest, if it wasn't for Mark, I doubt I would ever have attended college.

As Mark and I got closer, he introduced me to a new church called the Federated Church of East Springfield. The pastor, a man named Wayne Augustine, was characterized by his seventies leisure suits, Elvis-style sideburns, and a deep desire to serve God and preach the gospel *hard*. Pastor Wayne was all about Jesus and what He'd done for us, which I hadn't really heard in my Methodist church. I began attending that church every Sunday morning and evening, and sometimes on Wednesday night too. The message was just so… alive. Like God really was involved in our lives.

Many nights, I'd ride in the back of Mark's girlfriend's dad's whale of a Mercury. I'd hear Mark and his girlfriend's family singing all of those great, old-school church songs, and in that car, for the first time I experienced a very deep and genuine love. I continued to experience it at The Fed (as we called the church,) and slowly it began to dawn on me that there was something more to this life than just going through the motions, or seeking one's own happiness and fulfillment. I began to deeply desire what these people had, I just hadn't fully realized it was the personal relationship with Jesus Christ Mark had spoken so often about. But I had a hunch.

I began to ponder all of the "born again stuff," and wonder where I would end up if I were to fatally crash my hotrod Cougar. After experiencing that "something more" at The Fed, I slowly began to realize I hadn't been truly "saved." As always, however, I was stubborn and would never do something purely in response to outside pressure. As it turned out, this was the best attitude in the world for me, because I knew in my heart if I were to ever make a decision to live for Jesus Christ, it would be forever.

On the morning of Sunday, February 3, 1980 *EUMC* held what we called a "Youth Service." This was a special, once-a-year service where all the high school and college students performed a specific role, carrying out various duties. My job, predictably, was to lead the hymns while my sister, Beth, played the piano accompanying the young choir. None other than my best friend, Mark, preached the sermon. At first, although it was exciting, it felt like nothing more than any other Sunday. I didn't feel anything particularly special was about to happen, so I just sat there, enjoying the novel aspect of all us young people leading the service.

I sat right up front, next to the pulpit, and at the close of his message, Mark gave an altar call; something Pastor Ron *never* did. Suddenly, the weirdest thing happened. As I sat there thinking about the message, it was as if someone lifted me right out of that pew and carried me over to the prayer railing. Without realizing it, I found myself in front of the altar. In a moment of epiphany, I fell to my knees, weeping and begging for forgiveness for a lifetime of what I knew were my rebellious sins against God. One might have thought I was Hitler the way I sobbed. A deep yearning within me unleashed a sorrow of repentance, as I knew I needed Jesus Christ to save my life. I knew I was about to dedicate my life to Him, and it would be forever.

Through all eternity, I will never forget the waves of love and joy and hope that crashed over me as I knelt there weeping. I submitted my life entirely to my new, loving Lord, Jesus Christ, and He personally touched me and made my spirit alive again. Suddenly I was electrified; I finally knew what it was to be born again! I felt literally brand new, innocent again like a little child, washed in pure holiness and love while my soul was made clean and white as new-fallen snow. I wept and laughed and rejoiced with every ounce of joy in my heart. I hugged my friends, and looked gratefully into my laughing friend's eyes; he had led me from an unknown eternal death, to glorious eternal life.

Finally, I knew what had been missing all my life. It was my Savior's love; the love that even a parent can't match. It was total and unashamed acceptance and forgiveness for all my mistakes. I knew I was a new creation; this was what Mark had been talking about! My journey with my Lord had just begun, but I knew no one could ever separate me from Him.

In that moment, it felt like I could leap over the tallest mountain with ease, and soar to the heavens. *I wonder if life could be like this forever?* I thought to myself. *You know what? I don't see why it can't.* I determined in my heart to lead my entire family to a real relationship with Jesus, and share with them the joy and hope and love I had just experienced.

I wish I could say it would all be glorious, but my first opportunity to discuss eternity with my family would arise much sooner than I'd expected. Well, all but one of them…. and under circumstances I wouldn't wish on my worst enemy.

Chapter 4

Burst Cloud Nine

O ver the next few months, I felt so light and free, not a thing in this world could bring me down. I loved everyone! My new fraternity brothers, my coworkers, my sister… even my mom's new boss, who was a "suit" through and through; the epitome of oil to my water.

A couple of years before my salvation, my mom had retired from teaching and started working at the downtown office of Marine Bank. Diligence being her forte, she quickly worked her way up the ranks, until she headed up the HR department under the impeccable, if ostentatious, Bob Ross. Bob was the downtown branch's Vice President, characterized by his immaculate suits, shiny shoes, and sparkly new Buick every two years. To say it politely, Bob was a fan of money. Needless to say, when my mom started working at the bank, it was a bit of a change in our house, but I suppose she had always been destined for the corporate sector. It didn't affect me much, except for the extra cash we had on hand and, of course, when I'd go in to visit her at work. When I'd roll in rocking my bib overalls with ripped out knees, a pierced ear, tattoos, and long hair (all pretty wild for 1980,) I could feel Bob's condescension crawling on my skin. He was one of my first encounters with what appeared to be a truly judgmental person—what the kids call a "hater" these days, but once I was saved, I even loved him.

Although I still worked my shop job at OTM, I hung out with Mark and my new fraternity brothers more often. All I wanted to do was learn about Jesus, and I was all questions for the first few weeks. Mark, of course, was overjoyed I had given my life to the Lord, and was thrilled to teach me. I devoured the New Testament, and continued to grow in spiritual leaps and bounds.

While I've never been pushy, I was also eager to share my faith with my family. I figured my mom knew a good deal about the Lord since she was a little more devout than my dad, but because he and I were so similar, I knew if I could get across to him my perspective on this whole born again deal, he would be hooked. I'd never felt such liberation in my life before, and I knew it would appeal to my dad, who was also a free spirit.

Dad still taught at the middle school, and still loved every minute of it. April was the height of volleyball season and dad's current obsession was fearlessly leading the Lady Lancers girls' volleyball team. Dad had coached the Lady Lancers through a tremendous, near-undefeated season, and on Friday, April 18, they were headed to the District Ten Championships.

Dad was known to be passionate about his teams, and as they arrived at the school in the nearby town of Meadville, dad got the team into "game mode" with one of his famous pep talks. Believing they could climb Everest barefoot if they had to, the team then piled off the bus, and got ready to warm up. They practiced a few drills and pretty soon it was time to start the game. Dad gave them a final rallying cry, and it was go-time. The Lady Lancers surged ahead quickly, but within twenty minutes, the opposing team began to creep back up.

Dad knew what was on the line and wasn't about to let the girls slack off. To say he could get intense is an understatement, and he paced furiously back and forth beside the court, yelling instructions and making the referee's life a living hell. By intermission dad was blood-red in the face and hoarse from yelling, but the Lady Lancers had the lead. He gave them another motivating talk, with specific instructions and plays, then he walked off toward the other team's locker room. When someone asked him where he was going, he stopped, looking a little confused, then he just mumbled something about a cigarette and headed toward the exit door.

When the end of intermission was called, the Lady Lancers were ready to rock. They filed out onto the court to the cheers of a gymnasium full of Edinboro fans who'd made the drive to support them. Everyone looked around anxiously for their fearless leader, but my dad was nowhere in sight. The ref asked where their coach was, and confused, they said they didn't know. Someone shouted he was last seen heading outside to have a cigarette, and must have lost track of the time. But that was very unlike Dad. One of the girls on the bench ran out to find him, and the ref started the game.

The young lady ran out the side door toward the home team's locker room, through the corridor, and to the exit. As she stepped outside she screamed. Sprawled on the ground, my dad lay face down with a burned-out cigarette between his fingers. The girl, crying nervously, went up to my dad, crouched down and cautiously shook him, calling his name. He was unresponsive. Panicking, she ran back inside and frantically alerted the first adult she could find.

I'd been hanging out with my friends late into Friday night, as I always did. I came in through the back door, and walked into the family room nonchalantly. I was startled to see my mom sitting on the couch in silence. As I got closer I could see she was visibly shaken.

"Mom, what's up? Why are you awake?"

"Mark, something has happened to your dad and he's at the Meadville Hospital," she said, visibly trying to remain calm.

"What happened?" I exclaimed in fear. "Is he okay?"

"They don't know yet. Apparently he collapsed outside the gymnasium at the volleyball game." My mom was clearly distressed but also, as is her way, remaining calm. I figured it couldn't be too serious.

"Well, should we go to the hospital?" I asked.

"Well, I'm not sure what we can do right now. Apparently they have him sedated, so we can all go tomorrow."

The next morning, I got up and went into OTM for four hours of overtime. I worked from eight until noon, and when I got home one of my dad's closest friends, Walt Stafford, was in the family room, talking to Mom; he had stopped by to see how Dad was doing. When I walked in, Mom told me they had transferred my dad to *St. Vincent Hospital* in Erie during the night. She then told me Dad was not in great shape, and I needed to hurry and get showered so we could go and see him.

Freaking out a little and feeling guilty, I ran down to the basement to shower. Before I could get undressed the phone rang. I ran back upstairs and I could tell by my mom's face it was not good news. It was the hospital telling us to get there immediately. I panicked.

Walt decided to drive us since my mom, sister, and I were all approaching hysteria. Even though I wasn't an experienced Christian at the time, I prayed at the top of my lungs. I began speaking to the situation in Jesus' name and praying that my dad would recover immediately, and that we would take him home that very day. Everyone else in the car remained uncomfortably silent but I didn't care. I kept praying. After an eternity in the car, we finally arrived at the hospital.

We dashed up to the fourth floor, and spoke to the front desk. They paged Dad's doctor and he arrived within a minute.

"Mrs. Morrow, please come and sit down for a moment."

"What?" my mom begged. "Why do I need to sit down? Where is Ross? I want to see him right now!"

"Mrs. Morrow, you can see Ross in a moment, I just want to inform you of his prognosis. Please, can we go to the waiting area, and talk?"

The doctor, wearing a professional poker face, led us over to an adjacent room.

"Please have a seat," the doctor waved toward the chair. My mom started to cry, as he nodded to Beth, Walt, and I. I refused to sit, and stood where I was, staring at the doctor, beginning to get angry because he was making my mom cry.

"Tell us how my dad is doing?" I said firmly.

He inhaled deeply, and looked at my mom, "Mrs. Morrow, your husband has experienced an acute cerebral aneurism. I don't want to candy-coat this for you: it is extremely severe, and major damage has occurred to his brain." He sighed. "I regret to inform you that… we don't expect him to survive the day."

The words hung in the room like a dark mist. The doctor examined the floor with an apologetic expression. Then I reacted. "*What?* How do you know that for sure? Where is he? Where is my dad?"

"He's in an intensive care unit down the hall. I'm so sorry I don't have better news for you," the doctor replied stoically. My mom was sobbing now, as was Beth, while I simply stood there in shock.

"I can take you to see him now, but please be quiet and gentle," the doctor said. "Any noise or stress could ruin any slim chance of recovery. Also… you might want to say anything um… important to him, now." A boiling tear slid down my cheek.

We were escorted into the curtain-lined room, and a shadow of my father lay on a hospital bed. A million tubes snaked out of him, and all around, machines chirped and whirred and blinked little red and green lights. My dad looked serene but was white as lilies on a grave. Beth walked over to the far side of the bed, and I shuffled to the near side. Tears filled my eyes, but I was determined to be strong and not stress my dad out any further. Beth was already whimpering, and I scowled at her. My mom stood at the foot of the bed with her hand over her mouth; tears forming a rivulet down each cheek. It seemed neither my mom nor sister knew what to say to him.

After I was saved, for Valentine's Day my mom had given me a new, cross necklace on a silver chain. I wore the cross every day but as I stood there, I slowly pulled it over my head. I draped the chain into my hand, and then placed the cross over my dad's heart, and prayed loudly. "Dear God… Father in Heaven…." I wiped my eyes with my free hand. "If he hasn't yet, my dad needs to ask You for forgiveness of his sins. He isn't a bad man Lord, in fact he's about the best man I know. But we have all fallen short of Your glory and kingdom…" I took a deep breath, and tried to keep my voice from breaking. "Dad, please…" I continued. "I know you can hear me. Right here, right now… please make Jesus Christ the Lord of your life. I know you went to church every now and then but knowing *of* Jesus and *knowing* Him, are very different experiences. Please make Him the Lord of your life right now."

The room stood silent and the nurse shifted uncomfortably, seemingly unsure of whether I was disturbing my dad or not. I kept praying.

"Dear Father in Heaven, please reveal your love to my dad right now. He needs You more than ever and I just love him with all my heart. In Jesus' name. Amen…"

I looked down at my dad, still unresponsive. I lingered for a second, and then realized my mom and Beth were weeping. I picked up my cross from his chest, put it back around my neck, turned and walked out. I knew I would never see my dad alive again.

Within two hours, he was gone. When the doctor told us the news we all expected, my body went completely numb. My dad was the only one in our family

I was close to. He had modeled the carefree, happy but hard-working spirit for me. Now he simply wasn't there, and suddenly my mom and Beth felt like strangers. I got up and walked over to the payphone, dropped in a quarter.

"Hello? This is Mark."

"Hey man, this is Mark."

"Mark! Where are you? I heard your dad's in the hospital. Is he okay?"

I was silent for a second. "I'm at the hospital. My dad just died."

There was a surprised pause. "Mark! Oh my gosh, I… I'm so sorry man. I don't know what to say… what happened? Are you ok?"

"I guess I'm okay. He had a cerebral aneurism. Please pray for us man."

"Oh my Lord, I'm so sorry. That's terrible! I'll pray, of course brother. Oh man… Is there anything else I can do? Can I come down to the hospital? This is surreal."

"Thanks bro. I'll let you know. I prayed over my dad before he left. I'm sure he heard me. I believe he gave his life to the Lord right there. That's why he could go in peace."

Mark sighed. "Praise God. That's great to hear, Mark. I'm sure he's with the Lord now."

"But you know what's funny… even though my dad is gone, I strangely feel at peace. I know my Heavenly Father will take care of me, and will never leave or forsake me." I was surprised at how powerfully my faith had surged out of me.

"Amen, Mark. That's the absolute truth… You sure you're okay though?"

"Yeah…" There was an awkward silence. I didn't know what else to say, I just wanted to hear a friendly voice.

"Can I come down to the hospital? Are you guys going to be there for a while?"

"Nah… I appreciate it bro, but I think we're headed home in a bit. I'll give you a call when I get home, but I may just want some alone time if you don't care."

"Of course, man. Wow… this is unreal. Again, I'm so sorry, Mark. Whenever you need me brother, I'm here for you."

"Thanks buddy. Okay, I'd better jump off. I'll call you when I get home."

The rest of the afternoon was spent in quiet contemplation. Every now and then a surge of emotion would rush over me, and I'd cry quietly, but as the afternoon turned to dusk, and the dusk turned to night, the house became eerily quiet. I had never realized how lively my dad was, and how I really only interacted with him. Eventually I left my room to make something to eat, and now my mom, sister, and

I didn't really have anything to say to each other. My dad had been the family glue and common denominator. How could we begin talking now? This new awareness disturbed me as much as my dad's death.

To that point, I had never set foot in a funeral home. I had been given a couple of chances but had never taken the opportunity. Once in the eighth grade, during football practice, my friend, Danny Woods, was called away by the coach. Coach spoke to him for a minute and then Danny had walked away. I learned later that Danny's brother had died in a farming accident at their family dairy. My mom asked if I wanted to go to the funeral home to pay my respects but I refused. I had absolutely no desire to see a dead person, be around death, tears or anguish.

Another time, in high school, my friend, Greg Lucas' dad, died of cancer, and again Mom asked if I wanted to go to Glunt's Funeral Home to pay my respects and support Greg. I refused again. I wondered, if I had gone to either of those viewings whether it might have made my dad's funeral a little easier.

The next day, I was led down, with my mom and sister, into the basement of the funeral home to help choose a casket. As we descended, I began to cry. It was awkward, as my mom and sister aren't the nurturing types, so I just cried and cried as they stood with me stoically in a room full of caskets. But I'd always worn my heart on my sleeve, and I wasn't about to stifle the emotions I felt for my dad.

Everyone in Edinboro was shaken up by my dad's death. Pretty much the whole town turned out to the funeral, and the girls on the volleyball team were especially affected. They ended up winning ten games in a row in Meadville. Their former coach, Kay Prichek, who had been watching the games from the stands, stepped in to help after the ambulance took my dad to the hospital. They would go on to the state championships just days later, but sadly, they lost, undoubtedly doing their darnedest to win for Coach Ross. Clearly they were severely emotionally distraught by his passing. It was a dark, sad time for our community, but one that made me realize what a wonderful and loved man my dad was. That didn't help the sense of emptiness and aloneness I felt.

I wore sunglasses to the viewings and the funeral because I'd seen people do it on TV, plus it made sense to hide my tear-stained eyes and cheeks. At the funeral my two favorite uncles and my favorite aunt did their best to console me. Aunt Toni and I had bonded early in my life, and I looked up to her husband, Bill, like a second dad. He was a warm, kind-hearted man with a huge smile and an even bigger sense of humor. I quietly thanked God for Toni and Bill gathering around me, on one of the most bitter days of my life. I truly don't know what I would have done without them.

As we embraced, I felt another warm hand on my shoulder. I turned around to see Mom and Aunt Toni's brother Jim looking down at me with deep compassion. I hugged him tightly. Jim was Burt Reynolds' doppelganger and was about the coolest uncle a kid could have. He was smart as a whip, wore his disdain for authority like a badge of honor, and rode a fast, Triumph motorcycle. Not surprisingly, Jim was also a real lady's man. But as tough and cool as he was, Uncle Jim had deep love in his heart; he stood and cried with me until I couldn't cry any more. This was more of a comfort than a thousand condolences from the rest of the town. There is no doubt I would not have made it through the funeral without the three of them.

After the ceremony, I just went back to work at OTM. I had no idea what to say to anyone, so I said nothing. Once the funeral was over, and the reality of a changed life was upon me, I was surprised to experience a sense of residual shock which resulted in more numbness. Strangely, at the same time, it carried with it pain and bewilderment.

For the next few weeks, life became a sort of surreal blur. The reality of the first death I'd experienced didn't quite sink in for some time. I suppose this was because in the past, I'd experienced short periods of time away from my dad, so the reality that he was gone from this Earth was still only a mental one. The moment it really floored me was a few weeks later, at softball practice. I got out of my car, and grabbed the baseball glove my dad had bought me for my birthday the previous year. As I walked out to the field, I had a startling realization, "Man… I don't have a dad anymore." It hit me like I'd run into a concrete wall. I bit my lip, looked up to the sky and dug my thumb into the webbing of the glove. "I love you dad," I whispered. "I miss you so much." I wiped away a tear and kept walking.

———

I wish I could say my life cataclysms had ended, but they were only beginning. As it turned out, our family wasn't the only one with sorrows. It so happened that Bob Ross, my mom's boss, was a recovering alcoholic. A year or two before my dad died, Bob had admitted he was a functioning alcoholic, and had taken personal responsibility to quit drinking. From what I heard, AA meetings and the Big Book became his best friend, and Bob was able to conquer his addiction to alcohol and cigarettes. Bob's unfortunate wife, however, was soon to discover, in his sense of renewal he had decided to make a fresh start with a much younger, attractive lady whose corporate ambitions were more akin to his own.

Chapter 5

Times, They Are A 'Changin'

A person rarely plans to mature rapidly in a short space of time. Some say God sends suffering to accomplish this crash-course maturing, but I don't believe God killed my dad. When the events that followed my dad's death completely upheaved my life, I never got the sense God was doing so to punish me, or any of my family. I believe it ultimately comes down to decisions we make that affect those around us. But I cannot deny, I matured far more than I would have without these events; I simply had no choice.

I've heard many people get angry at God, and tend to question their faith in the face of tragedy. I'm not exactly sure why, but that has never been me. My dad smoked two packs of Pall Mall a day. A cerebral aneurism wasn't unthinkable in the realm of possibilities. My dad was one of the most genuinely cool people you will ever meet, but he made choices that affected his health, and as brutal and unfair as a father's death may seem to a family, that's life sometimes. Maybe if my dad was a praying man, God would have been able to show him he was in severe danger. Regardless, my faith remained strong; in a way, it had to. I didn't realize it at that time, but God would soon be all I had left.

If anything, my faith was strengthened by my dad's passing. I had such a powerful experience in conversion—probably because I committed entirely to Him when I accepted salvation, I knew my Father in Heaven was never going to let me down. In fact, I would even come to testify that my dad's passing was a powerful demonstration of the reality of God's hand upholding me in my time of mourning.

Don't get me wrong, it was never easy. But after a few months went by, Mark Terwilliger and I decided to, again, start a Christian band to get my mind off things, and more importantly, *to share the gospel.* We called our new band *Now Is the Time,* and we knew it was blessed of the Lord because we quickly gathered a strong following. We began playing in churches located within a two-hour radius, and soon we had gigs booked every weekend through the summer. We had a total blast, and it really helped me escape my emotions, even though one of the ways I shared the Word was using my testimony of God's hand upon me after my dad's passing.

Another silver lining was I began thinking about going to college. I wanted to make my dad proud, even though he was no longer present with me. In hindsight, that may not have been the best plan, and time would reveal that going to college to please someone else is *not* a great idea. It did, however, get me to start the journey. My dad passing also got me thinking about how, at the end of the day, we really are responsible for our own lives, and believing that we can ride, even our parents' coattails, is a delusion. I had no money and had no idea how to get the money for college, so I began researching.

By early fall, I was coping with my dad's passing pretty well, and trying to remain positive about everything. It was still different and awkward being around my mom and sister without my dad. That may sound weird but I truly had no significant connection with them. We managed of course—we weren't aliens to one another—but at the end of the day, we all just went about our own business.

One evening, my mom surprised me by walking out of her bedroom wearing a beautiful cocktail dress. When I asked what the occasion was, she glibly told me she was going out for dinner. I suddenly realized she'd been in her bathroom for over an hour.

"With who?" I inquired, frowning at her dress.

"With a friend," she replied flatly.

"What friend?"

"A friend from work, Mark." She snipped, and turned to give her hair one final inspection, in the hall mirror. She wasn't annoyed but she made it clear she didn't want to elaborate.

I was lost for words as she strolled out of the front door and left. *Surely she wasn't going on a date?*

I didn't see my mom the next night as I was working late, and then I went to band practice with Mark. The next night, when I heard my mom clattering around in her bathroom again, I knew something was up. She came out in one of her business-but-attractive dresses, and I demanded, "Mom, who the heck are you going out with?" I wasn't about to be brushed off this time.

Beth was sitting at the dining room table and made a face at me like I was handicapped, "Bob from work, you dummy. How could you not know that?"

"WHAT?" I blurted. My eyes widened like an astonished owl's.

"Mark, my personal life isn't really your business."

"Are you kidding me? Bob Ross? The freakin' *suit* from work? Your *boss*?"

"Mark, I'm not discussing this with you." This time she was annoyed.

"How long has this been going on?"

"Mark! Chill out!" my sister called loudly. "Mom's allowed to move on if she needs to, okay?"

I was about to protest but again, was lost for words. I just let my mouth hang open and raised my hands as if to say *What the heck?*

"There's roast chicken and potatoes in the oven, and I'll see you two later. Beth, please get that English assignment done tonight, okay?"

Beth nodded and called out a playful "Yes'm," then my mom grabbed her purse and left.

I turned to Beth.

"You knew about this?" I growled.

"Mark, you'd have to be blind not to see it."

"How long has she been seeing him? How can she do that… what about Dad? It's only been six months!"

"Mark, everyone has their own way of grieving, okay? Mom mourned for Dad. This is good for her."

I sat and gazed at my sister as though an alien had just popped out of her head, not believing the words that poured out of her mouth. She pretended not to notice, and carried on with whatever she was doing at the table. I got up, and stormed off to my bedroom before I said something I knew I'd regret.

I lay on my bed, never feeling more alone in my life. I prayed quietly, and after about fifteen minutes, I became so desperate I began to cry out to God in pain. Almost instantly I felt a warm comfort wash over me, but I couldn't stop crying. I kept praying and after thirty minutes, I began to feel a lot better. I had an idea, and decided to call my aunt, Toni. She and her husband, Bill, were some of my favorite people in the world. They'd know what to do.

Bill was a sharp guy. He headed up the Radiology department at a small hospital north of Edinboro called Erie Metro. Uncle Bill had been married before, but sadly, his first wife died before they had any children. After grieving for several years, he met and married my lovely aunt, Toni. She was a lot like my dad—warm, loving, and carefree, and I got along with her as well as I had with my dad. Maybe even better, since I had actual conversations with her. I got up, walked to the kitchen and dialed Aunt Toni. They were just sitting down to dinner, but I explained I was feeling a little bummed out, and she told me come on over right away. I smiled and jumped in my car.

At the time I was driving a sporty brown metal-flake, 1971 Mercury Cougar. It was beautiful, fast, and being my first car, I adored it. As I opened the door to get in, I was ambushed by a memory of my dad that came flooding back. Dad loved my car too, and would sometimes borrow it to go to *Perkins* or *Crossroads Dinor* for breakfast, making the car look infinitely cooler. The Cougar really matched Dad's personality well; fast and powerful, yet understated. My eyes welled up with tears again, but I jumped in and took off to Aunt Toni's house.

"Hey kiddo!" my uncle Bill called out jovially as I walked into the kitchen, through the back door. He was beaming his signature smile that instantly made me feel better.

"Hay is for horses!" I kidded.

"Oh listen to the fancy, educated young man!" he bantered. "I thought I heard a tank rumbling up the driveway!"

"More like a rocket…" I quipped.

"Ah, indeed," he conceded, with his signature smile. "You hungry?"

"Starved." I was joking but the look on his face changed to one of concern.

"Nah, I'm kidding. Well… I am hungry. Mom made roast chicken for dinner, but she went out on a date and I didn't feel like sitting around the house." It didn't take me long to sneak in the tattletale about my mom's date.

"Your mom's on a date?" Uncle Bill raised his eyebrows. I nodded my head.

"Who's on a date?" Aunt Toni poked her head into the kitchen.

"My mom," I looked at her mournfully.

"What? With who?" she demanded.

"Bob Ross!" I squawked. Her expression said everything.

"Isn't he married?" Uncle Bill said.

"Separated I believe," Aunt Toni glanced at my uncle who shook his head slightly as if to say *Let's leave it alone, it's none of our business.*

"Well get yourself some dinner," Aunt Toni sighed, changing the subject, perhaps more for her sake than mine. "I've made honeyed ham, green beans and mashed potatoes." I knew all about Aunt Toni's honeyed ham, so I didn't have to be asked twice.

I dished up huge portions of each for myself and sat down at the kitchen table. I was so happy to relax and be able to be myself. Halfway through dinner, another rumble was heard in the driveway. I grinned excitedly and watched the door in anticipation.

"Oh, the trouble knew where to find you, Mark!" Uncle Bill laughed. The door swung open and my Uncle Jim stood in the doorway as if the party had just arrived. And it really had.

"I thought I saw a slow, old *hoopdy* in the driveway!" he ribbed.

"Haha, Uncle Jim! That hoopdy will smoke that loud Triumph any day of the week."

"Oooh, these whipper snappers today," he shook his head at Uncle Bill and high-fived him as he walked into the room. "No respect for their elders, I tell ya!"

"Old is right" I laughed again, and Uncle Jim broke into a huge smile, bent down and pulled me into him for a hug. I squeezed him back, and my eyes fell on the hippy burlap hat he was wearing. I'd been bugging him for ages to give it to me, but to no avail. He'd bought it from *The Snooty Fox*, a hippy-dippy head shop in downtown Edinboro. It was the coolest article of clothing I'd ever seen.

"Look at this kid, calling me old, then eyeing my vintage stuff," he complained.

"You should just give it to him. At least he doesn't want your Triumph." Uncle Bill replied wisely. Uncle Jim nodded as if in sincere thought.

"Actually, I would *love* his Triumph too, if it's up for grabs," I had to clarify.

"You see? You see what I mean? You give 'em an inch…" Uncle Jim protested, as he grabbed my head and rubbed his knuckles on it. We all laughed as Uncle Jim released me and grabbed a plate out of the cupboard. He dished up for himself knowing he needed no invitation.

Uncle Jim sat down and rolled his eyes in pleasure at a forkful of honeyed ham.

"Seriously though, how's that pretty Cougar running?" he asked with his mouth full.

"It's ok, but actually there's been a weird pinging noise in the engine just this week." It had been concerning me for a while, and I'd been meaning to ask Uncle Jim about it. He was a really sharp guy. Apparently he had an IQ through the roof, but worked as a union welder for GE. Not that a welder isn't a respectable technical trade, he was just a true genius who could have worked anywhere he wanted to. I'd heard he struggled to work under direct supervision, however, or with peer interaction in an office setting, so I concluded he *was* working where he wanted to.

"Well, bring it over and I'll take a look at it. You working tomorrow?"

"In the morning."

"Well, come over in the afternoon. Around three work for you?"

"Yes, that will be perfect! Thanks Uncle Jim!" I smiled happily. He just continued munching on his dinner and winked at me.

After dinner, Aunt Toni suggested we break out a pack of cards, and play a few games of poker. When I was a kid, I'd visit my grandparents over in Corry, Pennsylvania and I'd be eating breakfast when Uncle Jim would come in from working the third shift at G.E. He'd sit down, have a cup of coffee, deal out a deck of cards and teach me how to play. Those were some of my favorite memories as a boy. I thought it was so cool how Uncle Jim had different, catchy names for certain hands, like a "Pair of Ladies" or a "Pair of Cowboys."

We played more hands than I could count, and if I had been betting real money instead of the jar of pennies we divvied up, I would have probably lost my Cougar. It was one of the best times I'd had since my dad died, and every now and then, just for a moment, it was almost as if the sadness about him being gone had passed. Eventually, however, I had to get going, and I hugged each of them goodbye.

"Tomorrow at three? Don't leave me hanging now!" Uncle Jim said pointedly. I assured him I would be there.

"Now if only I could trick you into giving me that hat!" I said as forlornly as possible, as I headed for the door.

Uncle Jim narrowed his eyes at me, and for a moment I thought I'd annoyed him one too many times about the hat. But as I was turning to leave, he took off the cool, burlap hippy hat and tossed it over to me.

"It's yours kid," he smiled compassionately.

My eyes lit up, but I was really surprised. I never thought he'd actually give it to me. Then I felt kind of bad.

"Uncle Jim… I was just messing with you… you don't ha—"

"We both know you know you want the hat buddy. It's a cool hat, and it suits a cool cat like you. It's yours!" His eyes were full of love and Aunt Toni put her arm around Uncle Bill, and put her hand over her mouth. I put the hat on, smiling broadly, and walked over to him and hugged him for fifteen seconds.

"Thanks Uncle Jim. You're so awesome." I looked around at Aunt Toni and Uncle Bill and said "You're all so great. Thank you so much for being there for me."

Aunt Toni grabbed me, and pulled me into her arms, giving me a giant squeeze. Her eyes were glistening as she said, "We love you so much kiddo." Uncle Bill rubbed my shoulder and flashed his warm smile at me. I wiped away the first happy tear I'd had in ages, and left feeling better than I had in a long time.

———

Over the next few months, to my dismay, it became apparent that my mom and Bob Ross' relationship was moving quickly. Before Christmas my mom announced she had invited him over for Christmas dinner. My heart sank; it all felt so terribly wrong. I used to love Christmas, and now I dreaded it.

From the moment Bob arrived, his presence was just so weird and unfitting in our house; uncomfortable was an understatement. Bob had two daughters, Carol and Diane—both a lot older than me—which meant he had no idea how to relate to a young man. I was a twenty-year-old who modeled his carefree dress, attitude and lifestyle after my dad's, while Bob was fifty-seven and my mom was only forty. I guess it would have been okay if he had tried a little more to relate to me but as I said, I guess I was water to his oil. As if that wasn't bad enough, even that very first night at our house, he awkwardly tried to take my dad's place. A few times he inquired as to what I was doing with my life, and was brazen enough to make some suggestions. It's safe to say we began to clash.

I felt bad for my mom, who was obviously in a new predicament, with two kids, a mortgage, and bills to pay on her salary alone. I tried to keep in mind that Mom was a mid-level bank administrator and Dad had never taken out a life insurance policy, and she faced some very real financial problems. Dad had always told her "Hey, I'm not wasting money on a life insurance policy, that's why you got a Master's degree." Mom had almost no money when he died, so here's a guy who's wealthy, is putting the moves on her, and even divorced his wife to marry my mom. Of course, there's a big difference between an excuse and an explanation, but the financial pressure was almost instantly removed. Despite this, I think she rushed into the whole thing. To make it worse, Beth was taking a real shine to Bob. I could see why, in a way; he was ambitious, successful, drove luxury cars and owned a newer home in a wealthy neighborhood. But what about our dad? It had only been about six months, and I still missed him terribly. I began to feel like a stranger in my own home.

I endured, as my mom's relationship with Bob flourished, but I grew more and more distant from the three of them. I hung out with my buddies more, worked more and spent as much time as I could with my uncles and aunt. The times were definitely a'changing, and it wasn't all good. The one thing I clung to was something no one could shake, and that was my deepening relationship with God. I prayed every day, and read His Word studiously. I also fellowshipped with Mark T. and the other young believers at our church, and any Christians I could find, to be honest. I also boldly shared my testimony with non-believers where possible; how my Heavenly Father was carrying me through the difficult time of losing my Earthly dad. Even I was amazed at times how, during the struggle and time of mourning in my changing circumstances, I grew and grew spiritually.

The world kept moving along; sometimes without me it seemed. Spring rolled around, and my mom invited Bob over for dinner one night. They were all dressed up, as usual, and Mom had made three elaborate courses, with a special dessert. The table was even set with our good dinnerware and cutlery. Although it wasn't even Easter yet, Mom really went all out, and I almost felt bad not dressing up. All the formality seemed a little unusual but I didn't think too much of it. I just chalked it up to my mom showing off a little for Bob, in their new ultra-chic lifestyle.

As dinner began I smiled through clenched teeth, while Beth, wearing a lovely spring sun-dress and cardigan, beamed at Bob and chattered away. My mom dished up the starters, then proclaimed she and Bob had an announcement. My stomach flipped.

Mom cleared her throat and held up her glass. "Mark, Beth," she nodded at each of us. "Bob and I have a very special announcement to make." She looked at Bob with a smile, and he nodded his encouragement. Her smile quickly faded when she looked back over to me. Bob caught my reaction too and coughed uncomfortably.

"Bob and I know there is no-one in the world who makes us happier than each other, sooo, as such, we've decided to make our relationship an everlasting one. Bob and I are to be married. Kids, Bob and I are going to sell our homes and buy a new one together!"

The words ripped through me like a hail of fifty-caliber slugs. She said '*we*,' as though Beth and I had any say in it at all. Adrenaline surged through my being as I sat there reeling from the revelation. It hadn't even been a year since my dad died. I must have been glaring, because Beth nudged me as she congratulated them.

"Mark, aren't you going to say anything?" My mom asked.

I looked over at her, and said "Yeah, I was going to ask if I can be excused." I pushed my chair out, maintaining eye contact for as long as possible but as I turned to leave without permission I burst into tears.

I ran out of the front door, jumped into my Cougar and sped over to Mark's girlfriend's apartment, which was only about three hundred yards away. I banged on the door until she opened.

"Morrow, what's up?" she asked, as I hyperventilated.

"My mom's selling my dad's house!" I squawked through a river of tears. "She's marrying Bob and moving in with him. Where am I supposed to go? I can't live with them."

"Oh Mark!" Phyllis sighed, and gave me a huge hug. "I'm so sorry my friend. It'll work out, don't worry. You'll be okay."

I wasn't okay. Nothing about it was okay, and I didn't believe it ever would be.

Chapter 6

The Last Role Models

My mind reeled from the revelation of my mom's whirlwind marriage to her boss, but as I lay on my bed that night, telling myself to "man up" I quieted down and became resolute in what I knew I had to do. It was all suddenly clear as ice: yes, I missed my dad painfully, and I was becoming increasingly estranged from my mom and sister, but I had to live with them. For the moment. My closest friends, whom I now considered my family, were Mark, and my fraternity brothers, so I decided to sign up for the fall semester at *Edinboro State College* that Monday. I had no money and no real source of income but I counted on two things: working and taking enough classes to be away from the house for all but sleep, and getting my degree in record time… for my dad. The incentive burned like a coal in my chest, and it alone was the reason for my calm. I wiped my eyes, smiling to myself. I had a plan and I would make it happen, no matter what the cost. I was done being a victim of circumstance.

That Monday, after work, I drove over to E.S.C in my roaring Cougar, and collected all the necessary information. I submitted financial aid applications right there on the spot, and registered as a potential student. I was fortunate to get a meeting right then with the guidance counselor and we agreed that Speech Communication sounded like the major I was most suited to. Things were just falling into place, and I was starting to get excited by the end of the day. Whenever I thought of my mom marrying Bob the Banker, I became even more determined. Within a week I had signed up for minimal student loans, and had received confirmation of some Social Security benefits from my dad's death. Things were definitely looking up, but I still didn't have enough money to get by each month. My shoulders slumped as I came to terms with the only way I could get some cash to get through the first semester. This would be the first test of my faith and determination.

I called up the local newspaper and placed two ads in the classifieds. One was to sell a lightly used, but quality Peavey PA system I owned from Now Is the Time. The other was an ad for one powerful, gorgeous, V8 big block, 1971 Mercury Cougar. Bitter-sweetly, both sold within a week. The Cougar was purring like a kitten after Uncle Jim tuned her up, and when the new owner quickly gave me the cash, snatched the keys and roared off, I tried to be tough but I couldn't hold back. I burst into tears, staring after one of the remaining connections to my dad, as the Cougar became smaller and smaller until I was alone on the empty road. I tried to tell myself it was a necessary sacrifice to go to college for my dad but I suddenly wondered if I'd make it, with so many physical connections to him slipping away faster and faster.

It was an adjustment walking to work, but I didn't care; I was enrolled in classes for the fall semester, and finally taking control of my life. Besides, we only lived about three hundred yards from the University campus, so the campus commute wasn't exactly tedious either. And if I really needed a ride, I had Mark Terwilliger and a couple of fraternity brothers who could hook me up here and there. Despite all the change, I began to feel a little more secure, if slightly overwhelmed.

That week a crazy storm chewed through the town and a huge branch from our backyard oak tree crashed to the ground, just missing our house. Uncle Jim was summoned (Heaven forbid, Bob work with his hands) and he came growling up on his Triumph. He slid off his bike like something out of a James Dean movie, carrying his chainsaw in a big bag; even doing household chores, Uncle Jim looked cool.

He fist-bumped me. "Hey, buddy! How's life in the fast lane?"

"Oh you know better than me, Uncle Jim!" I laughed. He grinned and nodded, conceding my point.

"Hey, your dad have a gas can?" he asked as though my dad were just at work.

"Umm yeah, there should be one near the lawnmower. Might be a bit dusty back there… you want me to get it?"

"Yeah, if you don't mind," he replied, stiffening, almost imperceptibly.

"Of course!" I ran off to the shed. When I was little my mom told me Uncle Jim had claustrophobia but I had never realized how severe it was until one day when Uncle Jim visited. He went into the bathroom and shut the door, and for some stupid reason the light switch was placed outside the bathroom door, and the door locked from the outside. I thought it would be hilarious to lock the door and switch the light off. Well Uncle Jim went completely berserk. He screamed like he was being murdered and started kicking and pounding on the door. Terrified, I just stood there, frozen in shock. Before any of the adults could get there, Uncle Jim had kicked the door out in splinters, and burst through it, panting and staring at me with huge, bugged-out eyes. I had never been so freaked out in my life. After they'd calmed him down, I was sternly reprimanded, and felt terrible but confused about the incident. When he'd left for the evening, my mom told me when Uncle Jim was a little boy living in Centerville, Grandpa Armstrong would punish him by locking him in the chicken coop, which was pitch-black and filled with cobwebs. I remember being astounded an adult could do that. Knowing all of this, I quickly volunteered to run and get the gas can. It was a curious Achilles' heel to my otherwise, extremely tough uncle.

As always, I enjoyed any bit of hanging out I got to do with Uncle Jim. As we were cutting up the branch, I suggested we go over to Uncle Bill and Aunt Toni's house again, and play cards.

"Yeah, maybe next week would be better, buddy," he replied.

"Why next week? I'm free tonight or tomorrow night?"

"Umm, ol' Bill's not uh… doing too well at the moment."

I frowned. "What do you mean? Is he sick?" That's all I needed; for one of my favorite uncles to be sick as well.

"No… He's just—he's going through a tough time right now."

I was surprised at this, and even more surprised at the cryptic explanation. Uncle Bill was always smiling so I kind of figured he was just—albeit a bit uncharacteristically—dealing with some stress or something. *How bad could it be though?* I thought to myself. *He's so successful in his job at the radiology department.* I wondered if it was some heavy adult stuff that I really didn't want to know about. I was already struggling to keep up with the recent changes in my life, so I figured I'd just visit them after studying on campus one day. I nodded to Uncle Jim, and we carried on cutting up the branch and cleaning up the debris.

Time flew by and before I knew it, I had begun the semester and was cranking through my 101 classes, enjoying every minute of them. I began to suspect I was going to love the college experience; so many people to talk to, so many new friends to make and *so* many pretty girls! *Hopefully at least one of them was a Christian.* I thought. *And hopefully she likes lead vocalists!* As the semester progressed, I tried to minimize time around my mom and Bob. I did about the same with Beth, and life actually started to work out relatively smoothly.

I made it through the first semester pretty well, spent most of a pretty awkward Christmas with Mom and Beth and Bob, then I began the winter semester. Thankfully, time rocketed by again, and after enduring a wedding where everyone else was happy, and I was miserable, I moved to the new house Bob and my mom had purchased.

Neither of them wanted to live in Bob's former marital house and the same went for our family house. So in July of 1981, they started clean and they started *big*. By now, my mom was making good money, and of course, Bob made exceptional money. You might think life would have been at least a little better with more cash flowing around but I realized at that point how little money matters when you're like chalk to your family's cheese.

I started to clash with Bob first; often and with intensity. I just couldn't deal with a stuffy, old guy telling me what to do, even though I was living in his house. It was all just way too much way too soon. That, of course, would set my mom off, and Beth was no haven of comfort, so I lasted two months.

My fraternity brothers helped me find a cheap apartment on Meadville Street, right next door to my childhood best friend, Scott Nanns. I basically grew up in his house so they were an instant surrogate family for me. The apartment was also right across the street from campus, and I shared the upstairs unit with Dick Burchard, a music major and brother in Phi Mu Alpha Sinfonia. I had no idea how I was going to make ends meet, but I honestly didn't care. I knew there was no going back to my mom's house, so I would find a way to make it work.

I absolutely *loved* that apartment. I went from the epitome of a nightmarishly uncomfortable living situation to being surrounded by like-minded friends, with all the freedom I needed. Suddenly the future was filled with all sorts of possibilities. The first order of business was a job. I managed to find a college work-study job paying minimum wage, working twenty hours a week. I worked as a maintenance helper, carrying tool-boxes for older *ESC* carpenters, running a jack hammer, doing some cement work and other basic maintenance around campus. Despite this, I was usually broke, often not having enough to eat.

I did, however, also land a gig deejaying a Christian music show on Sunday mornings for the college radio station, WFSE 88.9 FM. It didn't pay anything, but I did have a plastic milk crate full of my Christian rock albums. I'd walk over to the radio station with my milk crate, play a heck of a set, then walk back to my apartment and hang out with all my friends. The best part was, it was all about us just hanging out and fellowshipping. There were no drugs, no smoking or sex; we were all just into God, music, and growing spiritually. The next two semesters would be some of the best times of my life.

Then came November 4, 1981. It was a Sunday, and I'd finished a set at the radio station, and had come home to relax before taking a look at my homework. I saw the answering machine light flashing its message for me. My mom's voice anxiously told me to call her right away. Something wasn't right.

"Mom?"

"Hi Mark…" She sounded drained.

"Hey, I got your message. What's going on?"

She sighed, and my stomach sank. "Mark… your Uncle Bill has passed away."

What? My mind shouted, but my mouth couldn't say a word. An awkward silence followed, which my mom proceeded to fill.

"Mark… we're not sure why but Uncle Bill took his own life yesterday."

This time my voice worked.

"What?" I cried.

"I'm so sorry, but it's true. I spoke to Aunt Toni myself. She's beside herself."

Everything became surreal around me. I wouldn't believe what I'd just heard. I nearly dropped the phone.

"That can't be right, Mom!"

"I know, it doesn't make sense. Apparently there were some things that we didn't know about."

"What kind of things?" I realized tears were streaming down my face.

"I don't know exactly… your Aunt Toni said something about stress from an investigation at work or something." My mom's voice also betrayed her tears. I didn't know what to say to that. My mind raced. *Why would an investigation cause my uncle to take his own life? And what kind of investigation was it? It didn't make sense!*

"I can't believe this is happening," I whispered hoarsely, succumbing to the dark, heavy cloud. I crumpled on a chair next to the phone. Thankfully, my roommate wasn't home to see me crying. My stomach had that familiar, sick, empty feeling, and the emotional pain began to become unbearable.

It's not fair! First my dad, and now one of my favorite uncles! I began sobbing into the phone.

"It's not fair, Mom… why would he do that?"

It was more than my mom could handle. She was crying openly now too.

My mom eventually regained her composure and said, "Mark, we're going over to Aunt Toni's house at six. I would like you to meet us there, please."

For a second I reeled selfishly at the thought. The last person I wanted to deal with was Bob, but I quickly realized I had to be there for my aunt. I couldn't imagine how she must be feeling.

"I'll be there, Mom, but you know I no longer have a car." I said.

She let out a sigh of exasperation, "Okay Mark, we'll pick you up in a half hour."

I sat on the chair staring into space for about twenty minutes before I went to my bedroom to see if I had anything other than ripped jeans and a U2 t-shirt to wear.

The visitation was heart-rending, but a few days later, as I attended another role model's funeral, my heart was crushed. It had been just eighteen months since my dad had died. This time I didn't wear sunglasses. I wanted everyone to see my pain. The day before, my aunt told us the FBI had been investigating one of my uncle's colleagues in the radiology department on some serious allegations. He'd been accused of interstate trafficking of stolen goods, as well as placing a murder contract on another doctor. My uncle believed the FBI thought he was guilty of collusion with this colleague. Aunt Toni said he felt if the FBI didn't believe him, nobody would. Being the gentle soul he was, the stress and perceived shame was just too much for him. Aunt Toni said she had evidence he was innocent, and was filing a claim against the hospital, but of course, that didn't bring my uncle back. My head contorted and spun with grief and questions. *Why was life getting so crazy?* In less than two years, my entire world had been flipped upside down.

I walked up to Uncle Bill's casket and laid a hand on it. I gazed at his still face, and shook my head. He wasn't smiling. That wasn't my Uncle Bill, it was the body he once lived in. Uncle Bill would be smiling. *Why did this happen? Why did the world always find a way to kill the good things in it?* Tears poured down my face, but my face was deadpan. I felt numb but I was determined not to let life get the better of me. I couldn't help the tears but I could help my expression, and I wouldn't be beaten.

When I got back to my seat, Uncle Jim came over and put his arm around my shoulder. We stood like that for several minutes while everyone paid their respects to my Uncle Bill. We just stood in silence, but I was glad for the comfort. I silently thanked God at least my Uncle Jim was still there for me. He was so much like my dad, and had unwittingly become my last male role model. Uncle Jim wasn't perfect, but he was pretty awesome, and I was sure as heck grateful for him. He knew me well, even if at times it was in the same strong, silent way of my dad. He leaned over and spoke quietly but his voice was surprisingly troubled.

"Say Mark… being a church-going kind of guy… where do you think people go when they commit suicide?"

I was a little taken aback by the question, even though I had been wondering the same thing since I'd heard the news.

"Well… I obviously don't think suicide is right, and I don't think God ever wants us to resort to that, but I honestly don't think it's an unforgivable sin." I looked up at him and he just kept staring ahead but nodded slowly in acknowledgment. I studied his face for a second, then looked away. He was really distressed. After the funeral, Uncle Jim and I stuck to Aunt Toni like Velcro. I knew she appreciated the comfort.

The weirdest thing about a funeral is trying to resume life as normal the next day. At least, you're supposed to. A few people in my Communication classes had heard the news, and expressed their condolences, but everything pretty much just continued. What was even stranger is, I felt like I *was* starting to get used to it.

The days and then weeks passed slowly, and I spent my time trying to focus on school and work. Since I didn't have my own car, I couldn't visit Aunt Toni as much as I wanted, or see if she needed anything. When I could go, the house was eerily quiet without Uncle Bill. At first, family and friends brought more food than an entire village could eat, so I ate well at that time. People offered help, and swung by at random times for the first little while. I could tell she was happy for the company at times, yet sometimes she just wanted time alone. Or at least, she wanted to grieve with those closest to her. I could tell it was exhausting for her, although she would never say so. In time, however, the visiting slowed, the meals became fewer, and the calls dwindled. After a month, Aunt Toni was back to life as normal… except nothing would ever be normal again without my Uncle Bill in the house.

I found that being with my aunt whenever I could, helped me release some of my pain and anguish too. Just sharing the struggle with her helped, and I could tell she appreciated it too. Uncle Jim visited frequently with his new girlfriend. Actually, she wasn't exactly a new girlfriend per se, she was his high school sweetheart that he had recently reunited with. Uncle Jim made himself surprisingly available, considering the fact that he too had just been through some life-changing events. Uncle Jim's wife had left him, taking their daughter and his wife's son, whom he'd raised as his own. And this was the second time a wife had left him. Uncle Jim's first wife, whom he met during an Air Force stationing in England, moved back with him to the States. They had two children, but his wife became terribly homesick, and ultimately, had returned to England with the kids. Uncle Jim didn't betray much emotion, but I could tell he too was struggling with all of the change. And all of this on top of his second wife leaving him. Overall, our extended family had taken some severe hits.

I finished the semester, doing what I knew to do, just hanging out with my Christian friends, playing the Sunday morning show on the radio station, and trying to keep up my grades. Keeping up the grades was becoming increasingly tough, though. I *was* maintaining my GPA enough to remain in college, however, so I kept at it. I finished the fall semester, and tried to enjoy the holidays but I found myself missing my dad terribly, and longing for my simple, innocent life, that I had enjoyed only two years ago. To take my mind off things, I hung out with

Aunt Toni when I could, and my Uncle Jim came over every now and then too. He had been in a really good mood the last few times I'd seen him, and insisted on playing blackjack and poker as much as possible. He was getting ridiculously good, and at one point I noticed him staring at the cards and muttering to himself. Aunt Toni saw me looking at him quizzically.

"He's counting the cards honey," she explained with an amused frown.

"He's doing what?"

"It's easy kid," he said. "You just keep track of which cards have been played, and you can deduce the odds quite accurately concerning what is going to be in someone's hand, based on the played cards, and what's in your hand."

"Wow!" I raised my eyebrows. That seemed impossible to me.

"He's going to have to be more discrete about it though," Aunt Toni said, with a look of genuine concern. I looked at Uncle Jim in confusion.

He rolled his eyes and said to Aunt Toni, "Obviously I'll be discrete when I get to Vegas!"

I looked back at Aunt Toni.

"He's planning a trip to Vegas, to beat the house at their own game. I've advised him against it, but he knows better, of course."

"Kid, I'm gonna be rich. It's too easy, and I tell you what—when I win big— like real big, I'll buy you another Cougar. How about that?"

I looked at Aunt Toni, who just shrugged. I had to admit, it sounded pretty exhilarating.

"Why do you have to be discrete?" I asked.

"Because it's illegal to count cards!" Aunt Toni admonished.

"Not if they can't see you doing it," Uncle Jim replied with a wicked grin.

I smiled nervously, but didn't say any more. I was a little concerned but didn't think too much of it.

———

As the spring 1982 semester began, I was determined to get my grades up, and work as hard as I could to get my life balanced. It felt at times, like Sisyphus, the character from Greek mythology, pushing the giant rock up the hill, only to watch it roll back down the next day. Despite that nagging feeling, I continued trying to enjoy my life as much as possible, and finish my schoolwork. I was taking a pretty heavy course load, and tried to reassure myself I was making headway.

As April rolled around, and the semester was starting to wrap up, Uncle Jim became really excited about his upcoming trip to Vegas. We played cards several times again, and he had become amazingly good. I couldn't even keep up, and was glad we weren't playing for real money. He left, and told me to look forward to that new car when he got back, and not to worry because he was going to "hit up Atlantic City" after Vegas. I laughed, high-fived him, and wished him the best of luck.

On April 6, 1982 I was at home in the evening when the phone rang. My roommate answered it, and then quickly gave it to me.

"Dude, it's your mom," he said with a concerned expression. I grabbed the phone.

"Mom?"

"Mark..." she was crying again.

"Mom, what's going on?" My stomach dropped to my feet but I told myself there just couldn't be another tragedy in my life.

"Mark, your Uncle Jim–" she started sobbing.

"What?"

She kept sobbing.

Mom! What about Uncle Jim?" I yelled.

"He died Mark. He... he... shot himself." I nearly dropped the phone.

"Oh my God! Don't tell me that. Please tell me it's not true, Mom. Please..." I begged, my voice cracking into sobs.

"I'm so sorry Mark. I don't know what to say. He left a note saying something about meeting a man he didn't like in Vegas. Apparently he lost big, and couldn't forgive himself."

"This can't be happening!" I wailed. "Not again! *Not again!*"

My roommate, Dick, was visibly shaken and didn't know what to do. He just stood there with a sorrowful expression on his face. I turned away from him.

My mom was still sobbing. I didn't know what to do with myself. I felt like I wanted to crawl out of my skin.

"Mom, I've gotta go."

"Mark!" she protested, but I slammed the phone down and grabbed my head, groaning and wailing.

"What the hell is *happening*?" I screamed. My Uncle Jim—my awesome Uncle Jim was now gone too. What did I have left?

This couldn't be real. Why was this planet so messed up? Why did people keep dying around me? What was going on?

I ran to my room and threw myself on the bed, groaning and screaming into my pillow. I became lost in the moment and was consumed with rage at the world. Grief swallowed me as I sobbed and sobbed into my pillow.

After a short eternity I had nothing left to scream so I just lay face down, catatonic. All I wanted was to fall asleep and escape my horrible reality. But sleep would become a luxury that escaped me that night and many nights to come.

Chapter 7

Aimless

When I started college, I had the noblest intentions, but was truly surprised by the amount of fun I was having each day. I soon realized I was tailor-made for the college experience; I'm social, energetic, and I love people. I even enjoyed studying (when there wasn't a whole lot of other fun stuff going on.) But I think I didn't really admit to myself how much subconscious strain I was carrying from my dad's death, and my two uncles' subsequent suicides.

My faith is what carried me at that time, and as I said, once I committed to follow Christ, I was all in. Well, for the time being, at least. During my first year at college, I lived for hanging out with my friends, and as the semesters progressed our little group grew bigger, with more and more great people. Tuesday night Discipleship meetings and Thursday night "Celebration" nights were my favorite times of the week. These nights—facilitated by Campus Ministers Dave and Ginger Weeber—plus hanging out on the weekends, was our week-in, week-out routine. In fact, without this group of friends, I don't think I would have made it through that time.

I was a complete wreck after Uncle Jim died, but only a scarce few knew it. I'd become a master at concealing my emotions, and socially, I succeeded. The gargantuan stress, however, manifested in my grades. I even kept it all above board, spiritually speaking, but I struggled to care about what my academic future held. I never hung out with people who did drugs, smoked, had sex or drank excessively, so I felt I was managing everything, except my grades. But I had no idea about the toll that the stress of losing my only three male role models was taking on me. I'd never had to deal with my pain like that; I just didn't know what to do with it. I suppose as a "fight" instead of "flight" reaction, I actually ended up getting even more radical with my Christian radio programming gig at 88.9 FM WFSE, *The Fighting Scots of Edinboro*.

Bear in mind, I was the first person to ever do *any* type of Christian programming at *E.S.C.* But I also had long hair, purple Lennons, an earring (wild for the time,) and was playing nothing but Christian Rock & Roll. And I did this on Sunday mornings during church hours (gasp!). The campus radio station was just across the street from the community of Edinboro, and even though we didn't have a ton of wattage, the town could easily pick up our signal. Needless to say, I began to ruffle a few feathers. Especially when I started turning up the controversy with catchphrases like, "You're listening to Jesus Rock with your Born Again Jock!" or "You're listening to Mark Morrow, your host with the most, the Father, Son, and Holy Ghost!" I guess I sort of became the Howard Stern of Edinboro's Christian radio show. I wasn't swearing or being obscene but people were wondering who on Earth this guy was, playing hard rock, talking about Jesus but acting like Wolfman Jack.

The station began receiving complaints that the show was sacrilegious. That, of course, only spurred me on. I wouldn't admit it, but the show was becoming a vent for my trauma. All that pressure of my dad dying, my mom remarrying, my uncles dying… but I still wasn't being offensive. It was all Christian material, I just knew Jesus would have no problem with me being me. I played hard-hitting groups for the era, like *Resurrection Band, Servant, Larry Norman, Mylon and Broken Heart*, and I stuck to my guns. I guess it worked out because I was voted *WFSE* Disc Jockey of the month. *The Spectator, E.S.C's* campus newspaper, even published a lengthy article, and a picture of me sporting a bushy afro, full beard, and my signature purple Lennons. Yeah, those were good times.

By the time the summer of 1982 rolled around, however, I had become completely unfocused on school. Call it stress, call it ADD… whatever it was, I just wasn't feeling the excitement any longer. After Uncle Jim died, something changed. I felt like I needed to "find myself," although I had no idea what that meant. Even though my friends were a good support system, I still felt like I didn't fit in very well with many of the people around me. They weren't *family*. I missed my dad terribly, and missed my uncles almost as much. I just felt like I wanted to belong somewhere again. It seemed like everyone around me knew what they were supposed to do, but I was spinning out into space.

Despite swearing I never would, I actually decided to move back in with my mom, Bob, and Beth. After the spring semester was done, much to my mom's chagrin, I told her I was going to take some time away from college. So I gave it another shot living with them. It was humbling to say the least.

In June, Beth graduated from General McLane High School, and had barely missed being Valedictorian, *but* she was voted Faculty Choice to speak at graduation. As a straight-A student and a straight-as-an-arrow record, Beth had her pick of colleges to attend. She chose Grove City, an elite higher education institution which unsurprisingly happened to be Bob's alma mater. All summer long, while I tried to figure out what I was doing with my life (and pay back my mounting student loans,) Beth was excitedly preparing for her Ivy-League experience as I tried to convince myself I wasn't bitter.

I tried so hard to assimilate into what was supposed to be my new family, but I soon realized why I'd left in the first place. I don't know what I expected when I moved back in; I guess I was desperate. Desperate for help. Desperate for direction. Desperate for a family again. The ensuing clashes with Bob, my mom, and Beth, however, led me straight to one decision. *I had to get the heck out of Dodge!* In September, while my mom and Bob got Beth all moved in to her new dorm room at *Grove City College,* I booked a one-way Greyhound bus ticket to Grants Pass, Oregon.

The Highway Missionary Society was located in the thick mountains of Grants Pass, and was the headquarters for a Christian hippy commune. The residents had committed to follow the model of Biblical living laid out in Acts chapters 2 and 4, where all property was shared, and all activities were focused toward the common goal of serving the Lord.

The idea of a surrogate family who were completely sold out to the Lord really appealed to me. A similar, but more well-known group was Jesus People USA, based out of Chicago. Where bands like *Rez Band* flourished at *JPUSA*, the band *Servant* was a primary ministry tool at *THMS*. As soon as I heard about *THMS* from my friends, I decided I was the perfect candidate for this lifestyle. A free spirit who loved music and hanging out with Christian friends, what could be better than that?

When my greyhound arrived, I was picked up from the bus station by believers from the commune. I immediately hit it off with them, as they told me a little more about the community. *THMS* owned several acres of land right next to a lazy, winding river, deep in the mountains of Oregon, and the views were breathtakingly idyllic. Married couples lived in small A-frame houses, and the singles lived communally in a large farm house, with bunk beds in large rooms. The bathrooms were large and shared among everyone. Everyone served in various ministries, like sending teams up to Washington to plant apple trees, kind of like Johnny Appleseed. I didn't feel led by the Holy Spirit to do that, but what did intrigue me was helping dig a basement out from underneath the farmhouse. This is where the group planned to build their own recording studio for *Servant*.

Everyone was assigned jobs of various sorts, and whatever money we had, we'd put together to buy food, supplies, utilities, and more. The men worked, while the women typically prepared the next meal, cleaned up, and took care of the kids. It was a very Woodstock-ish kind of atmosphere, but Christ-centered, and obviously without the drugs. The part I really enjoyed was being with believers in Christ who wanted to live together, work together, and share all they had in order to proclaim their worship of Jesus Christ.

Servant was the largest ministry *THMS* pursued; the band had several albums out, and primarily focused on touring the country holding large concerts. A couple of the band members would share their testimonies of drug abuse, and subsequently finding Christ and being completely set free. They touched tens of thousands of lives and it was a very, very cool experience to be part of. For the most part.

After about a month, however, the reality of *everything* being communal wore on me. The hippy commune sounds really great in theory, but I think most people enjoy a fair amount of personal time. There was little-to-none at *THMS*. Being a somewhat private person, and enjoying alone time to recharge became an issue. Don't get me wrong, at first I loved hanging out with other believers, even for extended periods of time. But when there is no escape from that, the novelty wears off. As I've said, I never was much of a team player and by the time October rolled around, I couldn't take it anymore. Since *Servant* was getting ready to leave on tour again, I thankfully told the leadership I had bided my time, and I needed to move on.

Despite some people's imaginations, it really wasn't some sort of Jim Jones cult, so when I decided to leave, everyone wished me well, with no guilt trips whatsoever. In fact, I asked the band if I could hitch a ride on their tour bus to Los Angeles, where my friend, Mike Rocca, lived. They said "No problemo!" so I started packing my things. It was then I realized I hadn't communicated with my mom the entire time I'd been at *THMS*.

We cruised down to L.A. having so much fun, I almost wondered if I was making the right move. I had to remind myself that living at *THMS* was *not* touring with *Servant*, as awesome as that would be. They dropped me as close as possible to Mission Viejo, where Mike was waiting to pick me up. I hugged my new brothers and sisters in Christ, and wished them a thousand new souls won to Christ each concert. They thanked me, and then pulled off, heading for their next concert destination.

I was really excited to see Mike. He'd graduated high school a year before me, and was an outstanding trumpet player. He was also a sports fanatic and played on the varsity tennis team and golf team with me. We'd also bowled together Saturday afternoons at the Edinboro Lanes in the Teen league for years. We hugged and I hopped in Mike's sweet ride, as we began to catch up.

Mike had a roommate named Dave, but neither of them minded me crashing on the couch for a while as I planned to help out with rent. Mike was really laid back, and his roommate was cool too, so we all hit it off right away. They even landed me a job at Irvine Toyota, where they both worked. Mike sold new Toyotas while Dave was the head of the service department. I was hired as a lot attendant, mostly removing the plastic off the inside of new cars, and using a heavy, highly toxic cleaner to wipe off a thin coating of rubber sealant that was sprayed on the outside of the car to protect it from the trip from Japan, across the salty ocean. I'd also drive cars from various point's A to point's B, and sometimes even travel with a group to deliver or pick up cars.

I learned Irvine was the largest Toyota dealership in the U.S. at the time. This meant Hollywood celebrities, the *L.A Rams*, or *L.A Express* from the *USFL* would often come to the lot to purchase new cars. One of the highlights of my tenure was when Florence Henderson came to the dealership, and I washed and detailed her car. She wrote me a personal letter, thanking me for doing such a good job, and I beamed with pride. It was a fun gig for a twenty-two year old; it kept me busy and I was able to make a few bucks while working mostly outside.

What I really loved about L.A. was the weather. On a clear day, you could see the mountains, over fifty miles away. Of course, even back in the eighties, on other days it would be so smoggy that you could barely see across the street. That part wasn't great, but we just wrote it off as "life in the big city." At the time, *MTV* was just starting up and I can remember when I wasn't working, I was utterly mesmerized by the cool music videos. All the new music that was coming out was just mind blowing to me. New Wave was putting classic Rock to bed, and weird, fresh new groups were taking the music scene by storm. I was especially blown away by artists like *Missing Persons*, *A Flock of Seagulls*, *The Cure*, *Tears for Fears*, *Billy Idol*, *Duran Duran*, and *Adam and the Ants*… I could go on for days. Little did I know it would be the glory years of Music Television, and I loved every minute of it! I remember speaking to some of my pals back home, and they had yet to hear of many of these bands I was hearing every day on the radio. That was another cool thing about L.A.; hot music would start out there and slowly but surely move east across the country. I had a leg up on what was hot way before it landed in Edinboro and Erie, and that was pretty darn cool.

But pretty soon I started feeling that familiar sense of emptiness again. I was having fun, but I still felt as though I wasn't on any sort of real path. I'd been living with Mike and Dave for almost two months at that point, and sleeping on the couch was getting old. Also, while they would never have admitted it, I'm sure they were secretly looking forward to having their living room back. The problem was, I wasn't making nearly enough money to get my own place in L.A., let alone buy a car and pay for utilities and all that.

When Thanksgiving came around, a friend of Mike's invited us over to her family's house for a traditional dinner. At the dinner table, while I kept up a happy appearance, I couldn't shake how alone I felt. My journey to the West Coast had been exhilarating but I was really starting to miss my friends and even my family a little. Most of all I missed my dad, but I knew he wasn't coming back. I mulled over what to do practically the entire Thanksgiving, and eventually decided to write my mom a letter. When we got back to the apartment, I poured my heart out onto the pages, telling her while I had had a great experience, I was probably going to head back to Edinboro soon, to continue my college career. As more of a formality than anything, I asked if I could crash with them until I could get my own place, and back in my groove. I knew my mom would be happy at the news of having her boy back safe and sound. I mailed the letter, and told Mike and Dave of my plans, while thanking them for all they'd done for me. They said it had been a pleasure.

The next day, I gave my notice at the dealership, booked my Greyhound ticket back home, called Mark T and a few of my other buddies, and told them I was heading back. I started to feel a sense of purpose again. My adventure was about to continue, and I now felt a sense of peace that I had gotten whatever it was, out of my system in Oregon, and on the West Coast. I knew who I was now, more than ever. I was ready to get back to college, and build an exciting life for myself.

About a week later I received a letter back in the mail. What I read floored me. In her letter, my mom explained that in the last few years I had quit the Air Force, dropped out of college, lived in a hippy commune for a couple of months, slept on someone's couch for a couple more months, and now I wanted to come home and continue my cycle of meandering. She basically said, "Mark, you've quit this, you've quit that and you're continuing in your cycle. Until you get some stick-to-itiveness, you'll never amount to anything." That shocked me but what she said next shook me to the core. "Unfortunately Mark, you are not welcome to stay with us. Bob and I cannot have you. Son, it's for your own good."

I was stunned. *Wow!* was all I could think. Here my sister was able to attend Bob's alma mater, because she was essentially cut from the same cloth, and simply because I was *not*, I was considered a loser and dropout. After losing my father, my childhood home, and just about every family member that had been an inspiration to me, I was now being given no quarter and told it was because of "tough love." If stuffy, old, money-making Bob hadn't been in the picture I might have bought it, but I knew better. I burst into tears.

I was thankful no-one was home, and wept on the couch, for what had to be twenty minutes. I couldn't stop crying. Huge tear drops swirled the ink as I read the letter again and again, trying to make sense of it all. My life had been turned upside down and I just couldn't get a break. I began to physically tremble from the vulnerability I felt; I was homeless, and worse, I was totally alone, with no family whatsoever to back me up. I had already told Mike I was leaving, had given my notice at the dealership, and there was no way I could tell him about the letter. Yet I knew when I got back to Edinboro, I had no place to go. No place to call home. Not only was my heart torn apart that my mom had told me I was not welcome in her home, I now carried a deep sense of shame. I wrestled with options but there was no way I could tell anyone about the letter. I had already booked my Greyhound ticket, but as I sat there on the couch, I experienced a spinning, spiraling sense of aimlessness. That sense of purpose had vanished, and more than ever, I now belonged nowhere.

Chapter 8

Rock Bottom

I took a deep breath and sighed. I lifted my hand to ring the doorbell. This was going to be tough. I knew they'd be home, but prayed they weren't asleep yet. When I walked up, I was relieved to see lights were on inside, or I would have been in a real quandary at ten o'clock on a cold, snowy evening. I pressed the bell and in a few seconds heard a shuffling in the hallway. The lace curtains were pulled back from the side window and my grandmother's anxious face peered out at me. She disappeared then I heard the deadbolt, then the chain then lock open.

"Mark?" She asked, confused.

"Hi Grandma!" I said cheerily, but could only clear my throat when she glanced down at my duffel bag and backpack.

"I thought you were in California?"

"Uh yeah... I guess I was. I'm back now." I cleared my throat again. "I uh... I was wondering if I might crash... um, sleep here for a week or so? I'm kind of in between places at the moment." That's when she looked perplexed.

Suddenly she realized I was standing out in the cold and waved me inside. "Come on in, Mark."

"Oh, okay. Thanks." I grabbed my bags and followed her into the living room, closing the door. I placed my bags next to the couch.

"Ross! Mark's here!" she called out to my granddad. He came shuffling in from the kitchen, tilted his head down, and looked over his reading glasses at me.

"Well hey there son," he said, stopping at the doorway. "I thought you were in California."

"He was," Grandma informed him. "He's back."

"Oh well good to see ya. How is life treating you?"

"Oh, not bad, thanks. California was fun."

"I'll bet…" My grandpa noticed the bags on the floor, and glanced at my grandma. The awkwardness was tangible.

"Mark is between places to stay, Ross."

"Oh…" The question of why I wasn't staying at my mom's hung in the air. I gave an uncomfortable smile, and shrugged. I didn't really want to explain.

"Well, the attic still has a bed in it," my granddad said.

"Oh…? Would that be okay if I slept there for a few days? I don't want to impose."

"No, no, you wouldn't be imposing. It's probably dusty up there, but you're welcome to it."

My dad's parents had lived in the same house for nearly sixty years, and were like a real-life Edith and Archie Bunker. They were retired but upheld their old-school conservative values with pride, and I knew they wouldn't turn me away. I had never been super-close to them but I was desperate, and tried to convince myself that after my dad's death, it might be good for them to see more of me too.

"That's really great, granddad, thanks! I can vacuum it or whatever."

My grandmother asked if I was hungry, and I quickly said yes. She said if I took my bags upstairs she would make me a sandwich and pour me some Kool Aid. I thanked her and headed up to the attic-slash-bedroom. I sighed again as I turned on the dim light. *Boy this room is creepy.* I tried not to be ungrateful, but knew I needed to figure out another plan as soon as possible. This was going to be tough.

———

The next morning I woke up suffocatingly hot, with a dry, scratchy throat. For a few seconds I had no idea where I was, and was stupefied until it all came back to me. I sighed again. Several thoughts flooded into my head at the same time: I had to get a job. I had to find another place to stay. I had to get back into college. The room smelled faintly of mothballs. *Man, how did my life end up like this?*

I threw on my torn jeans and a *Def Leppard* Union Jack t-shirt. My grandparents kept the house at about eighty degrees, so despite the snow outside, inside was like a furnace. I made my way down the twisted, creaky stairs and saw they were both in the living room, watching *Let's Make A Deal!* The couch was covered in a heavy plastic protective covering, the kind that some people also put over their front car seats in the 60's.

"Good morning!" I said, rubbing my eyes.

"Hey there, buddy! How did you sleep?" Grandpa smiled up at me.

"Pretty well, thanks."

"There's some coffee in the pot. It may be cold by now but you can heat up it in the microwave."

"Oh… cool. Thanks." I turned into the kitchen, and poured the dregs of a pot of coffee.

"How is your mom?" Grandpa asked.

"She's okay, I guess," I replied. I wondered if a minute would be long enough to heat the coffee and hoped my grandpa would leave the question at that. I really didn't want to discuss my mom, but I knew they were wondering why I wasn't staying there. They knew my mom had remarried pretty quickly, so I was hoping they'd put two and two together. The silence that followed relieved me, but then brought a fresh air of awkwardness. I knew more questions loomed: *What are your plans? Are you going to get back into college? How long are you going to stay?* I didn't want to deal with it, so unless they asked, I sure wasn't going to bring it up. I still had no idea what I was going to do for money, or work.

"Mark, if you need to take a bath, I put a green towel out for you in the bathroom." I had forgotten they didn't have a shower. I groaned, and then caught myself, hoping they didn't hear me.

"Okay, thanks Grandma!" I grabbed one of her world famous sugar cookies from a big tin, and headed back upstairs with my coffee. My mind was reeling.

And things never became much more comfortable than that. I made contact with my old college buddies, but that first Saturday night they were all heading out to have fun, and I had no idea how long I had to make my last $700 last, so I just figured I'd watch some TV with my grandparents or something. But they told me some of their friends were coming over to play cards. They offered me a spot at the table, but I respectfully declined and retreated back to my attic.

I took the first week off, spending it catching up with Mark Terwilliger and some other friends. I immediately felt better when we started laughing about all the good times we'd had. The first thing Mark said was that I needed to start taking classes again. I told him I needed a job first, and he said he'd keep his ear to the ground for me. By the second week at my grandparents, I was going a little stir-crazy, and I began to get the sense my grandparents were wondering how long I was going to stay. I also knew I had to make a plan soon to either start paying back my student loans, or get back into college to defer them. I started asking around about jobs, and looked in the newspaper classifieds. I had to use my grandparents' phone, and even though the calls were local, I still felt awkward using their phone in the dining room. Plus I wasn't getting anywhere in a hurry.

By week three, I was miserable and starting to despise little things like the small bathtub, and the sweaty plastic covers on the couches. By week four, my grandparents were polite but the questions about college and work were coming more frequently. By week five, I was trying to spend as much time at various friends' apartments as possible. I had also started playing a few shows at the radio station again, even though I wasn't making any money from it. I also wasn't a student either. It was, however, a welcome relief from the smell of mothballs, and sixty-year-old furnishings. I was trying desperately to be grateful but on the flip side of the coin, I knew my welcome was wearing thin at my grandparents' house. They had raised their four children nearly fifty years earlier, and I felt it wasn't really fair to them to have to feed me as well, on a limited income. By the end of the sixth week, I showed up on Mark's doorstep with my bags and lied that I had missed the bus home, and would he mind if I crashed on his couch. I suspected he knew the truth but he said, "Of course."

I imposed on Mark for three days before it was time to move on again. Next, I spent a snowy night at the radio station. I pulled two chairs together and used my heavy *Harley Davidson* jacket as a blanket. It wasn't ideal but at least there was a sense of freedom not having to walk on eggshells in someone else's home. The problem was that I could only sleep at the radio station after I deejayed a show, and I didn't want to make a habit of it.

The next day I called another fraternity brother and asked if I could crash at his apartment. He asked me to hold, and I could hear him persuading his roommate to let me just crash on the floor. They didn't even have a couch, only a couple of armchairs, so we laid some thin blankets out on the floor, and my *Harley* jacket came to the rescue again. It was okay though. At least I could shower in the morning. As I drifted off to sleep, I couldn't help but picture my sister sipping hot chocolate in her cozy dorm room, getting warm in a comfortable bed. Bob and Mom were proud of her as she drifted off to sleep, all ready for her next day of expensive classes. She'd find a great job, and have a great life. I didn't even wipe the tear that trickled onto the patchy blanket.

I repeated that routine for about another six weeks, until life was rapidly becoming unbearable. I would have rather died, however, than go crawling back to Bob and my mom. My friends could tell it was getting bad, but didn't really know how to help more than what they were doing. As things were reaching a point of despair, a saving grace appeared. I was introduced to Mark Feldkamp, who was the campus minister at *Gannon University* in Erie. Mark ran a big, Christian house called *The Kirk House* where Christian, male, Gannon students lived for only $100 rent per month. Mark's girlfriend (and future wife,) Laurie, ran the girl's house. Mark invited me to stay at *The Kirk House* and I gratefully accepted.

The problem, of course, was where to find $100 a month. I knew Mark would let me slide for a little while, but the last thing I wanted to do was mooch off a minister and a friend. One night after taking a shower, I dried off and got ready to brush my teeth. I examined the face that stared back from the mirror. I reflected on my life, and for the ten thousandth time wished my dad was a phone call away. He would know what to do. He too seemed to live by the seat of his pants, but he always had a solution for whatever life threw at him. I realized my mom never understood that. Or maybe she just couldn't deal with the volatility. Even in the tough times, I could never live a boring, mapped out existence but then I had to wonder if my mom and Beth and Bob weren't the ones who were truly free? A sense of dismay washed over me. *What am I doing with my life?* I wondered. I had to get my act together. What did that even mean? I had been trying, but had I been trying hard enough? I needed to get focused. But what did I *want*?

Suddenly something broke inside me, and I crumpled to the floor sobbing. Everything that was wrong in my life bubbled to the surface all at once. My dad.

My uncles. The abandonment. My vulnerability. My loneliness. I begged God for His help, promising to work as hard as I could if He just gave me an opportunity to get my life on track. All I needed was a break. I wept and wept, as the pain and fear and memories of the past three years burst from my heart and through my tears. I knew I had to make a change. I couldn't carry on living like this.

After lying on the cold floor until I was shivering, I felt a warmth wash over me. It was as though God was telling me He'd answered my prayer and already had everything taken care of. Kirk House was the first step. My breaking down and submission was the second. In an instant I knew things were about to change. I wiped my eyes, and shakily stood up, went to bed and fell soundly asleep.

The next day I awoke with a renewed sense of purpose. I couldn't exactly explain why, but there it was. Something had definitely changed. I saw Mark Feldkamp later that morning and asked if we could talk. I spilled my guts and he listened intently. Then he simply assured me, "It's all going to work out." And I believed him.

Over the following weeks, Mark's influence on my life became monumental. As my friendship with him grew, my spiritual walk deepened, and he quickly became like a brother to me. Mark was fun, but gentle in his handling of people, which I really appreciated. I never felt even a hint of judgment from him. In fact, I only ever felt love and acceptance, and I saw him treat all the other guys at Kirk House the same way. Because I had never wavered in my faith, despite my crazy few years of circumstances, I think Mark had a unique respect for me. Our discussions also consistently took a turn for the deeper spiritual things. After my second "come to Jesus" moment, and under Mark's positive influence, I began reading my Bible fervently for hours every day. I was also praying throughout the day and I began to find my identity in God.

It may sound clichéd but despite the difficult times, I was determined to be faithful to God. As a result, I began to spiritually soar. One of the most significant things Mark did was to help me get back into *E.S.C.*, to pursue my goals of finishing my Speech Communication degree. Before long I had my old job back at Sauer's Golf Course, and was hitchhiking to work six days a week. The most important thing was, I actually had a place to live and supportive Christian friends around me. It was hard to explain but once I signed back up for fall classes, I knew I'd found my purpose again.

Once I had the basics covered, I even started going out on the occasional date with a Christian girl. Needless to say, I was proud of myself for never having to ask my mom and Bob for any more handouts. I made up my mind to finish my degree no matter what life threw at me. I would prove a point to the naysayers, and with God's help I would become successful and rich, *and* be dating the most beautiful girl in all of Edinboro. If I could endure the last three years and survive, when life normalized, the sky was the limit. And I was about to shoot for the stars.

Chapter 9

A New Friend

A pickup truck blew by my little spot next to the on-ramp; another driver pretending I was invisible, as if I wasn't standing with my thumb outstretched, begging for a ride. *What would it hurt him to let me jump in the truck bed? Can't he see I'm just a kid trying to get to my freakin' job?* I restrained myself from flipping him the bird, instead muttering quiet abuse in his direction. Even with renewed purpose, the struggles of my daily life sometimes wore on me.

After an eternity, an old lady picked me up, which surprisingly happened more often than not. *Brave, compassionate old ladies with little left to lose*, I mused to myself. Maybe they were desperate for some company, which is what definitely appeared to be the case this time. She unleashed an uninterrupted stream of conversation on me, with space left only for a "Yes," or "Really?" or "How about that?" I didn't mind at all. I already knew I loved to talk but I had also learned I was quite a good listener too. But I was really just happy to have a ride. After ten minutes of one-way conversation, I thanked my still-chattering, sweet, geriatric chauffeur and walked down the dirt road, then up the path to the Pro Shop. I looked at my watch. Seven minutes early. *Sweet!*

My day was typical. I mowed the greens, tees, fairways, and rough, day in and day out. I re-filled the golf ball cleaners with soapy water, raked sand traps, cut cups, fertilized areas, and aerated the greens once a season. The golf course was owned by a lady named Mrs. Sauers, who would ask me to work behind the counter in the Pro Shop if she just wanted to get away and drive to the nearby Millcreek Mall. After her late husband Jim passed, life had become difficult and draining for this elderly woman. I first worked for both of them as a high school student, but since I had graduated, Mr. Sauers had died suddenly of a heart attack. I empathized with Mrs. Sauers, and knew life could kick anyone's butt at any time.

I couldn't wait for the day to be over. I was really looking forward to Bible study that night. I craved the community of like-minded believers, which was all I really had in life.

I was able to pick up an extra hour of work, before trudging back to the highway, smile on, thumb up, desperately praying for a quick ride back to Erie. My prayers were answered, and as I walked into the Kirk House, Mark was waiting for me. We shared some left over pizza and spoke about my day. He told me to keep doing what I was doing and God would bring good things into my life soon. A couple of hours later, I had a surge of energy as I walked up to the front door of the Bible study host's house. *Man, I love my group!* I thought to myself.

I let myself in and walked to the living room shouting my arrival. I heard a few "Yo's" and "Hey Mark's!" and smiled. I turned the corner and grinned as I looked across the room. Various buddies waved and grinned back at me. Then my eyes stopped on a young lady sitting in the old leather Laz-E-Boy. She was dressed entirely in black, with jet-black, obviously-dyed hair, which she wore long and covering half her face. I could tell she was cute though, and I tilted my head as if to get a look at her eyes from under her hair. She refused to look up at me.

"Mark, this is Lisa. It's her first week," our hostess, Ginger, informed me, smiling over at the girl.

The girl looked up for a brief moment and offered a fleeting nod.

"Hi Lisa!" I said loudly and warmly. She just darted her eyes back at me and this time offered a quick smile. I could have sworn there was a flicker of attraction. I took the seat next to hers, and announced "Man, I just *love* Tuesday night Bible study!" The rest of the group laughed and everyone amen'd enthusiastically.

As we got into the Bible study, I gave my opinion on all sorts of angles and interpretations of the passage we were reading; I think it was the Sermon on the Mount. I looked over to Lisa a few times, directing my conversation to her but she just looked down when the spotlight fell on her. I didn't force it. When the "formal" Bible study part of the night was done it was time for cookies and iced tea, or coffee or whatever refreshment of which you partook. I made a beeline for Lisa.

"You really don't want any of these cookies," I said chomping on a huge mouthful. "They're really gross… in fact, I'll do my community service and eat the rest of them so no-one has to be forced to suffer this terrible fate." She giggled and I held out a paper plate with a homemade peanut-butter cookie on it. She smiled at me from under her hair, and accepted it timidly.

"Thanks."

"You're very welcome, Lisa!" I replied. "Sooo… you're not from Edinboro, right? I think I'd remember seeing you around."

Looking at the ground she said, "I'm from Slippery Rock."

"Ah, Slimy Pebble, that's not too far. Your family still there?"

"My parents are."

"Well, we're glad to have you here," I smiled. She gave me another quick look from behind her hair, returning my smile and clearly betraying her attraction.

———

That Friday night, I caught a ride to Edinboro then walked to Lisa's apartment. She answered the door with a smile, wearing a long black dress and still addressing the ground while occasionally glancing up at me. It didn't bother me. I could tell there was something innocent in the eyes behind that jet black hair. I think it was her involuntary smile as I joked with her. I'd gotten her number shortly before leaving the Bible study, and when I called, we arranged to grab a bite and then walk to the Village Cinema to see *Blade Runner*: a new, futuristic thriller starring Harrison Ford. I wasn't a rich man, but I was working enough to pay for this girl's dinner and movie. She seemed to be in a similar state of student poverty, which took the pressure to impress off my shoulders a little.

"Hi!" she smiled shyly.

"Hey there!"

"You want to come in for a minute? I'm almost ready."

"Sure. Man, you look great," I grinned. She smiled widely again, and for a moment I glimpsed a bright, sunny girl beneath all the black. Then she was hidden again.

I walked around Lisa's living room, noticing her apartment was pretty sparse but way less sparse than my situation. A cross hung on the wall, and a picture of Jesus stood on a shelf. I really liked that.

"Grab some orange juice, or whatever you can find in the fridge!" she called out from the bathroom.

"I'm good, thanks!" I called back, as I continued to analyze her place. On another shelf was a single picture of what looked like Lisa's family, taken at least ten years prior. Lisa was easy to recognize and looked really cute, wearing little pigtails, and grinning mischievously. Her mom had an arm around her shoulder, but was not smiling, and her dad had her two siblings between him and her mom. He was smirking behind a rather large handlebar mustache, proudly displaying an equally large can of Pabst Blue Ribbon beer in his hand. Both of her siblings looked older; a boy and a girl. *Must be her older brother and sister.* As I studied the picture, she walked out of the bathroom smelling heavenly.

"You ready?" she asked the ground. I cocked my head and waited for her to look up at me.

"I was born ready," I chirped. It worked. That bright sunny girl cracked an involuntary smile again. I put my arm around her and we left.

We were both hungry so we walked to *Crossroads Dinor*, located smack dab in the middle of town. Everyone in Edinboro loved the food and atmosphere of *Crossroads*. Way back in 1958 when my mom was a student at *E.S.C.*, she waitressed there for fifty cents an hour, plus tips. *Crossroads* was pure Americana, like you'd see in a classic movie from the fifties. It had original glass windows in the front, with old school booths and a long counter, lined by swiveling, chrome and red-vinyl stools. Lisa wanted a burger (which I thought was awesome,) and she threw some serious hints for milkshakes so I went all out.

"Two cheeseburgers please, fries with both. One gigantic strawberry shake..." I rattled off as our waitress scribbled. "...and a gigantic... chocolate shake?" I asked Lisa.

"Umm, sure," she nodded quickly and the waitress scribbled.

"Sure?" I asked. "*Sure* doesn't sound sure. Are you sure you want chocolate? You're allowed to have something else," I smiled.

Lisa giggled and replied, "Actually can I have a peanut butter shake instead?"

"*No!*" I barked, and our waitress couldn't help but chuckle too.

"Peanut Butter it shall be," the waitress confirmed. I smiled at her and mouthed, *Thanks.*

"Sooo… you're from Slippery Rock, huh? What's a nice girl like you doing in a place like Edinboro?"

"Oh… just checking out the big city I guess."

"You think Edinboro is the big city?" I feigned dismay.

"It's bigger than Slippery Rock," she grinned.

"Seriously though, you go to *E.S.C.* don't you?" I asked.

"Yep!"

"Ah, so that's how you snuck into my Tuesday night Bible study!"

She chuckled again. I already knew I felt good about this girl. She broke out of her shell a little more each time I joked.

"So, you know we only have two choices right?"

"Two choices?"

"You can either be my partner so we can be the coolest people at the Bible study…"

"Or?" she raised an eyebrow.

"Or… you'll have to find your own Bible study to rule, Lisa," I replied with a straight face.

For the first time that night she looked me square in the face, her eyes widened a little, then at the last second a mischievous grin crept across her face.

"Well, I'm kind of growing fond of that Bible study…" she chirped. "So I guess we'll have to go the partners route."

I smiled broadly, nodded slowly, and raised my cup of water. "To partners in crime…" I announced.

"To partners in crime!" she grinned, and met my toast. "At the Bible study…?" I laughed loudly and I could see that made her night. She looked down immediately but I could see her shaking as she giggled quietly to herself.

"You're fun!" I said, as our waitress arrived with our shakes.

"Mmm, look at that!" she said, eyeing the cherry perched on a mountain of whipped cream.

"I'm going to steal your cherry!" I threatened, and made like I was going to snatch it off her shake.

"Don't you dare!" she squawked, and in an instant had her fork ready to stab any offending appendages.

"Dang! You're quick!" I protested. "I'll have to keep my eye on you!"

"Mm hmm" she nodded, enjoying the cherry.

We laughed, and I stole a huge spoonful of her shake.

"So tell me about your family? What's life like growing up in Slimy Pebble?"

A darkness fell across Lisa's face, and she looked at the table. After a second she just shrugged. "I don't know... it's okay, I guess."

"I'm sorry... I didn't mean to pry. I was just making conv—"

"It's okay," she offered a weak smile. "My family's uhh... a little jacked up, you could say. But whose isn't, right?"

"Yeah. Exactly," I replied. I shifted in my seat, not sure what to say next. "I... I saw the photo on the shelf. I was just wondering... you all seemed pretty happy in the picture."

"Well... you might have noticed my mom wasn't smiling," she said.

"I actually did notice that."

"Yeah... she's pretty sick."

"Oh... I'm really sorry. I didn't know."

"It's okay... how could you?" She offered a feeble smile again.

The atmosphere took a sudden, dismal turn and I had to think fast, to swing it back. This girl clearly had some emotional stuff going on, and I knew our first date wasn't the time to discuss it all. I felt sorry for her though. It seemed she carried the weight of the world on her shoulders.

"Well, my dad died. And then my two favorite uncles died," I said matter-of-factly.

"What? Oh, I'm so sorry." Her eyes widened, and she looked embarrassed.

"Ah, that's life, eh?" I smiled at her. "My mom also got remarried a year later, and I was homeless for a while because she wouldn't let me stay with them."

Lisa looked truly horrified, and put her hand over her mouth. Then squinted at me.

"Are you messing with me?"

"No, I'm being absolutely serious," I laughed. I could see she had no idea how to take me. "My dad died, my uncles shot themselves, and then my mom remarried her boss within a year—a rich banker who can't stand having a long-haired weirdo like me as his step-son. But what are you gonna do, right?" I was still chuckling.

Lisa half-smiled nervously and said, "I guess so…" My ploy had worked though; Lisa seemed to be more at ease.

"Yeah, don't feel bad, my dad's an alcoholic," she said suddenly.

"What? Really?" I said. "Man, I'm really sorry about that Lisa. That can't be easy."

"What are you gonna do, right?" she smiled.

"What are you gonna do!" I echoed, and raised my milkshake. She giggled and clinked my glass with hers again. I could tell this was helping her feel more comfortable.

"I also have a sister who's going to *Grove City College,* which is where my step-dad graduated from. Yep, she's got it made in the shade and I'm the rebel without a clue!

Lisa's mouth dropped open in disbelief. "No way!"

"Way," I replied.

"My brother is clinically depressed and often talks about ending it all."

I couldn't help but flinch from that revelation, but then I saw the look on her face. We burst out laughing.

"I'm sorry, Lisa… I'm really not laughing at your family's problems."

"You don't have to apologize," she said. "I'm laughing too! It feels good to laugh… as though I'm immune to it all. Sometimes you have to laugh at how crazy it all is."

"Exactly!" I smiled. I experienced an unexpected protective instinct over her.

"I wish I was immune to *all* of it though…" she sighed, reverting to her *world-on-the-shoulders* demeanor.

"All of what Lisa?" *What else could there be?* I wondered.

"Some things are worse than others," she said darkly.

I didn't want to pry, but I could tell something else was going on. Something beyond just family problems. But the time wasn't right to push it. I waited for a few seconds then said, "Well, if you ever want to talk about it, I'm here for you."

She looked up, almost ready to cry. But she smiled and said, "That's really sweet. I appreciate that, Mark."

"Anytime," I smiled back. *Whoa*, I thought to myself. *This date took a heavy turn*

"This milkshake is amazing!" Lisa said, taking a huge spoonful.

"Is it really?" She nodded emphatically. "Well I'm going to steal some." I lunged in with my spoon, scooping out three times as much as I'd intended.

"Aaah!" her mouth dropped at the blatant crime. "Give it back!"

I opened my mouth and slowly shoveled a quarter of her milkshake in.

"You little swine!" she laughed as her eyes narrowed in indignation. She went for my milkshake but I was too fast, and slid it out of the way.

"Too slow, honey bunny!" I taunted.

"Mark! You are going to return the half of my milkshake you stole. Right now." In a moment, she was ridiculously attractive to me. There was a scary tone in her voice, and I liked it!

"What if I don't?"

"I'm going to come across this table."

"That's all I've been waiting for."

She eyed me, trying not to laugh as I smirked, holding my milkshake just out of her reach.

"I don't think you want me to come across the table this way," she said, trying to sound mean, but her grin betrayed her love of this new game.

"I'll take it any way I can get it," I flirted. *Man, I'm on my A-game tonight*, I thought.

"With ice-cream, and whipped cream?" she winked.

I set the glass down, raised my eyebrows and dropped my jaw, grinning in mock horror. Quick as lightning she scooped out half of my strawberry shake, and ate it before I could even protest. She almost snorted it out her nose she laughed so hard, and I collapsed in the booth at the sight.

Man, this chick is something else. This is going to get interesting.

Chapter 10

A Crack in the Clouds

I realized I had actually seen Lisa around campus. I hadn't spoken to her, but she asked if I took a certain Communications class, and I confirmed I had. We'd seen each other as Lisa was waiting for her friend in my class. She was hard to miss, but I guess I hadn't been paying attention. Maybe it was because she was shy, and seemed to fade into the background a lot. She was definitely unique, in the way she dressed and carried her look. Everything black, dark makeup, jet black hair, really quiet. Like myself, she was not a follower of fashion trends, and I liked that. I think that's also what attracted Lisa to me. I was on the hippy-slash-art-major side of style, and she, although with a darker vibe, appeared to flow in the same non-conformist vein.

My sense of individuality had undoubtedly been handed down through my dad's DNA, and I suppose a good dose of nurture too. Of course, my life circumstances had magnified these independent qualities in me. I had been, according to my perspective, rejected and abandoned by my remaining family, and this somehow intensified my drive to honor my dad in my free-spirited ways. Lisa had also experienced more than her share of trauma, which had clearly created deep furrows in her psyche. This manifested in the poor girl's appearance and borderline vow of silence.

Lisa and I had been dating for a few blissful weeks when we went to *Uncle Charlie's Pizza Pub*. The Pizza Pub is connected to *Edinboro Lanes*, a bowling alley not more than ninety feet from the *Village Cinema*. Besides *Crossroads Dinor*, *Uncle Charlie's* was the place to hang out and enjoy excellent food. We sat on the same side of the table, goofing off and laughing like two kids, when she paused to study my face.

"Why do you wear those?" she asked, gesturing to my pair of purple Lennon glasses.

"Oh, I don't know... because I love *The Beatles* and I look awesome in them?"

She grinned, "You *do* look pretty awesome in them! Mark Morrow with his long, shaggy hair and John Lennon glasses."

I smiled back, accepting the compliment. Then I asked softly, "So... why all the black?"

Her smile faded and she looked away.

"I'm sorry. I didn't mean to... it looks cool, I was just curious."

"No, it's okay," she said, staring at the floor. "I just like the kind of gothic style, I guess."

"Oh yeah? Hmm..." I replied, trying to peek under her hair. She caught my glance and smiled weakly but looked away.

"You sure? Because you still love pretty girly things... like flowers."

She blushed and nodded. I had given her some pink carnations a couple of days before and she just lit up when she saw them.

"You don't wanna hear what I've been through, Mark," she said suddenly.

I took a second to process this, and then replied, "No, I really do. I care about you Lisa!" She looked away again, as if in pain. "Hey..." I gently turned her face to me. "No pressure but you can trust me."

To my surprise, a lone tear trickled down her cheek. I put my arm around her and she leaned into me. I had no idea what was going on, but I could tell it was extremely difficult for her.

"Last semester..." she began, and then her voice cracked. I just listened. "Last semester, I went to a frat party and had a little to drink." She paused, and I nodded, but I cringed inside, guessing where this was going.

"I kind of had a crush on one of the guys who lived in the frat house, so we went to hang out in his dorm room." Another pause. I just waited. "Well, another guy came with us, which I thought was weird, but both of them were pretty drunk so I just figured his buddy was either going to get the message and leave, or just hang out with us for a bit." I nodded but my face was grim.

"Well, we got to the room and the guy I liked started trying to make out with me, but I told him I didn't feel right with his friend being there. His friend just laughed and said he could join in." Lisa talked directly to the table now. "I began to feel really uncomfortable and said I wanted to leave. He grabbed my arm, and said it was okay, and I needed to relax." She swallowed hard. "I became terrified and thought about screaming, but I was so scared. I tried to pull away, to leave, but his friend blocked the door. I started screaming but the guy covered my mouth…"

My eyes widened in shock. I was speechless. Lisa didn't need to elaborate, and I wasn't about to make her.

"Lisa, I'm so, so sorry," I said, finally. Tears streamed down each of her cheeks. I drew her into me again, and she shook from her sobbing. I had never met anyone who had gone through anything like that. I felt terrible and had no idea what to do, but I was angry.

I almost asked if she'd gone to the police, but then I thought twice. She was distressed enough already. I would, however, ask her at some point.

"That's not all…" she said.

"What do you mean?"

"I was at a Laundromat one summer, in Florida… it was pretty deserted but a guy came in, cornered me, and sexually abused me." Her tears were flowing freely now, and I caught a sideways glance from our waitress.

"Oh my Lord, Lisa, that's horrible." I hugged her again. *Wow, this girl has been through it,* I thought to myself. Suddenly my problems seemed minimal. I also felt that sharing this trauma with me, was somehow cathartic to her.

"Hey… look at me." I got her attention. She looked up sadly, and I wiped her cheek. "It wasn't your fault." Her mouth turned up a little, and she buried her face in my shoulder again, sobbing. I just held her head and whispered again, "Lisa, in no way was it your fault. You can do no wrong in God's eyes. Or mine." She sobbed harder, but she clutched me tightly and I felt like something had released in her.

The waitress walked by again with a concerned expression, and I just nodded that she was okay. Lisa cried for another minute or so and then quieted down.

Looking at the seat she whispered, "Thank you, Mark."

"Anytime, angel."

———

A couple of days later I met Lisa for lunch at the student union on campus. She wore a long black skirt, with black shoes, and dark makeup, but her shirt was new, and a pastel pink that really brought out the color in her face. I thought she looked beautiful. She smiled shyly as I ooh'd and aah'd over her new shirt, and finally told me to stop it. I didn't. After a couple of months she was wearing colorful dresses, and after that she even started lightening her hair a little.

Lisa and I grew closer and closer, spending just about every free moment with each other. We were both taking heavy course loads, and we had our individual jobs, but we cherished our Tuesday night Bible studies and Thursday night Celebration in Hendricks Hall. Lisa really loved the Lord, which I believe was one of the main reasons I grew so close to her.

After a few months, I met her family, and saw for myself that her dad truly was an alcoholic, and her mom was a very sick woman. Lisa carried a great deal of stress and insecurity about her dad, but I kept reassuring her neither of us could control our family. I felt like I was helping her, but that was just half of the picture.

I had always been a pretty happy-go-lucky guy, and studying for tests was not something I did, even days in advance. I was, and probably always will be, a crammer. Well, one semester we decided to take a class together. After I reassured her I wouldn't distract her in the class, she relented, and I knew it was going to just be a great semester!

Lisa was a diligent student, and took her classes extremely seriously. I did too, but I guess in a different way. I managed it on my own terms, while Lisa got very stressed if she left her studies or homework too late. In that particular class, Lisa studied intently before an exam, and I would read over the material to keep up in class, but rarely gave it much thought outside of that. After Lisa had absorbed the information, we'd have a study night right before the test, and Lisa would help me catch up. I felt a little bad about this, but I figured it helped her review the material too. She'd grill me, and cram the info I needed into my brain late into the night. When it came to test time, I would do really well. In fact, I recall several times when I received higher grades than Lisa. Needless to say, this really got on her nerves, but in this way she really helped me overcome my weaknesses. As a result, our relationship became deeply symbiotic.

After we'd dated for about a year, Lisa and I grew so close we started to feel like we were practically married. Our parents weren't very involved in our lives, we managed everything ourselves and we made just about all our decisions together. With all of the changes in my life, I was also taking significant strides out of my desperate situation, which was very exciting for me.

Things started going from good to better, and in the fall semester of 1984, I applied for an exciting internship that was available at my home church, *Edinboro United Methodist*. I was accepted, and able to complete my internship credits toward my Speech Communication degree. My job was just to help out where needed around the office, and even preach on occasion, usually when Pastor Ron was out of town, or busy taking care of emergencies.

One of the primary focuses of my internship, however, was to plan and implement a youth group for the church. The elders had begun to notice several youth slipping away, and they needed someone who was "in touch" but also grounded in their faith. I was the perfect candidate.

I worked hard on the plan, hit the ground running, and soon our church had a thriving youth program. While I was doing all of this, I even took a certified lay-preaching course that was held at my church. I was the youngest person in the classes, with my companions being mostly older men and a few women in their forties, fifties and sixties. I was just a green kid but I had plenty of enthusiasm and a fresh perspective. During the course, I received many compliments from the instructor and all the other participants. They even went so far as to tell me I should go to seminary and become a pastor. I began to feel really good about myself, and my walls of self-doubt began to greatly diminish. After three months, I had earned nine credits, with a perfect A grade for the internship. And *E.U.M.C.* now had a growing youth group. Pastor Ron and the parents were so happy with what I'd done, he asked the board to create a part time position so I could expand on leading the youth.

This experience would be something new to me, however. First I had to be interviewed by the board, and I wasn't quite prepared for what came next. The board was comprised of some older church members, to whom I had never really given a second thought. I knew who they were, and greeted them cheerfully, but never really considered the gruffness I encountered with some of them. I guess I just chalked it up to "elderly" mannerisms. In my first interview, I received a rude awakening; I was interrogated about my long hair, earrings, wearing purple-tinted glasses, and (Lord save us!) neglecting to remove my hat in church sometimes. There I was, not touching drugs, rarely drinking alcohol, and when I did it was moderately—I was even still a virgin. But they insisted on giving me the third degree about my appearance.

"Why do you wear purple-tinted glasses? Does that mean anything?" they'd ask with raised, skeptical eyebrows. "Are you trying to cover up your eyes for some reason?"

Why don't you just come out and ask me if I smoke pot, I thought. *Sheesh.*

I was blindsided and more than a little hurt by their judgmental attitude, but ultimately I just shrugged it off and assured them I was not a drug user, and rarely even drank alcohol. Thankfully, there were more enlightened members on the board than judgmental ones because I got the job, and that was my first big break.

As I began to serve in this capacity I mainly preached at my home church when Pastor Ron would go on vacation, or if he would go out of town. Pretty soon, however, I was invited to preach at a few small, country churches in Crawford County too. There were even times I'd preach at three different churches on a Sunday morning: one at 8 a.m., one at 9:30 a.m., and the next at 11:00 a.m. I'd greet the congregation, lead worship, give announcements, take up the collection, do a special music feature, facilitate prayer requests, preach the sermon, and greet everyone on the way out. Then I'd zoom off to the next church to do it all again. I'd be working hard and I was told I did a great job, but by the time I got home, I'd be spent, physically and emotionally.

Chapter 11

Blowing Past Boundaries

Lisa often went with me when I preached, and people would sometimes assume we were married. This was both sweet but also awkward, because I knew there was no way I was ready for that yet, and Lisa especially relished those comments. By this time, Lisa had gone from wearing all black, to feminine pastels, and lovely floral dresses. She'd also started wearing her hair out of her face, and was a hundred times more confident. We were both working hard, and it appeared to be paying off. We honored God despite a few dark areas in our lives, and I believe this was how I was beginning to be blessed. But we still faced the challenges any young couple faces, most notably that of sexual temptation.

Lisa and I knew having pre-marital sex was against God's will, and we had both committed to abstain until we were married. And marriage had come up several times, even early in the relationship. At first it was sort of a joking, passing statement by Lisa, and then a few days later I'd tease her about it, and she'd respond, but the topic was there, and the intention was growing. Regardless, as far as sex went, we were pretty innocent. I remember hearing college friends or kids I knew from my classes who were having sex discuss it like it was normal behavior, and

I just couldn't believe students would be so reckless. Needless to say, I was very naive. I would write music with a friend of mine I'd performed with a few times at local coffee shops. One day we were hanging out in his dorm room and I was shocked to see some condoms on the shelf above his bed. I couldn't believe he and his girlfriend were "doing it."

For the first year or so, Lisa and I would just make out and when it started getting too hot to handle, we'd both stop and agree to cool off. That worked for a while. Every now and then, however, we'd slip and do something a little more but then we'd get really convicted, and feel terrible about it. But once those lines had been crossed, the next time temptation came, we always blew right past the old lines.

When it first started happening, we'd get out of an evening class and sneak downstairs in Compton Hall, where it was dark, and start fooling around. We never actually had sex but did a lot of stuff we knew we shouldn't be doing. Of course, there was a thrill to it. It was fun, somewhat dangerous, and I told myself it was from a place of pure love.

When I started preaching we chilled out for a long time. The problem was, it felt so *right*. *We* felt right. Lisa and I would attend Discipleship Tuesdays, Celebration Thursdays, Christian concerts, and one of the highlights of our year would be to attend Jubilee, a huge Christian college conference in Pittsburgh every spring. We'd meet other Christian couples, who were often into music as well, and together we'd forge new friendships, and bond even more deeply with each other too. I honestly did love Lisa and wanted to marry her but I would tell myself I didn't have the money for a ring yet, or we still had a few things to figure out.

One of the major sticking points was Lisa really wanted children, and I absolutely did not. In time it became such a point of contention, whenever it came up, I'd deliberately shut down and refuse to discuss having children any further. I could tell this would really hurt Lisa, but there was nothing I could do. The piece of me that should have been entering the "nesting phase" and welcome that sort of familial responsibility and fatherhood, was simply broken. I couldn't even fake it.

In spite of that issue, pretty soon Lisa and I were doing everything but having sex. We just felt so close and it often felt so right, we didn't know how to stop. We'd go past our old lines, feel guilty and then a few weeks later, go even further. And the cycle continued, on and on until only full-on sex was left. When I'd be up in the pulpit preaching, I would become intensely convicted of my sin, and it was usually after I preached somewhere, that we'd have a "cooling off" period. But soon after that, the temptation came back too fast and too strong, and we'd be back to fooling around again.

Astoundingly, despite this darkening secret, God continued to bless me. My second big break came in that same fall of 1984. I had enough experience in my college career to apply for a position at an organization called *Hermitage House Youth Services*. This was a place that took care of disadvantaged, abused, and at-risk youth while training them to be self-sufficient in the outside world. I landed the job, and began immediately.

I looked forward to the work, but a great value-add of the job was, it was a live-in situation. I shared a house with two boys, who were my primary responsibility. The house had everything I needed, including a washer, dryer, fully equipped kitchen, and my own private room on the opposite side of the house to the boys. Life was finally starting to get good!

I was finally making some money, and with rent and utilities paid for, I began to save like crazy. I'd also spend a lot more on Lisa, which I quickly realized was a huge turn-on for women. Everything seemed just about perfect, and the next time the marriage conversation came up, I had a proposal for Lisa. We were just joking around, and she ended up completing one of my sentences as we often did for each other:

"I'm telling you, we're just like an old married couple. We're starting to assimilate our minds," Lisa laughed.

"You know, we *could* be an old married couple someday," I replied sincerely.

"Aw, don't even play with my emotions like that Mark," she protested. I could see the glimmer of hope.

"I'm serious," I said. "Lisa I would marry you in a heartbeat..." Her eyes lit up but she sensed there was a catch."As long as you're okay with not having kids, I would like nothing more than to marry you."

"What?" She scowled liked I was playing a cruel joke on her.

"Lisa, I really care about you, but I just cannot have kids. I'm not quite sure why, but I simply have zero desire. In fact, even the thought of it stresses me out. If I can have a vasectomy before, I will get you the biggest, most beautiful ring, and we will get married." I smiled at her lovingly, expecting her to swoon. Instead she was about to start crying.

"What?" I asked naively.

"Mark, that's undoubtedly the most bittersweet thing I've ever heard in my life."

"Honey, we can have a great life together. We don't need all the hassle of kids. We can travel, I can speak in different churches. We would have it made." It was a perfect plan, but Lisa just shook her head, and wiped away a tear. I raised my hands up as if to say, *I'm perplexed.*

"Mark, we would never be a family without children. Just about every woman dreams of having a loving husband *and* his children. A house would just be a house without children."

"Well, what about us? Wouldn't we be a family together?" I asked, foolishly trying to apply logic to the discussion.

"Mark…" she shook her head again, and looked even sadder. "We'd be a couple. And nothing more."

I believe that was the night Lisa's heart was broken. You wouldn't guess it though; she always maintained a strange kind of strength. A bitter hopefulness that seemed to sweep the disappointment under the rug, and continue our relationship, as if I'd said nothing to shake her hopes of having a family.

So life continued as normal, at least as far as I was aware. I continued building the youth group, preaching occasionally, and Lisa and I kept working on our respective degrees. We really did care about each other, and we both knew it. We spent tons of time together, sending each other cards, notes, and little gifts. Despite her dark period, underneath Lisa was a really loving, caring, and feminine girl. She loved the mushy stuff like taking walks, holding hands, and talking a lot.

One of our favorite pastimes was taking mini road-trips together. We went all over the place. Kinzua Dam, Virginia Beach, Vero Beach, *Disney World*, camping in tents and, of course, a ton of top notch Christian concerts. It was the most intimate and mature relationship I had ever been in, and it was founded on a great friendship. All of our friends just knew we'd get married, and live happily ever after.

When the new year arrived, something felt special about 1986. Lisa and I were set to graduate with our bachelors', and we'd been devoted to each other for over two years. We were still fooling around, and the problem with doing "everything but," you know there is that one last place to go, and it becomes more and more irresistible.

One night, we were alone in my bedroom, and one thing began leading to another. Pretty soon we'd reached the threshold we'd stopped at a hundred times before, but we both knew we wanted more. In my mind I heard a voice saying "Hey, you love each other, so it's okay." I tried to resist, thinking *We've waited this long, we need to be strong,* but I'd begun down the road, and the slope was ridiculously slippery. "You've held out for ages. You've done great, but you deserve it now. No one will ever find out." I could tell Lisa was succumbing to the same thoughts.

The chance to run came and went. Before I knew it, we were having sex.

I was completely unprepared for what followed. When we had come down from the hormonal, and emotional high, we plummeted into the terrible "B state" psychologists know so well. Guilt crashed upon us like a tidal wave, shattering our bliss. We felt like Adam and Eve who had just partaken of the forbidden fruit. We felt like we'd *lost our salvation.*

Lisa started crying, and I immediately suggested we vow to each other to never to let that happen again. After Lisa had calmed down, we took a long walk, and on the way we prayed, asking God to forgive us. We also asked one another for forgiveness and swore we'd never allow that to happen again. We were entirely sincere. But once you get a taste, quitting is easier said than done.

Before long, it happened again. And again. And again. Soon we simply couldn't stop sinning. There'd be moments we didn't care and would just think nothing of indulging our flesh, and there were times a deep, holy conviction would fall so heavily on me or Lisa or both of us together, one would say to the other "Look, this is just not right, we have to stop this and go back to 'everything but.'" We'd go for a few weeks or maybe even a couple of months, but the boundary was long gone.

As we continued in this lifestyle, what really blindsided me is I was completely unaware of how severely my conscience was being seared. I continued to lead the youth group and preach, but I was beginning to lead a dangerously double life. But I was addicted. I couldn't stop, and the last thing in the world I was about to do was break up with Lisa. But I wouldn't propose to her without an agreement that kids were out of the picture. I kind of felt trapped.

Then May of 1986 arrived, and with it, mine and Lisa's graduation ceremony. Another milestone. Another point proven to those who didn't believe I could do it. A shot in the eye to those who turned their back on me when I needed them the most. *I had done it on my own.* Ironically, after I graduated, I decided to lop off my long hair, take out the earrings, and start interviewing for a "real" job. Here I was, looking the part and getting satisfied nods from the stuffy, old board members who had suspected me of being a druggie, while I was following Christ with all my heart. Now that I had my short hair and looked the part, they liked me better, but I was living a life filled with sin. I shook my head at the irony.

About a week after graduation, Lisa and I went to *Uncle Charlie's* for dinner, and she was unusually quiet. I asked her what was wrong, fearing she was slipping back into depression.

"Nothing, I'm fine Mark," she snipped.

"Umm, I don't believe that for a second." I always shot straight with her. I would never tolerate her passive-aggressive nonsense. It was the only way to shake her out of her doldrums, and she knew I wouldn't let up.

"Well… I sometimes wonder what your intentions are."

"My intentions?" I was suddenly anxious, and I had no idea why.

"Yes, Mark. We've been dating for a long time now. We've both graduated, and are beginning our adult lives. I just want to know where this is headed."

"Where what is headed?" I blurted like an idiot.

Lisa rolled her eyes, and said, "okay, Mark, listen, I told you I was fine."

"No, no… I'm sorry," I said quickly, feeling inexplicably ill. "What's up? Tell me."

"Mark, are we thinking about marriage or what?" Lisa said abruptly.

"Whoa… easy there, tiger," I grinned. "Marriage? We're still kids."

"Mark, plenty of people our age get married. We're not kids."

"Well yeah but…" I stuttered.

"Mark, we shouldn't be sleeping together if we're not married," Lisa said resolutely.

"Whoa, whoa, whoa. Let's not get crazy, okay?" I tried to joke my way out of the conversation. Lisa wasn't amused. "Wait, where is this coming from?"

"Mark, I just want to know where this is going. I really care about you, but sometimes it seems like you're just having fun."

"Oh, come on!" I smiled. "We *are* having fun, but that doesn't mean I don't care about you." She didn't return my smile. "Okay, Lisa, you know I'm still a little freaked out about the situation with my dad, and Mom remarrying and all that. I just... I have some issues you know."

"Well what about me, Mark?" she said, her voice cracking. "I have issues too, don't you think I'm scared?"

She started crying softly. *Oh great,* I thought, but I put my hand on hers. "Hey, listen... don't cry. Please don't cry. I mean, of course I'll be willing to marry you Lisa... it's just that...."

"You'll be *willing* to marry me?" her eyes widened.

"No... That's not what I meant?" I became confused.

"Not what you meant?"

"Listen... what I mean is, I'll marry you... but I won't want kids. Ever."

Lisa just stared at me. For the first time, I think she realized how screwed up I really was.

"You really don't want kids?" she asked quietly.

I shook my head.

"How can you not want kids?"

"I just don't." My statement was cold and matter of fact.

Lisa turned away, and gazed outside, but I glimpsed an emptiness in her eyes that made me uneasy. But I shrugged it off. We didn't talk much for the rest of the afternoon.

———

By October of 1986 I had landed an excellent entry level job with an organization called *Harborcreek Youth Services,* as a Child Care Counselor. I was to be stationed at their West 25th Street Intensive Treatment Unit for teenage boys. My experience as a live-in counselor to the boys at *Hermitage House* was perfect on my resume, as was my youth leader position and recent Communications degree. I was apparently the picture of wholesomeness and achievement, because they hired me on the spot. This was my third break, and life was about to get *really* good.

I took Lisa out for a celebration dinner. While we were eating I quickly calculated how much I'd be making between running the youth group, *Hermitage House,* and *Harborcreek.* It was *serious* cash for a young man. The best part was *Hermitage House* took care of most of the typical bills I'd have to deal with, so it was pretty much all disposable income. I knew there and then, I was going to save up and buy a black Corvette to reward myself for "making it." And to honor my dad.

I knew he would have loved to drive it around, the way he drove my Cougar. For a moment, I sadly wished he could help me pick out my Vette.

Lisa wasn't as fortunate as I was. She couldn't find any work, and she just hung around town, seemingly waiting for something. I was moving ahead, and didn't think too much about it. We were still having fun, but in hindsight, something changed after the conversation at *Uncle Charlie's*.

One day Lisa told me she had to discuss something with me, and I knew something was wrong. I suggested we grab some coffee, so we headed to *Crossroads Dinor* and sat down.

"Mark, I'm moving back to Slippery Rock."

"What?"

"You heard me."

"Wait, what are you talking about? What about us? Why would you do that?"

"I want to pursue another degree in Business. Things aren't working out for me down here."

"By things, you mean us?"

"Mark, I've been waiting and waiting, but it seems like you just want to cruise around in your car, have fun with your buddies, and focus on money. I can't wait around for you any longer."

"You're breaking up with me?" I was stunned.

"Let's just say I'm moving on, Mark."

"Wow! Can I do anything to change your mind?"

"You can marry me and have kids."

I threw her a *Come on!* expression, but she was serious.

"You're not kidding?"

"I've enrolled at Slippery Rock College."

"*What?*"

She just stared at me.

I was floored. After a few moments of awkward silence, Lisa said she had to go. I hugged her and walked her to her car, not really knowing what to think. My heart was torn. *What will I do without her?* I wondered. *She's a huge part of my life.*

But on the other hand, a seductive voice whispered. If she wants to play that game, you're now a free agent.

———

By the fall of 1987, life could not have been better. At least in my own opinion. The youth group continued to grow, and I was saving a ton of money working at *Harborcreek* and *Hermitage House*. Lisa had moved down to Slippery Rock at the end of summer, and was living with her parents while starting her new business degree. Edinboro's homecoming approached and I hadn't landed a date yet, so I called Lisa to see if she wanted to drive up for the parade, parties and "Whatever else might come up." I could tell in her voice she missed me, so I wasn't surprised when she agreed. She drove up and met me at my apartment. As soon as we saw each other, it was lust at first sight and we fell right back into our old pattern. The weekend was wild, carnal, and we must have been having fun because it flew by. On Sunday, Lisa drove back to her new life and routine.

A couple of months went by and the snow was soon falling. Mine and Lisa's paths grew increasingly apart as we busied ourselves with our individual lives, but we talked on the phone here and there. Whenever I saw it was her, however, I answered it. That day the phone rang, and her number came up on caller I.D.

"Hey babe!" I said cheerfully.

"Mark!" Her voice was filled with terror.

"Lisa? What's going on?"

"Mark, you have to drive down here right now."

"What's happening?" I said in fear, already getting my jacket and keys.

"Mark, I think I'm pregnant."

I froze. A two-by-four across the head couldn't have stopped me faster in my tracks.

"*What?*"

"I took a pregnancy test, Mark. It was positive."

"Why did you take a pregnancy test?" I asked stupidly, and instantly regretted it.

"Because I'm late…"

"Oh my dear God…." My chest tightened up and I put my hand to my head. I didn't know where to go.

"Mark, please come down as quickly as you can."

I snapped out of my catatonic state, and ran out the door. "Ok, I'm on my way."

My Corvette was waxed, detailed, and put away for the winter, so I jumped into my new daily driver, a four-door maroon Ford Escort. I started up the engine and floored it toward Slippery Rock. Two hours later I screeched to a halt outside Lisa's house. She was waiting for me and threw the side door open, grabbed my hand, and pulled me upstairs to her bedroom. Fortunately, both of her parents were in bed and were oblivious to me being there. Lisa carried a fresh pregnancy test in her hand and her cheeks were stained red from crying.

"Are you sure the last test was positive?" I asked.

"Pretty sure," she replied shakily.

"Okay, come into the bathroom and take that one. I'll double check it so we can be sure."

We went into the bathroom and she did as I asked, taking the home pregnancy test in front of me. I saw the last one on the bathroom sink, and sure enough they were faded, but there were two red lines screaming out my deepest fears. She put the second test on the counter top and she checked her watch while my stomach churned. Thirty seconds. One minute. Two minutes. Three minutes. I couldn't bear to look. Eventually she picked up the test and checked it. The expression on her face said it all. Lisa was, without a doubt, pregnant.

Chapter 12

The Point of No Return

We lay on Lisa's bed, sick to our stomachs. In an entirely surreal vortex of panic and catatonia, I searched my mind for answers. I was the good guy. I had clawed my way up from sleeping in a radio station and bumming rides to work, to being a respected youth leader and counselor at two major non-profits. No one would understand if it came out I was involved in this sort of scandal. I was a role model. But that wasn't the worst part.

The scandal I could deal with—people make mistakes. Everyone agreed Lisa and I were just picture-perfect. If they found out she was pregnant, the fallout wouldn't ruin our lives. I was almost positive the church would agree we could get married, raise the kid, work toward a three-bedroom house with two-and-a-half bathrooms and a white picket fence.

Except we weren't perfect. We were human, and we had major, major differences. And I was feeling especially human in that moment.

Oh yes, I'm the Great Pretender…

Lisa's parents were just feet away in the room below; a sickly, middle-aged woman, and an alcoholic. *At least he's a living alcoholic,* I thought bitterly. I knew my dad would have helped me handle this well if he were still alive.

We must have woken Lisa's parents, and it depressed me even more as I heard their muffled voices. I imagined how it would go down if we told them there and then. *Oh the drama!* There was *no* way I was dealing with that.

"Let's check the guidelines. Maybe we have it backwards," I proposed.

"I've checked it ten times, Mark," Lisa protested.

"Check it again!"

She grudgingly picked up the box, and we scrutinized the guidelines, the colors, and the stripes. I mentally stepped through the process she had taken, desperately trying to clutch my last hope as it poured through my fingers. The instructions confirmed Lisa had done each step by the book.

"What are we going to do?" I asked finally. "I don't know, Mark... My brain feels like scrambled eggs right now."

"Umm, that's not really an answer... we need to figure this out."

"Jeez, what do you want me to say?" Lisa snapped at me.

I tried to relax, and change gears. "Well, we're both intelligent people, with good DNA. What about adoption?"

Lisa sighed and stared blankly into space. "I can't believe this is happening..." she whispered.

Her helplessness irritated me. "Well it is... so let's try to focus, and figure this out. My aunt, Toni, might be an option..."

Lisa scowled at the ceiling. "Your aunt, Toni? Mark, she's great but she's a good deal older than us. Also, how hard would it be watching our baby grow up, but not being able to tell the child we're his or her mom and dad?"

"Hmmm..." I hadn't thought of that. It would definitely be tougher for various reasons. "I guess I see your point. Give it to someone we don't know, and make a clean break?"

That was enough to start the waterworks again for Lisa. I turned to her and begged myself not to get frustrated. But all I wanted was a game plan. To resolve this stress. "Aw, c'mon now. Don't cry... what did I say?"

"Mark, you're just being so... clinical. Our baby is not an 'it.' I honestly don't know if I could give the child up after carrying him or her for nine months. We're both educated. You're making pretty good money, and I could find a great job and move back to Edinboro. Why couldn't we make this work?"

I knew this was coming, and a suspicious voice in the back of my mind wondered if this wasn't the ploy all along. "Lisa, what about business school? You'll find a job. You've been looking for months now. That's why you came back to Slippery Rock. To attend your hometown college just a few miles from your house!"

Lisa continued staring into space. When she didn't answer, I'd had enough. There were lines I could not cross, and I had to make that clear. I hated this passive aggressive crap.

"Okay, look, if you want to have this kid I will financially take care of it, and do everything I have to…" She turned to me with a fearful expression. "…*But, I cannot be its father.*"

For the longest moment Lisa stared pitifully right into my soul. I watched in surprise as the light in her eyes slowly dimmed… then she turned away. "So what about marrying me? Now that I'm carrying your child?"

"Lisa… I'll give you child support…" I surprised myself by faltering. "…but I can't marry you."

The light in her eyes was extinguished. She sat up, slowly hugged her knees and began to gently rock herself. I braced for more tears but none came. After a couple of minutes I got antsy. Something in the room had shifted, and it freaked me out.

"Okay, listen, I have to go," I said quietly, "but I'll call you tomorrow, okay?" She didn't respond, so I grabbed my jacket and walked to the car. The drive home was lonely and excruciating.

When I arrived home I wasn't any less confused or depressed. Waves of anxiety tightened my shoulders at unannounced intervals. I tried not to think about Lisa descending into an emotional tailspin. It was all I could do to keep myself sane at this point. That was when I first surprised myself.

I wonder how far along the fetus is? I blinked. *Whoa… 'fetus.'* I reeled at having used the clinical term for my unborn child. But I allowed myself to continue. *Well it is a fetus. At this point, it's just a few cells that have come together.* My rationale felt wrong but at the same time there was a certain maturity along with it. A sense of an independent, adult thought process I was working through. I just wanted to consider all angles, but I proceeded cautiously. *That doesn't mean it won't become a baby if left alone.* A shot of anxiety through my shoulders. *But that doesn't mean it is a baby right now either.* I let that thought rest for a few minutes.

I cleared my throat and acknowledged the truth: I could tell myself what I was contemplating but the bottom line was, I knew what I was willing to do to get my life back. The question was, what would Lisa do?

The next day I woke up, and the last thing I felt like doing was getting breakfast ready. I woke my two boys and told them to hurry up, and get showered and dressed. I would often cook a good breakfast for us but today they got cereal.

"Make it snappy, dudes. I know you're on break, but you have a ton of chores to do today and tomorrow, before the party," I barked.

"Aren't you going to hang out with us today, Mark? You don't have to do any sessions, do you?" the older one asked.

"No, but I have stuff to do," I grunted. I caught the furtive glance they exchanged, and I didn't care. "C'mon... snap snap." I got them outta there and tried to focus on the few tasks I had for myself. It was futile.

Eventually evening rolled around and I dialed Lisa's number.

"Hello?"

"Hey!"

"Hi, Mark."

"What you up to?"

"Just sitting here thinking about how bright my future is."

"Oh, I thought you may be registering for new classes or something?" I tried to steer her away from the pity party.

"Umm, no Mark, I registered like a month ago. If I had anything to do I wouldn't be answering the phone."

"Okay, take it easy. Maybe you left registration late or something." My brain was cooked. Of course she had registered. Classes started in a few weeks. Her sarcasm irritated me though, even though I knew it was because she was stressed.

"Oh yeah, I should leave registration until the last minute so that way I could get crappy classes and invest a bunch of time into my education for nothing as well."

Okay, so it was clear she was mad. "C'mon Lisa..."

"Oh, sorry. What would you like me to do, Mark? How can I make you feel more comfortable during this difficult time?"

"Okay, you know what? I was going to drive down there to talk, but if you're going to act like that, I'm not going to."

"You can't come down. I have things to do."

"Aaalrighty then… well, it was nice chatting…"

"Why did you call?"

"Well, I wanted to discuss our situation."

"So discuss…"

I sighed. She wasn't going to make this easy on me. I had to be patient. "What are you going to do, Lisa?"

"What am *I* going to do, Mark? About what, exactly?"

"About the baby, Lisa! C'mon, stop busting my chops. I know it's tough, but it's tough on me too, okay? Just let me know if you're going to keep the baby, and I'll start making plans to get more money together."

I heard what I was dreading, and obviously I had screwed up again.

"Aw, please don't cry. I'm sorry. I'm so stressed out right now, I'm liable to say anything. I'm sorry… *please* don't cry."

I waited until she had quieted down.

"Listen, I told you I'll support you if you want to go through with this."

She sniffed. "I was looking through the phone book earlier." I waited. *Why was she looking through the phone book?*

"There's a place in Pittsburgh, about an hour south of here."

"What kind of place? What do you mean?"

"A family planning center."

I flinched. She too had progressed to using the "conscience friendly" terminology.

"Are… are you sure that's what you want to do?"

"I don't know, Mark…" Her voice cracked.

Please don't cry again! I begged silently. "I mean, I support you no matter what," I added quickly.

"What do you think?" she whispered.

I paused. "Well, I guess there is a lot to consider. You do have options if you would rather keep it, and I truly will support you financially. I'll make it work." A sudden flush of anxiety washed over me as I wondered for a second exactly how I *would* make it work and how much monthly cash I would be out.

"I don't know, Mark. To be honest I really can't face the thought of being a single mother. Did you know that single mothers are the demographic most at-risk for living below the poverty line?"

I did not know that. I felt sick again.

"I'm trying to get through business school. I mean, if we did this together… that would be a different story, but…" She trailed off and I stiffened. She sensed it.

"But that's not going to happen," she finished her own sentence, with a sigh. My shoulders turned to concrete. We sat in silence for a few seconds.

"I have $200. It costs $450. Have you got the rest?"

I swallowed hard. "Sure."

"Pick me up at my house tomorrow at 1:00."

"Okay."

Lisa hung up.

Chapter 13

Hollow Eyes

The entire drive to Lisa's house was silent. I didn't play any music, I just drove with my thoughts. And drove and drove and drove. When I pulled up, she opened the door and climbed into the car as her neighbor waved at us. I ignored her. The girl looked over at Lisa in confusion but I didn't care. Lisa didn't even notice.

The drive continued in silence. One look at Lisa told me she was in no mood to talk, which suited me fine. I asked her once, trying to be polite, if she was hungry.

"I can't eat for twelve hours before the anesthesia," she said blankly. I didn't say another word.

After a lifetime we pulled up. It was a storefront clinic in a not-so-new strip mall. In somewhat dilapidated signage I read, *Pittsburgh Family Planning Center.* That was when it dawned on me that Lisa had found this place in the phone book. There was no way to tell how qualified the doctors were. Or doctor. *She'll be fine,* I told myself.

I took a seat in the waiting area, and Lisa stopped and looked at me as though I were an idiot. I wracked my brain and then jumped up. I dug the $250 dollars out of my pocket, and handed it over. She walked up to the desk to fill out the paperwork. She tried three times before she could write her name legibly. I glanced over at three other girls in the waiting area. They all appeared to be about twenty-one years old. Two wore thousand-yard stares, while one snapped her gum and assessed the condition of her nails. Each was alone, and at least two of the faces reflected the burden and confusion that took two to create.

I looked up at the calendar on the wall. 12/31/1987. New Year's Eve. Time for new beginnings. A hassle-free fresh start for us, while it was the end for my unborn child, before life even began. I regretted not being more caring toward Lisa. I looked to see how she was doing, but could only see her back as she bent over the counter. The woman helping her was annoying the life out of me. She was too chipper and all smiles, acting like a life wasn't about to be taken.

I shivered and realized I was wringing my hands. *Why am I getting cold feet all of a sudden?* I wondered. *Don't sweat it man. You have to make sure you can get established first. Or take your time and decide if you want kids. You know you can't deal with a kid now.* I wanted to believe that voice.

Mark. This isn't you. Another, gentler but more powerful voice spoke. *Your girlfriend is pregnant and now she's about to kill your child because you won't man up. Mark Morrow, don't allow the abortion of your child.* I looked around desperately for any escape. *God help me!* I looked at Lisa with a crazy thought. She was still battling through the mountain of waivers. I could get up, take her hand and lead her the heck out of this place.

I was about to do it when I heard, *Your life will be ruined.*

At least take her and try to discuss raising the child with your support. It's all happening too fast! the other voice countered. I shifted in my seat, to see if I could maybe physically take the first step to stop this, but my legs had suddenly turned to Jello.

The door opened and another girl walked in, who couldn't have been a day older than eighteen. She walked to the counter, staring at the ground, and began the process of signing in. The uber-chipper woman began her surreal, chirpy, smiley routine. I had never felt such pure evil in my life before. The whole place had a glossed-over sheen of creepy, and I knew we should just run. But every time I tried to get up, something seemed to hold me in my chair. I'd given the money over already. We'd come this far. We were in the lion's mouth. It was my complacency.

My indecision. My selfishness. A door flung open and a nurse appeared. She addressed Lisa, and before I could make a decision, she was ushering Lisa back into one of the rooms. I wanted to protest, but again, I couldn't. I looked at the other girls, wondering why they weren't going first. They seemed to have no problem with anyone jumping the line. I looked back at the counter and Lisa was gone. I stared blankly into space for about thirty minutes.

Adrift in a world of my own…

What I heard coming from behind the door to the procedure rooms turned my blood to ice. A low guttural wail that turned to a piercing howl. I instantly knew it was Lisa. She wailed again, this time closer and louder, and I stood up, terrified. A doctor and a nurse, each holding one of Lisa's arms, appeared around the corner with frantic expressions. Lisa was hunched over, clutching her belly and her face contorted in grim agony. When she looked up, Lisa's eyes destroyed me. She stared right through me, her eyes desperate and cold. At first I couldn't place what was different, then she coiled over again, and uttered a series of chilling, tortured grunts. The chipper woman at the counter wore a panicked, horrified expression, while the other girls glanced at each other and shifted nervously in their seats.

"Miss Jamison, please try to remain calm… the painkillers will take effect in a minute," the doctor spoke. The translation was clear. "Stop. You're freaking everyone out, especially the other customers."

Instead, Lisa began crying loudly, and I lunged forward to take over and get her out of there. The reason I hadn't sooner was, I was wondering if she didn't need to remain in the clinic in case she needed more medical attention. But the second the thought entered my brain I knew I did not want to spend one more second in the place. Lisa's eyes gazed through me again. They were vacant. It struck me like an avalanche; the light and innocence was gone. Lisa's eyes were hollow.

The doctor held the door open, and offered me a weak nod but was clearly glad to get the disturbance out of the clinic. I wanted to offer my arm as support for Lisa but there was a new, awkward distance between us. I just walked next to her as we made our way to the car. I held the car door open for her as she sobbed like a trauma victim. I placed my hand on her shoulder, expecting her to lean into me, but she gingerly lowered herself into the car instead. I shut the door and walked around to the driver's side, deeply inhaling the icy air and looking up to the frozen, blue sky. I yanked the car door, climbed into the driver's seat, and cranked the engine. Lisa's sobs were loud and consistent. I revved the engine loudly and she looked up with startled eyes. I just stared ahead and thudded the car into gear. I cracked my neck to the side, and tried to relax as I pulled out of the parking lot. I turned on to the main road, trying to distract myself by mentally back-tracing the directions home. Lisa continued sobbing loudly and groaned.

"Lisa…"

I didn't want to be insensitive but it was as though my nerves were open and raw and every sob was a searing hot poker. I knew it was an emotional and painful ordeal, and I tried to comfort her but she ignored me. She kept sobbing and sniffed loudly. I couldn't focus.

"Lisa!" I said, raising my voice. I rounded a corner toward the outer limits of the town, and started picking up speed. Lisa whimpered and clutched the door handle, stiffening, but continued to involuntarily cry and sniff loudly. I couldn't take it.

"LISA CAN YOU GIVE IT A REST FOR A SECOND? I CAN'T EVEN THINK. HE SAID THE PAINKILLERS WILL KICK IN. JUST DEAL WITH IT FOR GOD'S SAKE!" Terrified, Lisa wailed but tried to cover her mouth to stifle her cries. I glared at her, clenching my teeth, and she shut her eyes tightly trying to shut out my rage. I stomped my foot on the gas and the car lurched forward. Lisa yelped in fright but I couldn't have cared less. She was terrified, but clearly not enough to shut her mouth. She began hyperventilating and jerkily snorted involuntarily, desperately trying to stifle the sobs. Sixty… seventy… eighty miles an hour….

"MAAARK, SLOW DOWN!" she shrieked. We bulleted toward a T-junction and for a moment, I thought about blasting through it, slamming into the ditch ahead, and damning us both. At the last second, I geared down and smashed my foot onto the brake, skidding the car to a violent stop in the middle of the road. I flung the door open, jumped out and ran.

I ran and ran and ran. Lisa's howls grew distant but I kept running. The further I ran, the more I sank into the muck and mire of my dying conscience. There was no escaping the condemnation of what I had just done.

Mark Morrow: Youth Leader. Mark Morrow: Sunday school teacher. Mark Morrow: Preacher, Worship Leader, Singer. Ross and Judy Morrow's son has just aborted their grandchild.

I ran and I ran and I ran, but maddeningly, my conscience grew louder. *What is wrong with me? How did I get here?*

Mark Morrow. Baby killer.

Chapter 14

Flirting With Disaster

I collapsed in the field, and screamed until my lungs burned. Then I wept for longer than I could gauge. Eventually, I picked myself up and trudged back to the car. I ignored Lisa's fearful, questioning gaze, and didn't utter a word to her as I drove her home. She had managed to stop crying by the time I got back to the car, and was probably too afraid to talk because she too, didn't say a word. What we both heard loudly and clearly, however, was that nothing would ever be the same between us.

I pulled up to the curb and Lisa struggled out of the car. There was a millisecond's pause—a moment in which I somehow felt her monumental burden of the unspoken tragedy she now carried in her own body. The irrecoverable possibilities of a near-perfect life together. She shut the door and walked away.

―――――

I think, throughout my life, pride has been a significant issue. I've always believed I was somehow better than others—more talented, less prone to dealing with the tedious details of daily living. Sure, I could nurture relationships when I wanted to. Be the gold-star youth leader. Take care of troubled teens... but when it came to any permanent impositions on my life, there was nothing that could sway me. It was me first, and no-one else. No manipulation, no tears, not even genuine heartbreak. And at the end of the day, that's all I had. I had no idea I was becoming a spiritual beggar. Surviving isn't God's plan for us. His plan is for us to thrive, yet we always seem to have a better idea of what that looks like. I learned the hard experience that is a very slippery and dangerous slope.

Little by little I became distracted. I justified myself because I had endured some sufferings that many men before me endured, and so will many men after me. Yet these sufferings are far less than I deserved, if we're discussing punishment for our sins. God placed that punishment on His only Son, and I knew that. So why was I continuing to sin? As I said, it was pride, first and foremost. And blindness. After the abortion with Lisa, something changed in me. You might have thought I would have repented. Come clean. No… Shame ensured I kept my sin a secret. And guilty relief soon began assessing the possibilities. I was about to continue on my way up the roller coaster, yet I was not considering gravity. All that goes up must come down.

———

Jenny was about five years younger than I was, and had also recently graduated from *E.S.C.* with a bachelor's degree in marketing. Jenny was a voluptuous brunette, which was *definitely* my type. She was bubbly and fun to be around but there is a certain amount of ego-boost when it's evident a girl idolizes you. Maybe it was because she was so young, maybe it was because she wasn't a challenge, or maybe it was because she indulged in the one habit that was a deal-breaker for me, but the infatuation was not reciprocated.

The spring of 1988 had finally sprung, the snow had melted, and that meant one thing: time to get my Corvette out of storage. I suppose in many ways, buying a black, two-seat was a sure symbol of defiance, which reflected my lack of desire to have kids. I thought I loved my old Cougar, but a Vette? This car was smokin' hot and turned heads everywhere, especially on the campus of *E.S.C.* Eight years earlier I had to sell my Cougar in order to start college. Now I purred around campus in a sleek Corvette. I had clawed my way to a *highly* sustainable income, and I was pretty pleased with myself.

My 1974 Stingray, large closet with fifteen leather jackets, and the prideful attitude had taken root after searing my conscience to a sin I knew was so heinous.

It all worked in favor of my flesh, and sadly, naive young women ate it all up. The weird part was that I still maintained I had a relationship with my Lord. It was just a little more distant. Like I was a naughty kid who just had a few little problems, but he was really A-okay. I figured He understood. Like a dad giving his knucklehead kid a noogie, grinning that he'll "grow out of this wild phase." But this "wild phase" resulted in the death of a baby. My ignorance of this fact showed how far I'd drifted from my Savior. One glaring cause was, I barely read my Bible at that time. If I had, I might've stumbled across Proverbs chapter 7, and heeded the warnings.

Jenny was a smoker. Practically a chain-smoker, and this was my deal-breaker relationship-wise. I just couldn't stand it. I had a saying; "If Suzanne Somers rang my doorbell and was totally naked, and she asked me to have sex but she was smoking a cigarette, I would shut the door and walk away." I had promised myself a long time ago I would never seriously date a smoker, and I felt very strongly about it. But that didn't stop me from sleeping with Jenny.

One evening, Jenny, myself, and some mutual friends were hanging out at my apartment, watching TV and chatting. As it got late the others left one by one until it was only Jenny and I. We continued chatting and watching TV when she reached out to hold my hand. I looked over at her with an "Oh really?" expression. She drew me closer and kissed me. Within days, we were sleeping together.

I'm not sure if I was Jenny's first, but it sure seemed like it. The funny part was, I knew I could treat this girl however I wanted to, and she'd just keep coming back. For three months it was purely physical. For me at least. Day in and day out, just sex. Once, in a moment of wild passion, the poor girl whispered, "I love you." My silence was deafening. In fact, in three months I had never called her my girlfriend even once. After her little confessional slip, I got bored, and much to Jenny's dismay, broke it off with her.

It happened so slowly, I was failing to recognize a growing void in my soul that was once filled with joy and peace. Because this void grew so slowly, over so many little compromises, I had no idea I'd lost something so precious. The scary part was, because I had played near the edge, and slipped on that slick slope, I now thought I could only fill the void with more sin.

While I was still "dating" Jenny, I had received an invitation to attend my ten year high school reunion. I started reminiscing about my high school friends, so once I'd broken it off with Jenny and I was on the open market again, I dropped in to say hi to a friend named Becky (this was long before Facebook and even cell phones.) Becky's little sister, Kim, answered the door and told me Becky was already married and living in another state. She even had kids. After getting over my surprise, I asked Kim what she'd been up to. Kim already knew me from when I'd come over to hang out with her sister on occasion, so I felt comfortable chatting with her. After feigning shock that I was getting so old my peers were getting married and having kids, I joked that all I had accomplished was making lots of money and buying a Corvette. Kim swallowed down the bait, and immediately asked if she could see the Vette. "Of course," I replied slyly, and escorted her out to my black beauty. We admired the car for a while, until I perfectly timed an offering to take her for a ride. "Yeah, that would be awesome," she replied giddily. I opened the door for her, and cranked the engine to life. Her eyes became a little starrier as I revved it. I pulled out and we cruised around the town on a perfectly star-lit night, talking, joking and listening to great music.

When we got back to her place, we stood by the car, talking, getting physically closer and closer. I had mastered the shy church-boy persona, but Kim wasn't shy at all. She leaned in and kissed me. That was all it took, and in a few days we were sleeping together.

For the next couple of months, Kim and I cruised around in my Vette, hung out almost daily, and thoroughly enjoyed the summer. Even though Kim was only twenty-one, she was super laid-back, and not clingy at all, which suited me perfectly. I came to find out the reason—Kim was actually in a long distance relationship with a guy in Columbus, Ohio, who was going to school to become a pharmacist. She didn't have a problem having sex with me, though. Even though my heart warned me, again, what I was doing was heading for disaster, my brain told me, "This ride is getting pretty freakin' amazing."

In late June, I went to grab a bite at *Uncle Charlie's* with Sherry, a mutual friend of mine and Jenny's. I guess I had my guard up a little, not wanting any vicarious Jenny-drama to seep through Sherry. Maybe I was being defensive but when Sherry said, "You know, Jenny hasn't been feeling too well lately. She's been sick to her stomach a lot," I quickly replied, "Well, if she quit smoking cigarettes she'd feel a lot better." That effectively shut the topic down so we simply continued having dinner and chatting, if a little awkwardly.

Around August, Jenny called me up and asked if we could talk. I groaned, wishing she would just let it go and understand I was never going to get back together with her. I rolled my eyes but agreed, determined to be polite but very firm and maybe she'd finally get the idea. When she came over I offered her something to drink, and we sat on the couch. The couch where only a few months earlier one thing began leading to another.

Jenny came right out and said it.

"Mark, you remember that one time we had sex at my place and you didn't use protection?"

My stomach flipped. "Yeeeah…"

"You got me pregnant that day." She bit her fingernail and her knee bounced wildly. She touched the outline of the pack of cigarettes in her pocket.

"*What?*" *Oh God, not again!*

"Don't worry," she said, strangely placid. "Since I knew how much you loved your Corvette and never wanted to be a family man, I went to a clinic and had an abortion." She looked at me as though I'd realize how much she understood me, and how she was still devoted.

I blinked at her. "Are you freaking kidding me?" I said in a hoarse whisper. Jenny looked confused. *How can you keep doing this?* I wanted to scream to myself. *Aw, not again, please God, not again!*

Jenny just stared at me, a little dumbfounded. Neither of us knew what to say next and to be perfectly honest, from that point, I don't really remember much of the conversation. I mean, what does one say after that? I know I didn't offer her any money. I never even gave her a hug nor showed any type of compassion. I just thought she was crazy, so I was simply cold to her. I just thanked her for telling me, but made it clear I was done with the conversation. She left quickly, her eyes welling up, but I just closed the door behind her and dropped onto the couch, with my head in my hands.

You're sleeping with a girl who has a boyfriend, and you're coming off your second abortion. Way to go, champ!

I play the game but to my real shame…

My heart churned, and the quiet voice assured me again that I had to change. But since I was already sliding halfway down the slope, this was a lot easier said than done.

Jenny was also not a quitter. After telling me she'd had an abortion, she spent a solid month trying to get me back. She'd found out I bought a king-sized water bed with a mirrored ceiling, so she managed to always find me at *The Hotel Bar*. She'd brush up against me while I was shooting pool and whisper how much she'd love to see (and use) my bed. But I was done with her. There was no more challenge, and the bitter taste of her casual attitude toward the abortion had destroyed even the novelty of sleeping with her; so forlorn, and very likely quite broken, she eventually gave up.

Around September, Kim and I had also kind of drifted and fizzled, as I figured we would eventually. I found myself wanting something new. *Maybe a wild redhead this time.* I was becoming a seasoned player, my emotions becoming less and less of an anchor, and my pick-up skills were improving drastically. I began frequenting *The Hotel Bar* more, and at first I would just enjoy a good game of pool with a buddy or two, but I knew what I was really there for. When I'd hang out with a strong Christian buddy, I would ponder my path, and occasionally even tried convincing myself to go cold turkey, and not even think about women. But to do that, I knew I had to confess my sins and I couldn't even approach that kind of crazy thinking.

The weird part was that I still professed my faith and trust in God, and really did my best to follow Jesus in every other way. I knew I had the Holy Spirit living within me. Deep down, I was a Christian for sure, I just wasn't living like one. I was living on "the edge" so to speak, and not in a good way. I was sitting on the fence, not hot, nor cold, and I often thought about Revelation 3:16, "So, because you are lukewarm—neither hot nor cold—I am about to spit you out of my mouth." It scared me, but obviously not enough.

There was just no real accountability. I rarely met with my pastor, and in the event I attended a Bible study, I knew enough Christian-ese to fake my backslidden condition. It was a filthy place to be, but when you put yourself in a position to start with a drink at a bar, and a girl you just know will sleep with you comes over, the flesh just bulldozes over you like an Abrams tank. You've already set yourself up for failure. Sure, during that time, I had thought it through a few times. I asked myself why I couldn't stop. The way I saw it, I had a heart problem. My stumbling block was marriage. I refused to entertain the idea of having children, but I had eased myself into the trap of pre-marital sex. Once I started down that road, it became tougher and tougher to come back. The flesh believes that it needs physical relief. The further down that road I went, the crazier the compromises became. I was like the proverbial frog in a pot of water, slowly being turned up to a boil. He doesn't know he's cooking, and all he has to do is jump out of the pot to survive. But he doesn't. He just sits there, thinking it'll all be okay until it's too late. I wasn't seeking the help I needed to deal with the commitment issue I had, therefore I just couldn't stop.

Chapter 15

Proverbs 16:18

W hen I was first saved and started attending church regularly, right after my dad died, I met a lovely girl named Heather. At that time, Heather was exactly what I looked for in a girl; brunette, voluptuous and innocently pretty. Heather, like me, enjoyed talking about God, music, and attending Christian concerts. We were both nineteen when we met and even though I was still grieving, a couple of months after my dad died I asked her out on a date. I still had my Cougar at the time, so we had fun cruising around, going to movies, playing miniature golf and, of course, eating lots of pizza. We dated exclusively for a short while, then Heather decided to transfer from *E.S.C.* where she had majored in film and media. She had been accepted to a well-known Christian University in California, so when she moved, with three thousand miles separating us, and no cell phones, e-mail or Skype, we lost touch.

Fast forward back to 1988. Through the grapevine I heard Heather had flown home for her Christmas college break. Because Heather was an only child, her mom and dad understandably wanted her to spend a significant amount of time with them, since she didn't get home that often. Nevertheless, I called her up, and after spending a few days with her folks, she agreed to have dinner in a mall restaurant. That was when I found out Heather had a boyfriend (whom her parents really liked.) But we fell right back into our groove, like we'd never been apart. Pretty soon we started opening up to one another and as our conversation deepened, she admitted she was sleeping with her boyfriend. I in turn, admitted to sleeping with a few girls. Strangely, although it started out as confessions of our struggles as believers, the whole conversation had an exciting, taboo sort of feeling. I think it was because it was a real eye-opener for us. We now shared each other's intimate secrets. Secrets which only our lovers knew. I asked her what she was doing on New Year's Eve, and she agreed to accompany me to a big, new dance club in Erie.

My Vette was once again stored away for the winter, which was a bit of a bummer, since it was my lucky deal-sealer. But I picked her up in my fully optioned Chevy Cavalier, which wasn't shoddy by any means. I had visited my mom that week and told her Heather was in town. My mom had met Heather years before, and remembered her as the lovely young girl she was. Surprisingly, Bob gave me fifty dollars to take her out to a nice restaurant, so I grinned, thanked him, and pocketed the cash.

Heather and I had a dinner straight out of a romance novel. Everything about it was refined and romantic, from the candles on the white tablecloth to the waiter in a suit. After enjoying each other's company and an outstanding dinner, I could tell Heather was ready to let her hair down. We hit the club where the energy was through the roof. Loud music pounded through huge speakers, while the best D.J. in the region spun some of the most awesomely eighties dance music known to man.

Soon we were dancing, flirting, and getting closer and closer. When midnight rolled around, everyone in the club shouted the countdown out loud together. As we reached zero, I yelled out "Happy New Year!" and pulled Heather into me and kissed her. When she reciprocated, we both knew she was coming home with me. We fled the club and headed back to my place. After a few hours of lustful, unprotected passion, I dropped her at home just before sunrise.

As I left, I thought back to *exactly* one year earlier—I was lying catatonic on my bed, having just left an abortion clinic, after terminating my first child. Since then, a different girl had aborted another one of my babies, and here I was, at it again. I pushed the thought to the back of my mind.

Heather flew back to school a week later, and life continued as usual. I was looking forward to the new year, as I had some lofty goals. I wanted to start graduate classes for my master's degree in the fall. I had some new programs lined up for the youth group, I had some preaching engagements lined up, and I had a great game plan for taking care of the boys in my care. At first, Heather wrote me a few letters, which I always enjoyed receiving, and I wrote back. We would discuss the passion of our one night, how amazing and yet how bad it was. It was fun talking about it but soon the novelty wore off. After a while the letters stopped coming, which was okay with me. I was beyond really being hung up on anyone.

One day around March, however, a letter from Heather surprised me. I opened it up, eager to see what kind of naughty stuff she was thinking, but as I started reading, I froze. In the brief note, Heather wrote that I had impregnated her that night. She went on to say she'd driven to Los Angeles and aborted the baby. The letter fell from my hands, and I stood in my bedroom, trembling yet numb.

What. Are. You. Doing? my mind screamed. *You're like The Sperminator, man. Every girl you sleep with gets pregnant!* Predictably, I jumped into my Corvette, which I'd just retrieved from storage a week earlier. I felt like driving until I ran out of gas. As I stared into the distance, with the highway flying by, I felt cold and dead inside. I could almost feel my heart was callousing over. I couldn't believe I'd been so stupid. I felt guilty, but this time, instead of resolving to stop sleeping around, I resolved to be more careful and always carry protection. I scolded myself for being so careless, and in the dark recesses of my mind, a familiar old voice said, *It's because you're trying to be all goodie two-shoes and deny that you're sometimes going to sleep with women. Just carry protection, man!*

I mailed Heather a card, a check for four hundred dollars, and a big, stuffed teddy bear. In the card I wrote I was so sorry about getting her pregnant, was praying for her, and if there was anything I could do to make her feel better, I would. I received no response.

It was at times like this that my conscience would seep through the cracks in the fortifications I'd built. As much as I tried to repress my sins, in my moments at church, or when talking to a solid brother in Christ, or not hearing back from a good girl who'd aborted through my refusal to take responsibility, I knew I was living two lives. In the one life, in all major ways except sexual morality, I was righteous, loving God, and serving Him. I ran the youth group, truly cared for those kids, and guided them in the right paths. In my ulterior life, I was a proud, immoral hypocrite who had no idea how lost he really was.

The weird thing was, every time I tried to stop, or had a crisis of conscience, I was presented with the opportunity to regress ten times worse.

Around April of 1989, I started seeing another girl, named Amy. Amy was really cool, and laid back. I'm not sure if Amy sensed intuitively not to push me into a relationship or was just taking it slow herself, but she wasn't in any hurry for commitment. After a few weeks, we weren't officially an item, but I think it was safe to say it was headed that way.

I had tried to avoid sleeping with Amy at first, but immediately my old flesh demanded more. Before long we were sleeping together. One afternoon in early May, I had been over to visit my grandparents, and they asked me who I was bringing to their fiftieth wedding anniversary. They were so proud that I was preaching, they had asked me to officiate when they renewed their vows. Of course, I accepted, and was really excited since I knew it was set to be a very special party.

Amy had to work, so I told my grandma I would probably just fly solo. My grandmother asked, "Whatever happened to that lovely Lisa girl?" I told her we still kept in touch a little, but I hadn't spoken to her in a while. "Oh, she's such a lovely young lady!" Grandma crooned. I hadn't seen Lisa in a while, and that was enough to spark the thought of *Why not?* I called her up and to my surprise, we had a really good conversation. She said she'd love to come. I didn't say a word to Amy of course.

As it turned out, Heather had just arrived home for the summer too. I was bored one night when Amy was busy so I called Heather up to see if she wanted to grab something to eat. She said yes, but she needed a little while to get ready, so I said that was cool and took the Vette for a wash. I knew it would be safe to hang out with Heather because of the abortion. We still hadn't discussed it, and I knew she was serious about her boyfriend, so I figured we'd just have a fun evening.

I picked her up in my freshly washed and waxed Vette, and we went out to eat. During dinner Heather announced she had something special for me. I didn't notice her bringing anything in with her, so I gave her a puzzled look. She looked around slyly, and then flashed a silky teddy she was wearing under her dress. My flesh melted like rice paper in rain, so I stuffed my dinner down, yanked her out of that restaurant, and drove my Vette around the back of a baseball field… and I gave in to my sinful desires. The next night I slept with Amy.

When Sunday rolled around I went to church in the morning, then got ready for a fun day with my grandparents. I had to admit I was a little excited to see Lisa. We both knew there were still feelings there. When she arrived, she looked stunning. She had really gone all out, wearing a beautiful, white sundress, flowers in her hair, and an elegant pearl necklace. Lisa had always gotten along well with my family, and more than a few people asked why we weren't back together. I knew I was in trouble the minute I laid eyes on her.

By that time, I was so steeped in my dual lifestyle, when she asked me where the iced tea was, and I followed her inside to show her, and she took me by the hand to one of the bedrooms upstairs, I was prepared with the condom. As the great Robert Burns said in not so many words, despite my best laid plans, the condom broke.

As I drove home that night, I couldn't resist smugly thinking what a crazy week it had been. Sure, I felt a little guilty for sleeping with three women, but I couldn't deny I had never felt cooler in my whole life. Because no one was confronting me about my sin, and I was extremely good at keeping up appearances, my secret life had become part of my identity. Kind of like a second job you maintained, except it was secret, which made it cooler. I knew the rules by heart now. I had developed an intuition for which situations would require more of a poker face, and how to attract the least amount of attention to my relationships. I was a veteran hypocrite.

———

Lisa and I never spoke much about that day, and pretty much just carried on our separate lives. So three months later when I was exclusively dating Amy, I was more than a little surprised to receive a call from Lisa.

"Mark?"

"Hey! Lisa… what's up? What have you been up to, stranger?"

"Oh, just school and stuff. How have you been?"

"Pretty good. What's shakin'?"

"Hey, umm… can I drive up to see you this Sunday?"

"Uh, not sure that's a good idea. My girlfriend and I are visiting my sister, and I don't know what time we'll be driving back? She'll be with me all day."

"Well, I really want to talk to you, Mark. Can you find a way to make it happen?"

I sighed. I didn't know what Lisa wanted to talk about, but I had a strong suspicion, after what had happened at my grandparents' anniversary. I suspected her feelings had become all fired up again, and she was going to try to convince me to get back together with her. It was easier to just meet her and talk her down, instead of risking her calling while Amy was at my place or something.

"Yeah, okay. Let me talk to Amy, and if she doesn't mind, that sounds fine." I waited for her to say something snarky about me having to get Amy's permission.

"Okay, well, let me know. I'll hopefully see you on Sunday then."

"Okay, cool." I couldn't believe I was getting off that easily.

"Talk to you later." She hung up.

Chapter 16

Of Mice and Men

That day in the park, when Lisa told me the news of our second—my fourth—abortion, I felt physically ill. Although I knew I was doing wrong, I was locked into a destructive rut that was beyond my power to escape. The truth is, I was completely in denial but couldn't see it.

In my heart, I knew Lisa would abort again. When she called me and told me she had just gone ahead and aborted again, I knew I was responsible. Again. So I did what I'd always done. I ran out to my car, dropped my foot on the gas pedal, and kept trying to outrun my horror until the world was a streaking, peripheral blur.

Except, this time felt different. Not just because it was the fourth abortion—it had something to do with it being with Lisa again. We had gone from being the model, innocent young couple devoted to God, to shipwrecked shells of agony and lies. Worst of all, we'd left two aborted babies in our wake.

Lisa looked so lovely in her sundress. I knew all she wanted in the world was for me to say I would marry her, and that we could be a family. That might have almost made up for the first baby. But I just couldn't do it. When I bluntly refused to marry her, I thought I could easily handle the fallout, but I was dead wrong. I could not get the image of Lisa's tears out of my head; I replayed her tortured whimpers over and over and over in my head. It was more than that though. It was the look of pure hopelessness, and even worse… utter regret as she climbed into her car. Her hollow eyes had almost flickered with hope again. This time, I'd made very sure they were cold, dead, and all hope was buried.

I slowly lifted my foot off the gas pedal, succumbing to the fact that I couldn't outrun myself. A crushing weight descended slowly upon me.

———

At a casual glance, life went back to normal. Then again, normal for me meant I still had a huge, gaping hole in my spiritual walk. I was still leading the youth group, still known as an outspoken Christian, and still hitting *The Hotel Bar* pool room, hunting for hookups. Oh, I was still telling myself I was just going to shoot pool, but women were always the bottom-line.

Pretending I'm doing well…

In hindsight, it was easy to see I'd crafted my life to lure and close the deal with women. I drove a Corvette, wore unique and expensive leather jackets, and knew how to land what I desired. It was safe to say something inside was very, very broken. I couldn't face getting married as much as I couldn't face not having sex. Contrary to the cataclysmic guilt I was stuffing down deep in my soul, pride oozed from every crack of my soul. In fact, I was so deceived, all I could ask when disaster struck, time and again, was, "Why is this happening to me?" I never once stopped to accept responsibility. I fully believed I was the victim, while I was victimizing women and innocent babies.

One positive thing I had going for me was starting classes at *EUP* in the fall of 1990, toward my Master's in Guidance Counseling. But of course, this meant girls and more girls. One of my classes was on the second floor of Compton Hall, which was where I had taken a ton of undergrad classes. Radio I and II, Television I and II, Advanced Public Speaking and more were all in Compton, so I already knew many of the students and teachers. The bottom half of the building was primarily Speech Communications and Psychology, but I happened to know many of the professors because I had gone to high school with their children. I was definitely in my element at that building, and a beautiful thing about graduate counseling degrees was, the students comprised about an eighty percent to twenty percent ratio of girls to guys, respectively. I thought I was in heaven.

I began the semester sitting outside my classrooms, waiting for the professor to show up, scoping out the girls. Soon I was on a first name basis with many of them, so I'd call them over to throw out my flirting A-game. One of my favorite classes was Group Discussion, because I was about the only guy in there. In that class, I was initially teamed up with a girl around my age named Jeannie. We were told to interview each other, as though we were in a professional setting. I grinned to myself because Jeannie was *gorgeous*.

I casually asked how old she was, and she told me she had just turned twenty-eight. *Two years younger than me.* She had pretty, long, blonde hair, hazel eyes, and a stunning figure. Best of all she had a beautiful, friendly smile, and a totally laid-back personality. I played it cool, obviously, and acted as if she were just another average girl but we hit it off immediately, interviewing each other.

I asked her about a little Asian trinket she had hanging off her purse and she explained she and her three-year-old daughter had recently arrived back from a trip to Tokyo. They were visiting Jeannie's older sister, Lynn, who was married to a Japanese man. I feigned fascination, but was already pretty much derailed at "three-year-old daughter." Jeannie was so beautiful though, with a matching personality, so just being curious, I let it play. I rambled about my Corvette, and dropped the obligatory comments about the money I made at my three jobs. Strangely, Jeannie was polite but maintained a poker face. Either that or she wasn't really impressed by my showboating. But that couldn't be possible, could it?

I now knew Jeannie's name, however, and a little about her, so I had an angle. The next day I saw her coming down the hall so yelled out, "Hey, I dream of Jeannie!" She couldn't help but laugh, so feeling inspired, I immediately started singing and dancing to the *I Dream of Jeanie* theme song. *Doo do, do do do doo do… doo do, do do do doo do!* She rolled her eyes but flashed her stunning smile, and instantly I knew I had a shot. I liked the challenge, even though I wasn't sure about the three-year-old. The other students laughed too, probably thinking *This Mark guy is pretty out there, but definitely uninhibited.* But I had her attention, and she definitely had mine.

The next class, the lecturer put us into small groups of six to eight people for a discussion assignment. We had to write down ten things we didn't like about ourselves, and wanted to change. The other students got to work quickly, scribbling down laundry lists of things they didn't like about themselves. I sat there and tried to think of something. I thought about whether or not I didn't like the fact I'd put side exhaust pipes on my Corvette, but I wasn't sure that qualified. I wracked my brain but couldn't come up with a single thing I didn't like about myself. I thought I was pretty well put together.

We went around the circle, and the other students shared their lists (which, honestly, was a little too personal for my taste) but eventually the group looked at me expectantly. It was my turn to publicly list my shames so the catharsis could begin and, more importantly, keep us on an equal playing field. My page was blank. I could not come up with one item. After double digits of women in my wake and four abortions, there was not a single thing I wanted to change.

"I think I'm pretty okay," I said with a grin. Jeannie stared at me incredulously, but I stuck to my guns. I had worked hard to get where I was, and I was happy with that. I thought that might have thrown Jeannie off a bit, so before everyone left, I threw out an invitation to the group as a whole. I'd been working out quite a bit and had been to a bodybuilding show a few months before. I found it an entertaining, if unique experience, so with another competition coming up, I extended an open invitation to meet me there. Jeannie was the only one to give me a call. I smiled as we talked, knowing she was my next girl.

Jeannie and my first date to a bodybuilding competition was definitely weird, but it actually turned out to be a really fun date. She met me there, and once we found our seats, we settled in and couldn't help cracking up at some of the dudes in their nasty little neon Speedos. I had to admit these guys were ridiculously shredded though, and I wondered if there was any way possible to get that big and ripped without juicing. Jeannie guaranteed me there wasn't, and said huge muscles like that were gross anyway. I smiled, winked and put my arm around her.

After the show we grabbed something to eat and again I was struck by how chill Jeannie was. I found myself opening up to her a lot more than I usually did with other girls, and even though she was gorgeous, she wasn't high maintenance. I had to admit I was getting along with her really well. *It's going to be a shame when I get tired of this one,* I thought to myself. I didn't feel a thing about my arrogance.

But Jeannie threw a curveball at me. She invited me over to her house for dinner. With her kid. My head said, "Heeeck no!" but there was something about

Jeannie that drew my heart in. She was warm and fun, but highly intelligent, too. And she wasn't desperate. I really liked that about her.

So I graciously accepted and drove over to her house that night. As the door opened I was greeted by the ever-cheerful Jeannie and an aroma of something phenomenal cooking in the kitchen. *Oh this girl is good.* I grinned to myself. Jeannie gave me a hug and said she wanted to introduce me to her daughter. My stomach bubbled.

I followed Jeannie to the living room and there sat the prettiest little girl with curly blonde hair, looking up at me with wide eyes. She was suddenly far more interested in this big, strange man with the weird glasses than in her cartoons. I smiled and waved.

"Hi, Ricque!" I said.

She glanced at her mom in consternation.

"Honey, this is Mr. Mark, my friend. Remember I told you he was coming over for dinner!" Ricque wasn't sold.

"Say hi, please."

"Hi."

I had to break the ice. "Is that Bugs Bunny? I *love* Bugs Bunny!"

"Yep," She nodded and turned back to her cartoons.

Jeannie shook her head and smiled, and led me by the hand into the kitchen. "Come and see what I've made."

On the kitchen table was a huge salad and fresh baked dinner rolls. Jeannie opened the oven.

"Oh, my gosh! Look at that chicken!" It smelled like heaven. I was starving and she'd roasted a whole chicken in some herbs or something that smelled like a Michelin star dish. Jeannie winked at me, and asked if I could help set the table. I gladly obliged, and in minutes we were all ready to sit down at the dinner table.

We started eating and I suddenly felt awkward. Ricque just stared at me, until her mom chastised her, and then she just looked down for a few seconds and picked at her food. Then she looked back up at me. The good news was, it seemed as though men in the house was a rarity. I tried smiling back at Ricque while I ate, but she eyed me up and down.

I could see the little gears ticking in her head. *Who is this guy, and why is he in our apartment?* I began to wonder the same thing. Jeannie started to make conversation, and I responded, but then uncomfortable silence filled the air again. It became a quiet dinner for the three of us, and the silverware clattered deafeningly on the plates as we ate. I wondered if Jeannie was having doubts as well.

After dinner I helped Jeannie clear the table, and Ricque started playing with some toys scattered around their small living room. Jeannie and I got back into conversation mode a little, but every time we'd start laughing or joking, Ricque would squawk something from the living room. Jeannie would go in and check on her, and then she'd be quiet for a while, and we'd start having a bit of fun again, and Ricque would ask for something loudly. I smiled patiently, but it was starting to wear on me.

After about an hour or so, it was time for Ricque to go to bed, and I muttered a prayer of relief. I waited downstairs and looked around the apartment as Jeannie tucked her in. Ricque must have insisted on being read a long story, because it took forever before Jeannie came back downstairs. *Finally!* I thought to myself, and put my arms around Jeannie's waist.

"Thanks for the awesome dinner! Man, you're a great cook!"

"Aww… thanks. It was nothing… you should see when I go all out." I was about to respond with a *Oh, whatever!* when we heard a scream.

"*Mooommmm!*"

"Whoa…" I said, startled.

"Oh, I'm sorry. Let me just go check on her. She's just over-tired."

Jeannie ran upstairs, and the screaming stopped. She came downstairs again, and we started talking.

"*Mooommmm!*" Ricque wasn't giving up without a fight.

"She'll quiet down. We just have to ignore her for a while," Jeannie assured me. I nodded, and tried to keep talking normally, but it was tough, as Ricque kept screaming. I had to laugh a little.

We sat there for a few more minutes, waiting for Ricque to give up, but she was determined. I knew it was because her mom was downstairs sharing her time with a strange man. I felt bad for the kid, but it was also something I wasn't used to on a date. *Was it even a date if the kid is here, too?* I mused.

Ricque just kept screaming and screaming and screaming. It was so loud and nonstop that Jeannie eventually suggested we take some plastic chairs and sit in the basement, near the furnace. We did, and sat chuckling about it. The funniest part was, we could still hear Ricque screaming for another hour.

So I had a dilemma on my hands. I *loved* Jeannie's company, but I was already seriously apprehensive about having children in my life. I mean, I was at least fifty percent responsible for four abortions. *And the kid was screaming her head off on our first date. That isn't a good start. How is this going to work?*

Then a strange thing happened. I realized I was curious. There was something about sitting around the dinner table with a little munchkin staring at me that I found amusing. I suddenly knew I wanted to give it another try.

That Saturday, Jeannie asked if I wanted to go and see a movie with them. She was taking Ricque to see *Teenage Mutant Ninja Turtles*, and I figured it couldn't hurt. I had watched episodes of the Turtles' cartoon with some of the boys at *Hermitage House*, and thought they were kind of funny.

That Saturday night, I came to pick them up in the Vette.

"Say hi to Mark, Ricque," her mom coaxed, as I stood at the front door.

"Hi," she grinned, and then ran away and hid her face in the couch.

"Oh, see… she's getting to know you now!" Jeannie smiled.

"Yeah! She knows to run and hide…" I laughed. Jeannie rolled her eyes and playfully punched my arm.

"C'mon baby, come and see Mark's cool car! It's a Corvette."

Ricque came trotting over curiously, not sure what a Corvette was, or why it was considered cool.

"You ready to go, Munchkin?" Jeannie said as she ruffled Ricque's blonde curls.

"Where's the Car Vet?" she asked with big eyes. We both stifled a laugh.

"It's a *Cor*vette, angel. And it's right outside. Come, let's go take a drive in it. It can go very fast but Mark promised not to go too fast."

Ricque eyed me suspiciously but was intrigued about the buzz of this car. She poked her head outside.

Then I had a brainwave. "C'mon… if you say hi, the Corvette will blink her lights and say hi back," I promised. *Where did that come from?* I wondered to myself. Ricque looked up at her mom who was grinning widely at me, and she nodded.

"Yeah, it's true," her mom confirmed. "If you say hi to the Corvette, it'll say hi back." Ricque took her mom's hand, and stepped out gingerly onto the porch to get a better view of the sentient car. I winked at Jeannie, and held the keyless entry remote in my hand.

"Say hi to the Corvette, baby," Jeannie prompted.

Ricque stood at the end of the porch and looked back at me. I smiled and nodded.

"Hi Car Vet!" she waved quickly to the car.

I pressed the lock button twice and the car chirped and the blinkers flashed. Ricque whirled around with eyes as big as softballs and jumped up and down excitedly.

"Mommy, the Car Vet said hi, she said hi!"

Jeannie laughed and said, "I know, sweetie. Isn't she a smart car? And she likes you!" Jeannie looked at me as if I had just won People Magazine's award for the most attractive man in the world. I felt a strange, sudden warmth I'd never experienced before.

"Hi, Car Vet!" Ricque squealed again, jumping up and down, waving excitedly. I pressed the lock button again and the car chirped and blinked. Ricque couldn't get enough of it and jumped around madly on the porch. We both had to laugh at how adorable she was.

"Ricque, do you want Car Vet to drive you to the movies?"

"*Yes!*" she shouted without a nanosecond of hesitation.

I laughed again, and said, "Alright! She'd love that! Let's go." Jeannie had to restrain Ricque from running out to the curb, but she smiled at me again with those dreamy eyes, and I was surprised at how good it made me feel.

After opening the passenger door, it suddenly dawned on me: *Mark, you idiot, this is a coupe! There is no room for three people, even if one of them is a little tyke who weighs less than forty pounds.* I looked at Jeannie and she looked back at me, and we both chuckled, while Ricque tried to scramble into the front seat. Jeannie finally suggested that we jump into her little Horizon. I felt terrible.

After no small amount of protesting by the munchkin, and a promise that I would take her for a ride someday in the Car Vet, we eventually got Ricque all strapped in the backseat of the Horizon, while Jeannie hopped into the driver's seat. Being 6' 4" tall, I contorted my large frame so I could fit into her passenger seat. We headed down to our excellent and affordable little Village Cinema to see the *Ninja Turtles. Huh… I guess this is what a little family feels like,* I thought happily for a moment. A strong wave of anxiety then forced me to chill out. I really did enjoy making the kiddo laugh, and it was great to see Jeannie's face light up… but in no way was I ready to step into the role of daddy.

We had a blast at the movies, even though Jeannie had to take Ricque out several times; she was too restless, the fighting scenes were a little too scary for her or she had to go the bathroom. I offered to help, but when Jeannie said she was okay, I just enjoyed the movie.

That Wednesday, I took Jeannie and Ricque out for ice-cream at our downtown Dairy Isle. This time I was smart enough to pick them up in my Escort. The next Saturday we played miniature golf, and I found it rewarding teaching Ricque how to putt the ball. When she became frustrated, I started a sword-fighting duel with the putters. I had no idea little girls could swing so hard, and her little plastic putter didn't tickle when it caught my knuckles!

The next weekend, we saw another movie, and then went for a drive in the country, singing *Sesame Street* songs as we wound along the scenic roads. I was outside of my comfort zone, but on most levels I caught myself actually having fun. I pondered over how Ricque had firmly weaseled her own little place into my heart. And the way Jeannie looked at me when I played with her made me feel, strangely, like more of a man. But the occasional waves of anxiety persisted, and I had no idea why.

I would also stay over at Jeannie's place sometimes. By this point, we were sleeping together, and although I was convicted about it, it almost felt a little "more right" because I was playing family. But the more we hung out, the more I began to figure out the waves of anxiety.

There I was, sleeping with a woman who had a child, getting myself deeper and deeper into a relationship which I knew would be tougher than usual to escape from. Without even desiring it, I wanted the *option* of something fresh, and I didn't want to deal with the fallout. When I was in the moment with Jeannie and Ricque, the world couldn't have made more sense… but thinking about committing to the future terrified me for some reason. I think it was at that point, I began to realize my issues were more about my insecurity, and brokenness, and… fear of failure. And ironically, my terror of failure had, this far, caused me to fail spectacularly. Four times. But Jeanie was so wonderful. If I had believed in soul mates at that time,

I would have told anyone without hesitation, Jeannie was mine. But a desperate, raving fear of commitment gnawed at my soul.

Chapter 17

How to Break a Tiny Heart

About ten weeks into our bliss, I told Jeannie I wanted to take her out to dinner, so she scheduled a babysitter for Ricque, and the two of us went out to have some fun. I took her to a great seafood restaurant in Erie, and we were having the best time when she looked at me and said, "Mark, I just love how natural you are with Ricque."

I chuckled, and remarked how great Ricque was, but anxiety knotted my gut. Then I asked, "You've never told me where her biological father is. Does he help at all? Come to think of it, you never talk about him."

Jeannie nodded as she weighed up how to respond. "Yeah, he's not around."

I frowned. "He's not in town?"

"He's in town… he's just out of the picture."

"Whoa. I'm really sorry about that. It must be tough."

"Yeah, it hasn't been easy. Especially financially."

Before I could stop myself, I asked, "Why did you have a child out of wedlock though?"

Jeannie reeled in astonishment, visibly hurt.

"I'm so sorry, Jeannie—I didn't—that came out completely wrong." I shook my head. "I mean, what made you think it was a good idea?" I groaned, knowing I was digging a deeper hole, so I stopped talking.

Jeannie wasn't happy. "Well, for starters, you know I'm Roman Catholic, so I've never believed in abortion." I flinched, but nodded as if to say, *Obviously.*

"Did your folks persuade you to keep the baby?" I asked, blowing my own mind at how blunt I was being. The words just kept coming out like that.

Jeannie replied, "Actually, Ricque's biological father tried to convince me to abort." She looked at me as though she hardly knew me. "He put a lot of pressure on me, but I wouldn't give in. And just look at Ricque..." she said with an edge of defiance. "My beautiful little daughter. He wanted me to kill her."

The mood at our table had completely changed. Jeannie was now sitting up straight, and leaning away from me. "You can't tell me that even though she was just a few cells at some point..." Jeannie made air quotes with her fingers, "... she wasn't going to become the beautiful child she is today." I nodded in obvious agreement but I thought I might throw up.

"Yes, it has been extremely difficult," Jeannie continued. "I've had to ask for help from my parents, for money, diapers, baby sitting here and there and they've paid for my car. I've been working myself to the bone, putting myself through school to better our life. I've had to rely on food stamps, the Women, Infants, and Children program, HUD Housing Assistance... all of that. But don't, for one second, think I regret my decision. Ricque and I are doing just fine." I kept nodding and finally kept my mouth shut.

"It's not the picture of the prince marrying the princess and living happily ever after that I dreamed of as a little girl, but I'm by no means unhappy," she concluded.

I was floored. I had never given even a thought to how difficult it was for single, unwed mothers. It dawned on me how astoundingly brave Jeannie had to be to make the unselfish decision to carry, bear, raise, and cherish her baby *and* fight to make a better life for the two of them. I had never felt like such a lowlife.

I'd been making decent money when I was dating Lisa back in eighty-seven, I mused silently. *Between the two of us, we could have easily worked things out.* I chewed my lip as I tried to add something up.

"Say... when was Ricque born?" I asked.

"September twenty-fifth. In eighty-seven. Three years ago."

Jeannie thought I was asking how long she'd had to fight so hard for survival, but I was counting back to when Lisa and I had conceived the first baby. *They were only three months apart!* My eyes widened; here was Jeannie, a confessed believer in the idea of Christ, but never really understanding the scriptures about what it means to be born again. Neither did she know much about having a personal, daily relationship with Jesus... yet she defied all odds to keep her baby. A dark, heavy shroud descended slowly over me. Jeannie noticed the change, and asked if I was okay.

"Uhh... yeah, I just feel terrible you had to go through all that," I half-lied. I did feel terrible for her, but I felt worse about myself. I was beginning to hate the person I had become.

After that, we tried to make light conversation, but despite how much I tried to cover it up, and how forgiving she was, I had offended Jeannie, and there was now an apprehension in her eyes. Then the guilt started to eat me alive, and all I wanted to do was escape. I told Jeannie I didn't feel well after all, and dropped her off. I called one of my buddies to see if he wanted to shoot some pool, and thankfully he was up to it, so I jumped in my car and headed to *The Hotel Bar*.

That night the itch returned with a vengeance. I honestly loved the time I'd had with Jeannie and Ricque, *But who am I kidding?* I told myself. *I could never really be a dad. Not after what I've done. You're always gonna be haunted. You don't deserve to play family. Jeannie is right to be apprehensive of you!* I figured even if I ever did want to do the whole family thing—which I didn't—I'd have to confess my sins and there was no way I could do that. And definitely not to Jeannie after I'd made her feel like total crap for having a child out of wedlock. *After all,* I thought grimly... *we're coming up on the three month mark.*

I started hanging out with my friends more. Shooting pool more. Flirting with random girls at the bar more. Jeannie soon noticed the difference in my attitude, and one day she phoned me and called me out on it.

"What's going on with you, Mark? Are you still interested in our relationship?" she asked directly.

I hesitated. "I don't know Jeannie..."

"What do you mean? You don't know if you're interested or you don't know what's going on?"

I sighed dramatically. I had this part down to a science. "Jeannie, you know I care about you… Hanging out with you is a ton of fun, and you're an awesome person, and I really respect you. But I must be honest… I just don't know if I'm cut out for this level of commitment. I'm really sorry." I braced myself for the waterworks.

"Are you freaking kidding me, Mark?" Jeannie said, matter-of-factly.

"Huh?" I replied, dumbly. *Wait, this is new. Oh Lord, I hope she's not gonna flip out on me.*

"Mark! Are you trying to tell me that the level of commitment to a rewarding relationship is a huge surprise to you?"

I was caught off guard. No girl had ever held me accountable for my selfishness before. "Nooo… I'm just saying, I don't think I'm ready to play dad at this point in my life." It came out defensively, and even I knew I sounded like a jerk.

"So you just now figured that out, huh? You're willing to sleep with me, tolerate my daughter, but as soon as you're bored, you're not ready to commit?"

"Jeannie… C'mon honey. Please let's not do this." I tried to palm it off on her. I was not ready to deal with this weird new accountability and… *logic!*

"Wow, I see. Okay Mark, that's fine. Do what you want to do, but I am not going to budge on this—you need to come and tell Ricque yourself! You haven't just played games with me, Mark. You know how attached she's grown to you, and I'm sure as hell not going to be the one who tells her you've decided that you had no idea what you were getting into."

"Oh come on, Jeannie! She'll understand." I was instantly terrified.

"Mark, she'll eventually get over it, because she's tough, but if you're not a punk and you want to retain a shred of honor, leading that youth group and being all involved in church, you will do the right thing and come and tell this little girl in person that you won't be with us any longer! And you can explain to her why, while you're at it."

Schizophrenically opposed emotions surged through my body. I was angry at Jeannie for having the audacity to say those things to me, but I knew she was right. Anger, guilt, shame, and… regret swarmed through my head and heart. I had to tell Ricque myself. I may have been a commitment-phobe, but I still had my dignity.

"*Fine!*" I barked. "I'll head over tomorrow tonight and tell her."

"Well, good!" Jeannie replied firmly. "What time should we expect you?"

"Around seven, after work," I said, suddenly feeling defeated.

"See you at seven!"

The next day was one, long, bad mood and I even grew irritable with my two boys at the house. The day dragged on and on in dread, as I desperately tried to figure out the best way to break a three-year-old's heart. Finally, six-forty-five arrived, and I left for Jeannie's house. I narrowly avoided a panic attack in the car, and walked up the sidewalk and rang her doorbell. I heard the scamper of little feet, then Ricque's melodic little voice demanded, "Who's there?"

I'd usually respond with something like "Cookie Monster! Me want *cookies*!" in a loud, gruff voice. Ricque would squeal and run around behind the door giggling and shouting that I was not allowed to have any cookies. But that night I couldn't say anything.

"Who's *there*?" Ricque insisted. I was about to ring the doorbell again but mercifully, I heard Jeannie's footsteps coming down the hall. The door opened, and there stood Jeannie, looking lovely as ever. Her eyes were a little red and puffy, but she kept a brave face.

"Mark!" Ricque yelled as she ran around her mom, and hugged my leg.

My stomach sank. "Hey, precious girl!" I said, and squeezed her shoulder.

"Angel, Mark has something he has to tell you, okay? Let's go sit on the couch." Jeannie cast me a disappointed glance, but bravely walked Ricque to the living room. I felt like the devil himself, and immediately wished I had just chickened out of this whole thing.

"Go ahead," Jeannie said as she waved to Ricque, who was sitting on the couch looking up at me with a grin, and big, curious eyes.

I knelt down next to her. "Ricque—" my voice cracked, and I had to clear my throat. My nose burned and my eyes welled up. *Hold it together, dude!*

"Ricque, angel… I ummm…. Mark won't be able to come around and hang out any more. It's not that I don't want to…" *Don't lie to her.* I told myself. *But I'm not lying to her. I actually do enjoy hanging out with them.* I argued with myself while Ricque looked at her mom, starting to get scared. *So why are you doing this, crazy?* I exhaled deeply. *Oh God, help me. My heart is about to be ripped in half.* Ricque looked back at me anxiously.

"I just won't be able to make it around anymore, okay?" I didn't know what else to say.

Ricque looked up at her mom, her bottom lip creasing up. Then she looked back at me, "But why?"

"Aw honey…" I wiped a tear from my eye. "I can't explain now… I just can't, okay?" My soul shattered into a thousand pieces.

"Why, Mommy?" Ricque persisted. "Why can't he come around anymore?"

I looked away at the floor, and sniffed too loudly. "I don't know, baby," Jeannie said honestly. I looked up at her, and realized her eyes were wet now too.

"Ricque, I'm so sorry my angel. You'll always be my friend and I'll always care about you, okay?" I had to get out of there.

She puckered up and looked back at her mom. "Mark, please don't go!"

That destroyed me. I started crying freely, but all I could say was, "I'm sorry, baby. I really am." I had never felt so ashamed in my entire life.

Ricque started crying as well, and Jeannie struggled to hold back her tears. The whole situation suddenly became way too heavy for me. I had to escape. I stood up and patted Ricque on the head. She jumped off the couch and clung to my leg. "Please don't go!" she cried again. I squeezed her little shoulder and covered my eyes with my other hand and sobbed like a baby. Jeannie bent down and gently pried Ricque off my leg, and picked her up. Ricque stretched her arms out to me. "Mark! Please don't go!"

"Do you have anything else to say?" she asked me.

I shook my head, completely defeated.

"I'm so sorry," I said again.

"Give Mark a hug before he goes, baby," Jeannie said, and held Ricque out to me. Ricque grabbed me and clung to my neck as if for dear life. I squeezed her tightly, sobbing into her little shoulder.

"I'm sorry, angel. I will really miss you. Maybe I can come visit some time, okay?" Ricque wailed and clutched my neck desperately.

"Come girl, Mark has to go now. Say goodbye," Jeannie said softly, taking hold of her little arms.

I let go of her so her mom could take her. "Nooo," Ricque wept, struggling to hold on to my neck. Jeannie gently pried her little hands away. When Ricque knew she had lost her grip she turned away from me, into her mom's shoulder and sobbed hysterically.

It was more than I could handle. I rubbed her little back, and desperately avoided Jeannie's eyes.

"Bye, Ricque. I love you sweet girl."

I walked through the front door with Ricque's cries echoing behind me. I stopped on the front porch and wept freely for a good minute. Then I plodded to my car, Ricque's wails getting fainter and fainter. I opened my car door, got in and drove away.

Chapter 18

Crossroads

The next day the severe guilt I felt irritated me. I had never met a woman like Jeannie before. A woman who held me accountable for dumping her, and to my face, showed me the fallout for my selfish immaturity. To that point, I had little idea I was so self absorbed, so Jeannie's actions really rubbed me the wrong way. My heart had been ripped out when Ricque had tried to cling to me, screaming and crying, and deep down I blamed Jeannie for that. With the abortions, it was horrible, but there was no coming back from those so you just had to get over it until you started sleeping with the next girl. But that was something you just put out of your mind. This was different. I almost missed Ricque more than I missed Jeannie, and one thing was sure: I never, ever wanted to experience that sort of heartbreak again.

With no excess of wisdom, I remained single for several months, and tried to live my old bachelor life. But I couldn't stop thinking about Jeannie and Ricque. I knew Jeannie was different. She had been such a positive influence on my life, and as much as I told myself the insta-family was in no way for me, I missed them.

One day I realized they had felt like my family—something I didn't realize I'd been longing for since my dad died. And all I could do was run from them.

The hardest part was seeing Jeannie at school. I'd talk to her occasionally, and she was so gracious she'd treat me cordially but never tried to make me regret breaking up with her, or try to force me to return. That made it worse, of course, because I could tell she still had feelings for me. Eventually I admitted I was still in love with her, too. After a few months of seeing other guys hitting on her, and doing my best not to throw books or chairs or tables at them, I eventually broached the topic of hanging out again.

Boy, Jeannie didn't make it easy. I had to really work for it, but I sensed if I persisted I could date her again. I tried and tried, and she said she just wasn't sure. Eventually I just told her I wanted to take her out for dinner, like the old days. She said, "Sorry, I don't think I could get a babysitter right now."

"Well, obviously I want to take you and Ricque out for dinner!" I replied.

She melted. I meant it sincerely; I fully intended to take them both out for dinner. I wanted to see Ricque's sweet little face. I only hoped she'd be excited to see me.

By this time, amazingly, I'd sold my cherished Corvette, and bought a 1973 Buick Centurion convertible. Like the B52's song, *Love Shack*, my new, classic car *was* "as big as a whale" *and we were about to set sail!* Jeannie must have told Ricque we were going out for dinner, because when I rang the doorbell, pandemonium broke out behind the door.

I laughed as my heart brimmed with joy when I heard little footsteps running around crazily. Ricque's little voice shouted, "Mark's here! Mark's here!" Eventually Jeannie came and opened the door and Ricque pounced onto me.

"Hey, beautiful girl!" I cried as I scooped her up in my arms. She threw her arms around my neck and hugged me.

"I missed you so much, Mark! And Mommy has missed you too!" she grinned. I thought my heart would explode with joy.

"Aw angel, I missed you, too… so, so much!" Jeannie smiled and gave me a knowing look.

"Where's the Car Vet?" Ricque shouted, looking over my shoulder up and down the street.

"Oh honey, the *Car Vet* is with new friends… but guess what?"

"What?"

"Mark got the Car Vet's big sister—a big ol' convertible for you!"

"A com…verta…bill?" she asked adorably.

"Yes! Just for you. We can take the roof off the convertible and drive around in the sun!" I knew I had to sell a very good reason for replacing the legendary Corvette. Ricque bought it.

"Yes!" she pumped her fist. "I want to drive around in the sun!"

I laughed. "Okay, even though the sun is going down, ask your mom if we can drive with the top down, okay?"

Jeannie rolled her eyes at my sneaky trick, but she was already giddy from the conversation. We both knew she couldn't say no, as Ricque was already pushing off my chest to get down and see the new car.

I took her to look at the car, while Jeannie got her purse and locked up the house. When we'd taken the roof off and strapped Ricque into the back seat, she declared she would like to eat at *Uncle Charlie's*. So that's what we did, and dinner was a total blast. I sat back, relishing how good it felt, catching up with Jeannie and Ricque. We fell right back into where we left off—well, pre-heart-wrenching tears that I couldn't hang out anymore. Ricque's sweet, unbridled, innocent charm made it possible. She climbed under the table several times, going back and forth to my side of the booth, then her mom's, wanting to be near each of us the entire dinner. It was too cute.

Before our dinner arrived, Jeannie and I took Ricque over to the claw machine so we could try to bag a stuffed animal for her. I stood Ricque on a chair next to the machine and reached into my pocket, pulling out a handful of quarters. I played a few times, getting it just right on about the fourth try! She eagerly reached into the hole, and dragged her prize out, shouting with glee. In that moment, I was nobler than any knight in the shiniest of armor. Jeannie laughed happily, and hugged her thrilled daughter tightly.

By the end of dinner, Ricque had worn herself out, and was lying down on her mom's lap, quickly falling asleep. Gazing at the two of them I took Jeannie's hand and said, "I can't tell you how glad I am to be back with you."

"Me too, Mark," she blushed.

After dinner, I drove them home and hung out at their house for a while, then helped Jeannie tuck Ricque into bed. We kissed her goodnight, and as she clutched her new stuffed animal baby to her chest she whispered, "I love you Mark!" A warmth filled my entire being and I told her I loved her too. I kissed her on the forehead and after turning off her light, we walked back downstairs to hang out.

I gave Jeannie a sly grin, and winked toward the bedroom.

"Not a chance, buddy," Jeannie said quickly. She wasn't having any of it. She walked to the living room and flopped onto the couch.

Oookay, I thought, and followed her. We started talking and pretty soon it just felt so good catching up, we ended up just talking and laughing for several hours. After a lovely time, I eventually had to leave, so I kissed Jeannie good night and walked to my car.

I was happy the entire drive home, I was happy until I pulled into in my parking spot, and I was happy when I went into my room. But as I lay on my bed, I realized I'd been pushing back a sinister, old, feeling all night. I groaned. I knew then I truly loved Jeannie and Ricque with my heart. But the demons were already beginning to howl again.

You can't do this.

You can't be tied down. It's too much responsibility.

What are you going to do when you meet another cute girl?

I forced those thoughts out of my head and reminded myself how happy I was to be back with Jeannie. They kept howling though. All night long, even waking me up several times.

Within three months, I succumbed to them. I knew it was the terror of commitment—the fear of being vulnerable and facing the pain I'd buried so deep in my past. I just didn't care. I couldn't handle it. There were too many temptations, too much self-inflicted pressure feeling tied down again, and I just wanted to be free and single, living life as selfishly as I pleased.

This time Jeannie was surprised. I sat her down again and told her I needed a break. I was dreading what would come next, and I hoped and prayed Jeannie would just let it go, but I knew she was a better woman than that.

"Well, Mark, you know the drill by now. You have to come and tell Ricque again," she said.

I shook my head, emphatically. "No way," I protested. "I can't."

"You can and you will, Mark," she replied, as serious as a broken back. "Unless you want a guarantee I will never, ever speak to you again?" I could see the pain in her eyes, but still she thought of Ricque first. Yet I could also see the scarring taking place. She was becoming calloused to my flakiness.

"Aw, come on!" I said, getting panicky.

"It's your call, Mark," she said. Somehow, Jeannie was holding it together this time.

"Fine!" I said. When must I come over?

"Tonight."

I groaned. "Fine, whatever. I'll meet you tonight at seven."

By the time I arrived at Jeannie's, I realized my t-shirt was drenched from anxiety. The scenario went down pretty much like the first time, except somehow this one hit me twice as hard. It was something in Ricque's eyes. Through her tears, the glimmer of hope—the belief that the world would actually turn out okay for a little girl who'd seen too much of it already—died a little. The only man she knew as her hero was breaking her heart. For the second time. The hero in me died that day too.

I drove home again, with my heart totally shredded. *Why are you doing this?* I silently screamed. I almost turned around to go back and shout, "Just kidding!" but what kind of cruel lunatic would that make me? I began to wonder if I really was insane.

I tried to return to my bachelor's so-called life, convincing myself I should be happy about it, but I was becoming a hollow, wretched shell. Deep in my heart, I knew something bad was happening. Something really bad. I could barely even hear the voice of the Holy Spirit anymore. And not only had I killed my unborn children, I was now betraying the most beautiful little girl I'd ever known.

Something, somewhere had definitely gone severely wrong. This was not how life was meant to turn out. I was making money, I was living the life I wanted. I was even still respected by my youth group and the church. Yet these terrible, terrible secrets were consuming me. Why did I always want more? When I was with Jeannie and Ricque, I was happy but afraid to commit. When I was on my own, all I wanted was to be with Jeannie and Ricque.

I was suddenly having trouble defining the "more" I was so desperately holding out for. I thought it was freedom or some ultimate shining dream, but what if I had the dream and I was killing it? What if the "more" was looking more like slavery every day? The terrifying part was I could actually see I was losing control, and I wasn't so sure I could stop my sinful life. And I knew *that* had eternal implications.

When I got home I picked up my Bible from the nightstand and wiped the dust off it. I flipped it open to a random page and read,

Matthew 11:28 "Come to me, all you who are weary and burdened, and I will give you rest."

Wow, I thought. *I wish I could believe that, but what did it really mean?* I knew mentally that God could forgive me of my sins, but I knew I could never admit them to anyone. I couldn't even admit them to God. I sighed and put the Bible down. I reasoned with myself, *I can't give this burden to God because... A. I could never admit to my sins and I'm sure God will require that. They are simply too horrific, and I've been leading young people while participating in taking the lives of my own children. And B. I have no idea how to stop my depraved mind from operating the way it does.*

Fear slithered around my bed, over my legs, up my body, into my chest, and finally coiled around my mind. *You'll never be free?* it hissed. I jumped off my bed and double-timed it to the kitchen to make dinner. I wondered if either of the boys were awake. I needed someone—anyone—to distract me. Yet in the middle of that gripping fear, another voice gently whispered, "Come to Me, Mark... I will give you rest."

––––––

For weeks I wrestled with God. One day I would be on top of the world, swearing to live a celibate life for long enough until I had proven to myself that I could go back to Jeannie—if she'd take me back. The next day I was at *The Hotel Bar*, eyeing up some full-figured brunette and turning on the charm. It was ridiculous. I flipped back and forth schizophrenically, knowing I needed to make a clean break with my secret life, yet having no idea how to do it in my own strength.

One particular day, right before fall semester ended and Christmas approached, I was having an especially bad time. I felt as though the Lord was starting to give up on me because I had let Him down so many times, and completely burdened down, I trudged to class. As I turned the corner I almost bumped the prettiest girl, in a colorful woolen hat and scarf, right off her feet. I was taken aback, and then realized it was Jeannie.

"Whoa, sorry... hey, Jeannie! Wow, you look beautiful!" I couldn't help myself, I just blurted it out. She gave me a weak smile, but I could have sworn her eyes fluttered a little.

"Hey, Mark."

"H-how have you been?" I asked.

"Not bad. How about you?"

"Terrible." I said with such a straight face, and knowing me so well, Jeannie couldn't help but giggle.

"Well, that's not good," she replied, her voice involuntarily turning soft and caring because it was just her nature.

I knew I was hopelessly in love with her, and had to have her back.

"Jeannie... is there any way on Earth you would want to give me yet another shot?"

She shook her head as her shields flew up. "Oh, I don't know, Mark..."

Before she could completely shoot me down, I said, "Jeannie... what if I said it was for the last time? That I would never, ever break up with you again? And I would be faithful and commit to you like I should have the moment I laid eyes on you?"

She sighed, and looked at the ground, softly kicking a little pile of snow.

"Mark... I want to believe you, but it gets so hard for me. It's even harder for Ricque."

"I know... I know." My heart stung with a pang of grief. "But if I swore on everything sacred to me... and you gave me just one more shot?"

Jeannie sighed, and looked into my eyes to see if I was serious. I had no doubt she could see into my soul. "Let me think about it, okay? And maybe I'll call you sometime."

I blinked and looked away, never feeling the wind knocked out of me so hard before. I genuinely thought she was about to agree. I nodded and cleared my throat, "Okay, fair enough," I said quietly. "If I don't talk to you before then, I truly hope you and Ricque have the best Christmas yet."

She smiled and my heart melted and ached again. "You too, Mark."

To my surprise, a few days later Jeannie called me.

"I have no idea why I'm doing this, but Mark, one way or another this is the absolute last time. Either we stay together, or we stay apart. Do you understand?"

"Absolutely!" I replied. I would have done anything. I would have signed my car over as a guarantee, I would have promised her my next year's paychecks as surety. All I wanted was to be back with my girls. Within the week, we were back together. This time, I humbly apologized to Ricque. For a moment, she looked at me as if she didn't understand me. She was in good company, because I think not one of us understood me. But then Ricque just came up to me and threw her arms around my neck, and whispered, "I still love you, Mark!"

At this point in time, my mom and Bob had been living in Vero Beach, Florida, for several years already, so although I booked a flight to visit them, I decided to spend Christmas with Jeannie and her family. I'd forgotten how magical Christmas was for a kid, and hanging out with Ricque brought all those memories flooding back. I had so much fun buying presents for Ricque, then watching her face as she tore open the gift wrap to reveal a Strawberry Shortcake doll, stuffed animals, Disney VCR tapes and more.

A thousand times that day, I counted my many blessings and told myself, *It just doesn't get better than this.* For a moment, I was tempted to ask Jeannie if she and Ricque could fly down to Florida with me at the last minute, but I knew it would be really expensive to get tickets for them on such short notice. Probably the only slightly negative feeling I had all day was knowing I'd miss them while I was away.

After New Year's, I flew down to Vero Beach to visit my mom and Bob. As the years had passed and it became clear I was succeeding on my own terms professionally, Bob had warmed up to me somewhat. Not that I cared a great deal, and I didn't spend a great deal of time with my mom and Bob, but at least it was easier.

The thing about staying with a parent is it's almost unavoidable to have feelings of reversion—like you're a kid again. I was taken back to when I was serving the Lord innocently and happily, and strangely found myself returning to an intense soul-searching.

It felt weird to be alone again so soon after getting back together with Jeannie, but I found comfort in the fact that I knew my love was at home while I was away. Throughout that week, as I walked the beaches and various piers, I thought deeply about what Jeannie and Ricque meant to me. The peace of the ocean quieted my soul, especially at night with the sound of the waves crashing on the beach, the crickets chirping, and the occasional seagull caw. Since I had committed to Jeannie,

I now found myself drawn to getting right with God. Or rather, fully committing to Him. I began praying again. Briefly at first, and quietly. And then more and more. I had forgotten how wonderful and energizing the presence of my Lord was.

One night, toward the end of my week in Florida, I was alone, standing on the board walk, looking out over the ocean and praying quietly about all the various aspects of my life. Suddenly, a rush of warmth washed over me as I heard the still, soft voice of the Holy Spirit whisper, "Mark, isn't it about time you came home to your Heavenly Father?" Tears welled up in my eyes. Through some strange and wonderful grace, my heart was finally pliable enough to allow the Lord to take it in His gentle hands and softly begin healing it. I wept quietly as I knew it was time to return to Him.

I prayed through sobs, asking God to forgive me for my long and winding *prodigal son* journey. I told Him I wanted to come home. On that boardwalk, in the serenity of the waves and ocean breeze, I broke down and submitted everything to God. I confessed my sins of abortion, of fornication, of lust, of greed, and a hundred other things. I repented of them all and knew I was turning away from my sins for good. As I did, I felt the loving blood of Christ wash me thoroughly and unquestionably clean. I fell to my knees, and began to worship the Lord. I had forgotten how wonderful and beautiful it was to be clean and pure and innocent in His presence. All my selfish deeds, those horrible sins like illicit sex, abortions, rebellion, selfishness, the lies... all were completely washed away by that royal blood. As I knelt on that boardwalk I knew without a shadow of doubt I was right with my precious God again.

The next morning I felt like my face was shining, and my body was as light as the wind. My mom and Bob must have noticed it, because they looked at me curiously, as I had woken up early, ready to enjoy the day.

"Couldn't sleep in today?" my mom asked, managing a simultaneous smile and frown.

"Heck, no! It's too beautiful a day."

"You're awfully chipper, aren't you? This trip has done you some good, I take it?" she said.

"More than you can imagine, Mom!" I sang, and kissed her on the cheek. I even winked at old Bob who smiled back nervously and quickly turned back to his newspaper.

"Wait a minute…" my mom asked suspiciously. "You didn't meet another girl down here did you? Oh Mark, you couldn't do that to Jeannie, after all you've told us about her!"

"No! No… of course not, Mom," I said, crashing my eyebrows together. "If you must know… I re-dedicated my life to God last night. I haven't felt so great in years!"

"Huh? What do you mean re-dedicated?" my mom replied. "I thought you're the youth group leader and involved at your church?"

I shook my head. "It's complicated, Mom. But trust me, I needed to come back to God, and I did." I paused, shaking my head. "And it's amazing."

"Well, okay," my mom said, looking puzzled. "I didn't know you needed to but that's great," she grinned. "How about Jeannie? Is she on board with all your church stuff?"

My eyes widened as my mom's words struck me. My mom didn't know enough back story to realize how much I really needed to return to God. I also think she didn't have a deep understanding of the salvation I had experienced, both when I was a young man, and now. But that wasn't why I was speechless.

When my mom asked me if my girlfriend was on board with my "church stuff," I realized I could no longer sleep with Jeannie. In fact, since I was returning to my devout walk with the Lord… I knew I couldn't date her anymore.

Chapter 19

New Beginnings

My newfound joy was short lived, as I wrestled with what to do about Jeannie. I knew I loved Jeannie, but I also knew I loved Jesus even more. My revival was evident to all around me, and even colleagues and other students who didn't know me well commented on the change in my countenance. Thankfully, Jeannie chalked it up to a restful vacation, and was happy we were back together. Of course, that was the worst part. I didn't have the heart to explain everything just yet… I knew the conversation would lead to where we stand.

I groaned, wondering why life couldn't be simple just for once. I always seemed to have to make tough choices these days, and it really bothered me. By the end of January, my procrastination in breaking up with Jeannie had begun to affect my spiritual progress. Jeannie had been wanting to be intimate and I was running out of excuses, fast. Second Corinthians 6:14 kept ringing in my ears, and I knew I had to speak to Jeannie. I kept hearing, *"Do not be unequally yoked together with unbelievers. For what do righteousness and wickedness have in common? Or what fellowship can light have with darkness?"* Boy, I wished there was another way out.

Of course, life's display of irony was, I had come to realize how crazy I was about Jeannie, while actually wanting to finally commit to her. I knew this time when I broke up with her, it would be the last. This time she would surely think me completely insane.

On January 26, 1992, Super Bowl Sunday, I went over to Jeannie's house to watch the game and knew I had to talk to her afterward. As the game kicked off between the Washington Redskins and the Buffalo Bills, I was so anxious I could barely even focus. By this time in my life I had perfected my poker face, so Jeannie was taken by surprise when I turned the TV off at halftime and said we needed to talk. Strangely, I could tell in her eyes that me breaking up with her was the last thing on her mind. *Dear Jesus help me*, I prayed silently.

"Jeannie, there is something I have to tell you, but first I have to explain a few things," I began.

Her brow furrowed in concern. "Sure Mark, you can tell me anything."

"Okay, here goes…" I sighed. "Basically, I'm not the person you think I am." She looked confused so I proceeded to explain. I started all the way back with my salvation on February 3, 1980. She knew when I rattled the date by heart, this was extremely important to me. I went on to explain how I used to be really radical about the Lord and how close I walked to Him. I explained how I remained a virgin for so long, and would never have dreamed of having premarital sex in my early Christian years. I told her about my Christian band, *Now Is the Time*, about my deep involvement with Tuesday night Discipleship meetings, and the Thursday night Celebration meetings. I also explained that I had been backslidden and living a lie for several years. I then recounted how, while I was in Florida, I had a deep heart-to-heart with God and had rededicated my life to Him. The only detail I left out, was the nuke. The four abortions. The last thing I needed was to break up with Jeannie and have her talking about all that. Not that I even believed she would, but you never know.

Throughout my dialogue, I tried to gauge her reactions, and she still seemed oblivious to the fact that I was about to break up with her for good. I braced myself, and delivered the conclusion to my sermon. "Sooo, you see, that's why, even though it's the last thing in the world I want, I don't think we can see each other any longer." I waited for the water works.

Jeannie heard me out and sat for a few seconds deep in thought. "Wow, Mark…" she said finally. "That's really something. I knew you were religious, but I had no idea you were so devout."

"Well, I was never really religious," I tried to explain. "I know that may not make sense but it's way more of a relationship with God than just a ritual religion I follow."

"How so?" she asked. I was surprised she wasn't focusing on my breaking up with her.

"Well…" I had to think for a second. I wasn't expecting Jeannie to ask me about my faith. "I guess at the core of my faith, I believe that Jesus rose from the dead. But wait, let me back up… you know that Jesus died for our sins, right?"

"Yeah," Jeannie replied. "Of course."

I nodded. "Okay, but do you know why?"

Jeannie gave a small shrug.

"Well, someone had to pay the price because we've *all* disobeyed God and even though our sins might seem trivial to us, one tiny act of disobedience makes us a rebel and completely wrecks His pattern for eternal life."

"Wow… I've never heard it explained like that."

At least I remembered how to share the gospel, I mused to myself.

"Oh yeah, but that's not even the best part. While God could have just thrown in the towel and allowed us to be eternally separated from Himself, He sent Jesus to pay the price of our sins… which, considering what some of us have done…" I paused, trying to blink away my tears. "…We really deserve the death penalty." Jeannie had that look of confusion again, at my severe conviction. I had to continue before I started crying, "But Jesus opted to take our place. Even if it was just me or just you, He still would have done it for either one of us individually."

It was obvious Jeannie was really moved, and something had struck a chord in her heart. "Huh… so that's what *saved* really means," she whispered.

"Exactly…" I squeezed her hand, surprising myself because I was actually trying to break up with her. "And Jesus said that when we receive Him as Lord and accept Him into our hearts—note the relationship part—He revives our spirit, making us alive when we were spiritually dead. That's where that term *born again* comes from." I smiled as I saw the light bulb go off in her mind, and her eyes well up with tears.

"Mark… that's just… that's what I've been searching for my whole life. The way you explained it. A relationship instead of following rules… is that real? Is all that in the Bible?"

"Every word of it," I promised her. For the first time, something began to dawn on me and I wondered how I could have been so stupid for the past few weeks.

"Aw honey…" I said softly, as I saw a little trickle run down her cheek. I put my hand on hers again.

"Mark, I've never heard it explained this way. It's like you really do know God."

"Jeannie, I'm nothing special, I promise you. All I ever did was accept Jesus as my Lord, and He completely changed me."

"Could I accept Him like that? I want Him to change me too. Would He make me born again?"

I smiled at the beauty and the innocence of her questions, and realized my own eyes were filling up with tears too. "Of course! He loves you more than I could ever hope to explain!"

"I want to, Mark. I want to be born again."

I took a breath, and squeezed my eyes closed tightly for a second, fighting the urge to weep. As I did I silently worshiped God for His mind-boggling mercy. His ways were truly being demonstrated as so much higher than my ways. I knew without a shadow of doubt, Jeannie's desire to give her life to God was sincere.

I opened my eyes, prayed with Jeannie and she repented in tears as though she were the lowest sinner on the planet. She vowed to turn her back on her past life, and gave her life completely to Jesus. We never did finish that football game, and I didn't care a lick. It was as if the noonday sun was shining right into the living room, and we hugged and celebrated as Jeannie couldn't stop crying and then laughing with joy.

Chapter 20

Easter Lilies and New Life

Over the following days, Jeannie had a ton of questions. It was as though we were walking on clouds, and throughout the week, I had to make sure I wasn't dreaming. I could hardly believe God had allowed me to lead the love of my life to Him. I only wish I had listened and obeyed sooner.

That whole first week was pretty blissful, as we stayed up late into the nights talking about God, what salvation means, and how wonderful it all is. I felt like I was back in my early days of college, so on fire for God.

The second week became a little busier, but whenever Jeannie and I were together we'd excitedly discuss the Word, and I'd share many scriptures with her. She couldn't get enough, and I was amazed at how she grew in leaps and bounds. It made me so proud to see her enthusiasm, and I realized I was actually leading my girlfriend spiritually—which was a first for me.

One night, however, after I left her house, I sat in my car and tried to pinpoint another feeling. I searched my heart, because I had decided I was going to be brutally honest with myself and not let anything get in the way of my walk with God again. It felt like... fear. No, even more than fear... I eventually admitted

I was terrified. *Aw man, what is wrong with you?* I chastised myself. I searched my heart a little more, and couldn't shake the feeling I was having. After some time I came to two conclusions: one, Jeannie and I hadn't slept together since my rededication (and her salvation,) and we would not sleep together. Two, I knew if I wanted to keep dating Jeannie, sooner rather than later, the question of my intentions would quickly become a central issue. *So what are your intentions now?* I felt the Holy Spirit gently bringing me face to face with an area in my heart that had freaked me out for years.

One of the biggest stumbling blocks for me was, Jeannie wanted more children, and that was something I just could not deal with. I didn't want to be alone, but the prospect of committing the rest of my life to marriage—even with someone as special as Jeannie—just shut me down for some reason. The good thing was, at least I was facing the issue squarely. After wrestling with it for some time in prayer I asked myself honestly, *Mark, can you commit the rest of your life to this woman and her little girl?* My mind reeled and I was scared to even answer, so I hung my head, started the engine and drove off.

The next morning, I woke up and the same question was the first thing on my mind. *Mark, can you commit the rest of your life to this woman and her little girl?* I had the same reaction as the first time. Sheer panic. I jumped out of bed and ran to the kitchen to fix something to eat. After I had some cereal, I grabbed some clothes out of my room as quickly as possible and went to shower. I didn't even spend any time in prayer, avoiding what I knew would surface in my heart. I got ready for work and left the house, but as soon as I was alone in my car, the haunting question echoed in my mind again.

That afternoon, I knew I had to spend time reading the Word, so I sat down and prayed, knowing what the Holy Spirit was about to bring up in my heart. And He did… *Mark, can you commit the rest of your life to this woman and her little girl?* I sighed, knowing my fear was crippling me. I adored Jeannie and Ricque with all my heart, but I didn't know what to do. So I desperately tried to put the question out of my mind. I didn't want anyone else, and just the thought of breaking up with Jeannie almost sent me into a tailspin. I was distraught and had no idea where to turn.

The Holy Spirit didn't ease up. Over the following days, I kept having the recurring thought with the same reaction. Eventually, I decided to pray about it.

I prayed and prayed and prayed for God to help me, but after a week it was the same question. I knew I already loved Ricque with all my heart, but the prospect of having more children tilted my brain every time I thought about it. And I knew it was likely a deal breaker with Jeannie, so I began to grow despondent.

One morning, I woke up knowing I couldn't carry on living a lie. I had to figure out what to do about my relationship with Jeannie. I bowed my head and decided to be honest with God. *Lord, I can't go on like this. I love this woman with all my heart, but I just can't seem to wrap my head around committing to her. It's not that I'm being selfish, I just don't want to commit to having children if I don't think I'll be a good dad.* I sat there on the brink of tears, when the question arose again in my heart… yet it wasn't like the first time I'd heard it. This time, I heard, *Mark, can you spend the rest of your life WITHOUT this woman and her little girl?* I sat bolt upright. The answer was a resounding, *NO!* I asked myself again, just to be sure. *Mark, can you spend the rest of your life WITHOUT this woman and her little girl?"* This time the answer was a loud, *HECK NO!*

My face fell into my hands and I started laughing hysterically. The laughter turned to relief, then into tears of joy, as I couldn't believe I finally had my answer. I had no idea what had just happened but one thing was absolutely clear—God had given me a supernatural shift in perspective and it changed *everything.* I worshiped God, singing to Him in joy. I was blown away that the answer had been right there in front of me for so long, but yet again… I had been too afraid to trust God. As I sat there, I knew exactly what I had to do.

Being an all-or-nothing type of guy, once I knew what I wanted to do, there was no stopping me. With Easter fast approaching, I began scheming and planning. Jeannie and I continued to have our late-night talks about the Lord, and the amazing work of grace, but she had noticed something different about me.

"What's happened to you?" she smiled at me one day.

"What do you mean?" I asked innocently.

"You're even more… happy… the last few days."

"Oh, I guess I'm just excited about Easter coming up, and all the fun remembering what God has done for us." I knew exactly what she was talking about but I maintained my poker face.

Jeannie nodded and returned my smirk, but she wasn't fully convinced. Over the following weeks, I helped Pastor Dean Ziegler and the planning team with the

Easter church decor and service arrangements. I added my own special touches here and there, and when we were done, one thing was certain, the church was going to look spectacular.

A few days before Easter Sunday, I told Jeannie we had to head in a little earlier, to help set up a few things. That Easter Sunday on April 19, 1992, I woke up early and began to get ready. I called Jeannie to ensure she was up and would be ready when I swung by to pick her and Ricque up for church.

"Oh, Mark, can't we just meet you there at service time?" Jeannie groaned from bed.

"Nope. I need your help with a few things." I was adamant, and knew Jeannie's heart was so giving she wouldn't say no.

"What about Ricque? She's going to get uncomfortable in her Easter dress for that long."

"Ah, you can bring some other clothes for her." Jeannie was being persistent. This was unusual.

"Okay, good idea. Maybe I'll just dress her in comfortable clothes and she can put on her Easter dress at church."

I had to think quickly. "No, I uh… I want to get some pictures of the three of us in the early morning light. It looks beautiful coming through the stained glass windows and the church will be all decorated."

Jeannie was silent for a second, and then sighed. "I love you, Mark!" she said finally. I breathed a sigh of relief.

"I love you too, Angel," I smiled to myself.

I picked the girls up and, *wow*! Did they look beautiful! I made a huge fuss over how lovely they looked, and Ricque put on a real show, doing little twirls in her dress for me. I clapped my hands and hugged her as she beamed with regal joy. We bundled the little princess into the car, and I kissed Jeannie on the cheek.

"This is going to be an awesome day!" I smiled. She smiled back curiously.

We sang all the way to church, worshiped the Lord, with Ricque singing the loudest. When we finally arrived, I ran around and opened the door for Jeannie first, then Ricque, and I escorted them into the church. My heart was racing.

As soon as we stepped into the sanctuary, Jeannie did a double-take.

Wow, Mark! Everything looks absolutely beautiful!" she exclaimed, clutching her heart. In the front of the sanctuary huge bouquets of bright, white Easter lilies were spread among gorgeously colored vases of other flowers like carnations and daffodils and roses. White bows and flowers adorned the ends of each row, while unlit candles were waiting on elegant stands, ready to shine their light at the right time for all to see. Most importantly, as I had predicted, soft rays of warm, diffused sunlight streamed directly onto the display in the front of the church.

"Wow!" Ricque shouted as she ran up to the stage. My heart pounded with joyful nervousness, overflowing into the biggest smile. I put my arm around Jeannie, as we watched Ricque dance happily in the sunlight.

"Hey, I forgot something I need in the car," I whispered, kissing Jeannie's cheek. "I'll be right back."

"Okay. Do you need any help?"

"No, I've got it, but thanks," I grinned and headed out the door.

When I got back, Jeannie and Ricque were holding hands, dancing in the sunlit rainbow of the stained glass window. Ricque's giggle was so contagious I laughed heartily with joy. I'd never seen anything so beautiful in all my life. And God had given them to me.

"Ricque! Come look here, baby girl." She stopped her giddy spinning and her ears pricked up.

"What?" she asked directly.

"Come here! I've got something for you," I waved her over. Her eyes grew big and she ran up to me. "Close your eyes," I said as I produced a long, narrow box out of my jacket pocket.

"Oh!" Ricque exclaimed, putting her hands up to her face.

"Here my darling. Happy Easter! This is from me and Jesus." Ricque opened her eyes, and not wasting time with false airs or graces she snatched the box out of my hand, and tore at the ribbon.

I laughed as Jeannie said, "Say, 'Thank you, Mark!'"

"Thank you, Mark!" Ricque squawked happily, halting her assault on the box just long enough to give me a kiss on the hand. My heart melted. Ricque eventually conquered the ribbon and pulled the lid off the box. Inside lay a sparkling, silver *Praying Hands* necklace. Ricque squealed with delight, "Put it on! Put it on!" she yelped. Laughing, I obliged, and she proceeded with twirlings befitting pure royalty. We both laughed and clapped, and Ricque strutted around showing off her new treasure.

Jeannie wiped a tear from her eye, and said,

"Mark, that is the sweetest thing I've ever seen."

We were standing right in front of the pulpit. Rays of soft, gorgeous sunshine streamed down on Jeannie's face as she was surrounded by pure, white lilies and swathes of other colorful blooms. I reached into my pocket and produced another long, narrow box. It was wrapped with the same white, satin ribbon.

"This one's for you, my love," I said, getting lost in her eyes.

Jeannie raised her eyebrows as if to say, "For me too?" and delicately took the box from my outstretched hand. Before she opened it, she hugged me tightly and gave me a big kiss. "Now I see why you wanted to get some pictures! You wanted to snap shots of us with our new Easter necklaces!"

I grinned sheepishly.

Jeannie undid the ribbon, and lifted the lid on the box. Inside was a paper note, folded over the full length of the box. She lifted it out to read it but when she saw what was beneath, she nearly dropped the box. Under the note rested a sparkling diamond ring. I dropped to one knee, and took my love's hand. "Jeannie. Will you make me the happiest man on the face of this Earth and marry me?"

Ricque looked over, knowing something extraordinary was going on and ran over to her mom. Jeannie had covered her mouth to hide the joyful sobs, but tears were already ruining her mascara. She nodded emphatically. "Yes!" she whispered, stifling her tears.

"Why is Mommy crying?" Ricque squawked at me. I laughed, scooping her up and hugged them both.

"Baby, these are happy tears!" Jeannie replied, falling into my shoulder. "Mark just asked me to marry him, Angel. And I said yes. We're going to be a real family!"

Ricque whirled around to get affirmation from me with her big, bright eyes. "Yes, honey. We're going to be a real family," I nodded, kissing Ricque's cheek first, and then my fiancé's. My face was shining even brighter than the streaming sunlight.

"*Yaaay!*" Ricque yelled, jumping up and flopping around in my arms so much I nearly dropped her. I laughed and set her down as she took off running, and gave Jeannie another long, tight hug. Jeannie continued to cry happy sobs into my shoulder, and I may or may not have shed a few tears of joy myself.

"You know this day is also special for another reason, right?" I reminded Jeannie.

"Oh, honey," she said remembering. "Today is the anniversary of your dad's passing." She looked at me, not knowing what to say next.

"It's very symbolic to me," I explained. "God has taken the saddest and most disruptive day in my life and turned it into the happiest, most blessed day of my life." Jeannie's bottom lip puckered up involuntarily again.

"And what's more is, where I lost a father… God is giving me the honor of becoming a father to the most beautiful little girl in the world, where she really didn't have one before." Jeannie burst into sobs of joy again and I pulled her into me, smiling and stroking her pretty hair. "Hey… it's the happiest day of my life," I whispered.

Ricque was looking up at me again with stern eyes because I kept making her mom cry. I laughed again and all I could say was "It's okay, Angel. I promise, your mom is just happy because we're a real family now!" Ricque wasn't convinced but her mom looked down at her and took her hand.

"It's true, baby. It's okay," she smiled. Ricque smiled back and hugged her mom's leg.

"Happy Easter my beautiful girls," I said. We all laughed and hugged with unspeakable joy.

———

After a wonderful service, and congratulations, followed by no small amount of ooh's and aah's from our friends when they saw the ring, I drove the three of us to my Grandma and Grandpa Morrow's house for Easter dinner. When Grandma opened the door I remembered when I had to live with them all those years before. How far the Lord had brought me. I introduced my Grandma to Jeannie and then to Ricque. To say Grandma was taken aback that I was with a woman who had a child was an understatement. I winked at Jeannie, and brushed it off as we went inside. When I told my grandparents and all of the other Morrows, however, that Jeannie was my new fiancé… let's just say mouths hung open in disbelief around the room. Nobody could say a word for an awkward several seconds. I broke the silence with a "Who knew, right?" and everyone laughed.

We had a fantastic dinner and everyone instantly fell in love with Ricque and Jeannie. I endured the "So why did you settle for him?" ribbing, and smiled as Jeannie defended me as her knight in shining armor. After dinner, we drove over to Aunt Toni and Uncle David's house to break the news, and show off the ring. They cooed and made a huge ordeal. Predictably, Aunt Toni's eyes welled up with tears too. Of course, Aunt Toni knew me so well, she asked Jeannie, "So, how did you convince this one to settle down?"

Jeannie cast me a loving gaze and said, "Actually it was all the hand of God."

Aunt Toni raised her eyebrows and gushed, "Really? Well, then I'm sure you two will be having many more beautiful little brothers and sisters for little Ricque?"

Jeannie swallowed hard and looked down at the ground, deferring to me. The change in mood was severe, and Aunt Toni immediately saw Jeannie's anxiety. Frowning she cocked her head at me.

"Uh… we're actually not going to have any more children, Aunt Toni," I said, as gently as I could.

"*What?*" Aunt Toni replied, not even trying to conceal her shock. She stared at me as I shrugged and nodded. "Oh, Honey," she swayed her head. "Sooner or later… things just happen." She was grinning from ear to ear.

I shook my head, "No. I'm actually going to have a vasectomy. We've discussed it and Jeannie's okay with it." I immediately felt guilty and I didn't know why. I knew Jeannie had reluctantly accepted my decision that if we were ever married, it would be on the condition that we didn't have any more children. I had come a long way but Ricque and Jeannie were all I ever wanted.

Aunt Toni looked over at Jeannie, who averted her eyes.

"It's okay… not everyone has to have fifty kids," I laughed, but Aunt Toni just frowned and gave me that look that said, *I don't buy it, Mark.*

I looked into the kitchen and said, "Boy, have you guys got any coffee? I could really use a cup after stuffing my face at Grandma and Grandpa's. I am *dragging*!"

After a long, disapproving pause, Aunt Toni replied curtly, "Of course." Then she asked my uncle, "David, can you put the kettle on for Mark? Anybody else want a cup?" She put an arm around Jeannie and squeezed her. Then she whispered, "God has His ways, dear." I pretended I didn't hear.

Chapter 21

My Girls

A few days after I proposed, Jeannie cautiously approached the "When?" question. I suppose in her mind, knowing my track record of flaking and fear of commitment, she was torn between wanting to be sure I would follow through and not wanting to freak me out. Of course, I had recommitted my life to Christ, and as she would begin to realize more and more, that made all the difference.

"Well, our first date was on 10/20/1990 at the bodybuilding show, so why not get married on the two-year anniversary of our first date?"

Jeannie looked at the calendar on the wall and said, "Mark, that's only six months away!"

"So?" I smirked. "That's more than enough time." I broke into a grin and she happily smiled back. It began to dawn on Jeannie that "all-in Mark" didn't play games.

After looking at the calendar again, her expression dropped. "Well… there's one problem though…" She looked at me forlornly. "October twentieth falls on a *Tuesday* this year."

"So?" I repeated, still grinning widely.

"Mark, who gets married on a Tuesday?" she smiled like I was a weirdo.

"Us, I guess?" I laughed. "C'mon… why not. It's so *romantic,* babe."

Jeannie chuckled and I gave her a big hug. I knew that was it. We decided to be married on a Tuesday night and if that surprised anyone, it really shouldn't have if they knew my nonconformist ways.

Two months before I proposed to Jeannie I had saved enough money to put down a payment and purchase a house. I'm not sure whether it was subconscious intent or mere coincidence but the house was literally the next street over from Jeannie and Ricque's apartment. As we started figuring out the million details of planning a wedding, the question came up about Jeannie's apartment lease. It was due to expire and if she re-signed, even for another six months, that would put us past the date of the wedding. It was a no-brainer to move Jeannie and Ricque into my house. I would just stay back at *Hermitage House.* We hustled and packed, I got Jeannie's brother Mike and a friend, who had pickup trucks, to help, and before I knew it, I got them moved in. I smiled to myself after the long day's work. *I'm already taking care of my girls.*

Around the same time in May, I reached another welcomed milestone. I received my Masters degree in Counseling, as well as a new Masters level Specialized Therapist position at *Harborcreek Youth Services.* With that new level of education came a substantial pay increase and a better work schedule. Things were falling into place like I couldn't believe—actually I could totally believe it, because once I submitted to God, His favor rested upon me.

Soon we were knee-deep in the business of planning the wedding. I had always wanted to get married with my toes in the sand, standing at the edge of the ocean. I always wanted something casual, yet near the edge of God, so to say. I was never one to believe that I had to be married in a church building, so after considerable (and painstaking) research, Jeannie and I chose a beautiful historic inn called *Riverside Inn.* It was located in Cambridge Springs, only about ten miles from Edinboro. The enormous old inn was built in the 1880's and is as magnificent in history as it is in charm. The building is a three-story wooden hotel on the banks of the French Creek. Back in the 1800's the nearby springs were said to have healing properties, to which thousands flocked every year, including a couple of U.S. Presidents. *What better place to get married?* we figured. So naturally with me being a youth group director, leading worship, and preaching, it made sense that I should be married in the church, right? Well, not according to Mark Morrow. I'm sure a few people raised their eyebrows, but I figured most just thought *Well, that's Mark for you.*

Pretty soon, we had recruited both of our entire families to meet the looming deadlines, and my excitement began to accelerate. The most poignant thing for me, however, was realizing how relieved everyone was that I had found my beautiful fiancé, and was settling down. Things started falling into place left and right, and pretty soon we had a semblance of a game plan. Aunt Toni had a friend, Barb, who was a professional photographer, and had actually photographed my sister Beth and her husband Randy's wedding four years before. Aunt Toni also had a friend whose boyfriend was a D.J., and since our wedding was on a Tuesday night, we had no problem getting the back of the inn. We were also able to book the formal dining room for dinner.

That took care of the ceremony location, the reception, photographer, and the D.J. Next were the guests. Jeannie's sister, Lynn, was booked to fly over from Japan, and Mark Feldkamp, now in Michigan with his wife, Laurie, was driving over as my best man. Jeannie's parents, Bud and Joyce, were part of the entire wedding planning. My mom and Bob were set to fly up from Florida, and my sister Beth and her husband Randy said they'd be there. In fact we had room to invite most of my family, and it dawned on me how blessed I was to have four living grandparents. Only my Grandpa Jim was unable to make it due to health issues. I was naturally sad about that, but understood.

Living on counselor's salaries, Jeannie and I decided to keep the wedding simple, rather than hurl ourselves into debt over a single day. Our rationale was that couples should put more emphasis on their actual marriage than starting off spending too much on the launch of their maiden voyage. The last thing we needed was the stress and financial strain associated with an over-the-top wedding, so we kept it to a hundred guests, and planned it to be elegant but simple. *But that doesn't mean it can't be memorable*, I smiled to myself.

Four months screamed by and at that point, Jeannie hadn't brought up anything about my desire to have a vasectomy. Oh, I'm sure she was praying about it and believing Aunt Toni's words, "God has His ways," *but* as the wedding day approached, I called up my primary physician and asked him for a referral for the surgery. Jeannie didn't say anything but I could tell the reality of my stubbornness left her heartbroken. For Jeannie, it became the most bitter of sweet moments; planning a dream wedding with the man who loved and treated her daughter as his own, yet doomed to never have any children together.

Two months before our wedding, I checked myself into Saint Vincent's hospital and had the procedure done. The irony of having the procedure after four abortions struck me. It was like locking the stable doors *after* all the horses ran away. I stuffed it way far down into my mind, hoping that thought and… guilt… would never come up again, and attempted to go about life normally.

It felt as though I blinked and the big Tuesday was upon us. I had moved just about all of my things from *Hermitage House* the days before, and that morning all I had left was a bag with a few clothes and toiletries. I hugged my boys goodbye and promised I'd still see them, then excitedly drove over to the inn. When I arrived, I was pleased to see everything was well underway.

We were set to have the wedding on the first floor of the *Riverside Inn*, in a great room at the very back of the building. A huge fireplace drew one's focus immediately, while elegant antiques and classic furniture from days gone by added to the memorable atmosphere. The staff had set out two columns of chairs, flanking each side of the aisle leading up to the fireplace. Pastor Dean Ziegler stood up front, reading over his notes. I smiled as I took in the fact that this was actually happening. *Who woulda thunk it?* I grinned happily.

I neurotically checked over all the details, and was in the middle of double checking the cake when my mom asked me when I planned to get dressed. I then realized the guests were arriving and I wasn't dressed yet. In what felt like a moment, I was then standing at the front of the aisle in my dapper new suit, with over a hundred friends and family in front of me.

I chewed my lip as I waited for my wife-to-be to make me the happiest man in the world. Dr. Gary Christiansen, my former *WFSE* radio instructor and advisor, was at the ready on a classical cello, along with his friend and classical pianist, Roger Held. Suddenly they struck up the most beautiful rendition of Mendelssohn's wedding march and my stomach flipped. Lynn, Jeannie's sister and matron of honor, came down first, followed by Ricque. That little girl was a picture to behold. She was grinning like the Cheshire cat, so visibly proud to be part of her mom and

Mark's wedding! She was wearing a gorgeous little dark blue dress, and hanging very deliberately over the collar was the praying hands necklace I had given her on Easter Sunday. My eyes instantly became afflicted by the onset of moisture, which I hopelessly tried to blink away.

Then, there she was. Jeannie appeared at the top of the stairwell like a radiant, angelic vision. She wore a simple, yet breathtakingly elegant, white dress, and carried a candle-burning lantern, adorned with flowers. My heart swooned and I fell in love all over again, yet a thousand times deeper. I stood with my mouth gaping, wondering how God had managed to give this woman to me. The joy and beauty of it all was written on Jeannie's face too; her dream of marrying a good man and starting a loving, Christ-centered family was coming true. Everyone rose to their feet as Jeannie paused at the top of the stairs, and I realized I might have been drooling a little. I saw Jeannie slightly giggle, then she floated down the stairs, down the aisle and then she was next to me. She gazed up at me with the beauty of a young doe blinking up at her proud buck. Knowing Ricque would be as much a part of the marriage as we were, it was only fitting she stood between us, giggling and smiling at us the entire time.

Pastor Dean led Jeannie and me in our vows, as we promised ourselves to each other before God and man. Pastor Dean reached the part where he said, "And if there is anyone here today who does not feel that this man and this woman should be joined together as husband and wife, speak now or forever hold your peace." There was a slight pause, and I slowly glanced over my right shoulder as if expecting more than one person to speak up. A couple of people spontaneously snickered, then the whole room burst into laughter. Jeannie just smiled, shook her head and gave me a healthy nudge in the side.

While Pastor Dean was new to our area and church, he had the genius, Spirit-led idea that Ricque and I come up with vows between her and myself. I stood there fighting that curious wet phenomenon in my eyes again as I gazed lovingly at the precious little five-year-old beside me.

"Do you, Mark, accept Jeannie's daughter Ricque to become your daughter? Do you promise to love Ricque as your own and guide her in the ways of Christ? Do you promise to make sacrifices for her and to be a loving husband to her mom?"

"I do," I said, my voice cracking.

"Ricque, do you take Mark to be the husband of your mom? Do you accept him as your father, and will you honor him and obey him and follow his guidance and direction in Jesus?"

Her tiny, sweet voice squeaked, "I will," and not a dry eye remained in the house. I believe that moment was the most beautiful I'd experienced to that point in my life. The woman of my dreams beside me, and willing to sacrifice for me. Even more than that was a certain redemption. Right in that moment, I knew I was becoming so much more than a husband—I was becoming a *daddy*. God was giving me a second chance. After makeup was ruined and eyes were dried, we lit a unity candle where Jeannie, Ricque, and I each had our own lit candles, then the three of us joined together in lighting a large one. We had just become a real family.

When the ceremony was complete, Jeannie and I left the room together and stood halfway down the hall, where we could greet our guests as they left for the reception area. It was such a day of joy, as everyone was so thrilled I had found such a wonderful woman, with such a precious daughter. We hugged and laughed, and I got more than a few doses of healthy heckling.

After a legendary dinner it was time for Jeannie and me to have our first dance. We chose, "I only have eyes for you," by *The Flamingos*. The song began, and as I danced with my beautiful, new wife I reflected on how content and happy I was with this one woman who could fulfill me more than anything I had ever known. I truly had eyes only for her. For several minutes, we were lost in each other's arms, the world around us invisible.

Eventually the track ended and together we gave a small bow. Then it was time for another special dance. Ricque stood on the side of the dance floor looking way too adorable in her puffy little blue dress. I shuffled over to her and scooped her up in my arms. The deejay queued *The Temptations* track, "My Girl," and holding Ricque in my arms, we slowly glided and drifted around and around the dance floor. I knew Ricque felt like the most special little princess in the entire world, and she was a hundred percent correct. I smiled from ear to ear, while Ricque glowed. To this day, that remains one of the most astoundingly beautiful memories of my life. As David Ruffian crooned the lyrics, the meaning of the words overwhelmed me while I held this formerly vulnerable little girl who now looked up to me as her hero:

I've got sunshine on a cloudy day.
When it's cold outside I've got the month of May.

I guess you'd say
What can make me feel this way?
My girl (my girl, my girl)
Talkin' 'bout my girl (my girl)

I've got so much honey the bees envy me.
I've got a sweeter song than the birds in the trees.

Well, I guess you'd say
What can make me feel this way?
My girl (my girl, my girl)
Talkin' 'bout my girl (my girl)

Hey hey hey
Hey hey hey
Ooooh

I don't need no money, fortune or fame.
I've got all the riches, baby, one man can claim.

Well, I guess you'd say
What can make me feel this way?
My girl (my girl, my girl)
Talkin' 'bout my girl (my girl).

I've got sunshine on a cloudy day
With my girl.
I've even got the month of May
With my girl
Talkin' 'bout
Talkin' 'bout

Talkin' 'bout
My girl
Ooooh
My girl
As long as I can talk about my girl[1]

As I glided around the dance floor, thinking how blessed I was to have these two gifts from Heaven, I had no idea I was about to be challenged in ways I had never dreamed possible.

---

1   *The Temptations*. My Girl on Gold, (Motown Records, a Division of UMG Recordings, Inc., 2005. CD.)

Chapter 22

The Power of God and The Punch of Mike Tyson

Married life was something I had completely underestimated, both in rewards… and adjustments. The bliss of being a family and doing it right was incomparable to anything I had known before. But I had lived as a bachelor for nine years, doing whatever I wanted, whenever I wanted. Needless to say, these adjustments came rapidly and they came painfully.

I quickly learned that even though I was making the right choices, I still had a lot of growing up to do, and I had to do it *fast*. As much as I adored Ricque, and wouldn't change anything about her for the world, the reality of becoming a father began to hit home pretty hard. I would do anything for Ricque, I just wasn't used to the demands of a little girl. It was entirely due to my rough edges, having shunned any and all prior interaction with kids, but it soon became apparent I had a lot to learn.

I even became frustrated when Ricque would say "sgabetti" instead of spaghetti, or wouldn't know her left from her right when it came to turning the bath water on or off. At times, I'm ashamed to say, I even got angry with her. It was astounding how little I really knew about children. Jeannie was so patient and would mediate, saying, "Mark, she's five years old! Give her a break," but it was still tough going for me. I had to face the sad reality that *I* was in fact, the one behind the curve.

Adding to that was the usual compromises, negotiations, and sheer adaptations of marriage. I knew I was no walk-in-the-park to live with, so I made up my mind to try really hard. I guess that was my one saving grace; once I committed to something, I was devoted. But even that brought its own issues. I had, by this point, worked at *Harborcreek Youth Services* for about seven years, and knew the importance of building a résumé. Jeannie on the other hand, had to deal with doctor's appointments, taking time off work, and taking whatever work she could get at times, so her work history was a little fuller than mine. I tried to explain that she needed to settle down and work consistently at something, like myself, or her dad, who had retired after over thirty years at General Electric. This, predictably, led to more than a few disagreements between us.

But in time, I slowly began to adapt. My love for my new family was stronger than even my selfish traits. Plus, I was determined to actually live like a godly man should. After a few years I began to see that Jeannie's life was hers, and she had a right to her way of doing things. I realized (shockingly,) God had a plan for her *and* a way to exercise that plan in her life using her choices as well. I also began to see that partly because of Jeannie's varied work experience, she was the interesting person who so powerfully attracted me. What's more, Jeannie was truly using her spiritual gifts, and using her own difficult experiences to draw on to help other people instead of wallowing in self-pity. That was often more than I could say. For a while she worked at *The Refuge*, a Methodist shelter for homeless women and their children. She also worked at *Meadville Medical Center* as an oncology social worker and counselor. She even worked as a family counselor at an organization called *Family Services*, and would venture into bad neighborhoods to help with family dynamics in underprivileged homes. In all of these jobs, Jeannie's past experiences of being a single mother molded her into a unique and highly effective counselor, as well as a humble and sincere Christian.

Around 1995, the timing became right for another decision I had made. I waited several years before beginning the process of adopting Ricque; the primary reason was probably because she was only five when Jeannie and I were married.

I figured she didn't understand the significance of a biological father who had no interest in her. I didn't really feel a need or rush to do it—I was her dad and that was that. Yes, it was terribly sad that Ricque's biological father had totally bailed on her and Jeannie, but I wasn't complaining. But the guy really was completely absent. He never saw Ricque, never sent cards, letters, or gifts. Jeannie made sure he paid a minimal $100.00 per month for child support, but that was it.

It was tough not to judge the guy, but I always tried my best to keep that opinion at arm's length. It wasn't just because I had suddenly become such a devout Christian either. The guy had wanted Jeannie to abort the pregnancy. The scenario was scarily similar to someone's I knew too well. I suppose it was true it had never been my idea to abort my other children, but the fact of the matter was, I had always been complicit. I didn't want the children and had placed their mothers in the difficult position of making that decision. Jeannie is simply one in a million. Yes, there was a very fine line between Ricque's biological father and I, and that thin line was called the *grace of God*. Not that he didn't have the grace of God available to Him, I was just blessed enough to know about and receive it. The problem comes, however, when a man has to admit he's been a deadbeat and let go; he will often takes offense and try to protest.

I contacted this guy's brother, explained who I was, and asked him if he would relay the message that I had married Jeannie and wanted to adopt Ricque. More importantly, I wanted to know if he would contest the adoption. I had been Ricque's dad for years anyway, but if the guy wanted to, he could really complicate matters. I hoped with all my heart we wouldn't have to fight it legally and prove he wasn't there anymore. If he contested the adoption though, it would be very difficult to win. I told him about the adoption hearing, and said if he was going to protest we'd like to know before the court date.

We had scheduled an adoption hearing at the *Erie County Court House*, and when the day arrived, Jeannie, Ricque, and I got dressed up in our Sunday best for the occasion. I had explained to Ricque what was going to happen, and how I had pretty much always been her daddy, but we were just going to make it all totally official. She was all happy smiles in her pretty white dress, and nodded the whole way through. As we walked into the courthouse, I looked around for Ricque's biological father. I had never met him, but figured I'd somehow recognize him if I saw him. *So far so good,* I thought, as we were called into the courtroom.

We went before the honorable Judge Shad Connelly, a tall, broad man who, when outside of the courthouse, wore cowboy boots and a giant Stetson. Judging from his demeanor, his typical docket included criminals, cases of abuse, neglect and worse. So when he saw Ricque's adoption, it certainly appeared to make his day. He began by asking me a few questions like, "Are you aware of the responsibility you're accepting? Are you committed for the long haul? Are you aware this makes you financially responsible?"

I explained our circumstances and how I had been the only man in Ricque's life for years. I told the judge how much I loved her and had always been her dad, but wanted the official piece of paper. As I was talking, I got a little choked up and had to pause for a moment. In that moment, I believe Judge Connelly knew instantly I was fully aware of what I was doing and wanted this, with no doubts. I remembered Ricque's biological father, and looked around the courtroom nervously one last time but saw no-one. Judge Connelly then gave a formal little talk, smiled broadly, and told us it was official. Ricque was legally my daughter.

More than a few tears of joy were shed as I hugged my little girl, then kissed her mom. The strange part was, I had absolutely no anxiety, and didn't even wonder how I had reached this point. A few weeks later we received a lovely judicial certificate, stamped, sealed, and signed. Once we had that, we applied for and received a new birth certificate, showing me as Ricque's indisputable father. I *really* liked that.

It may seem strange that there were no explosions in the sky, no dramatic revelations, or God waving His hand to make my situation miraculously turned around. Instead I had simply responded to the gentle voice of the Holy Spirit back in Florida years before, and began taking the right steps. I kept taking them and life just kept improving. I was beginning to realize obedience—as scary as it could be at times—was producing the miracles. And they didn't stop there.

––––––

In 1996 I bumped into Ron Raymond, a good friend of mine from college days, whose wedding I sang at in 1983. He told me he was working at a Christian radio station called *WCTL* and invited me to come check it out some time. I did exactly that, and right there and then he asked if I might want to do some voice-over work for them and get a little money on the side. I told him he didn't even have to give me any money, I'd just help him out as best as I could. I said if he wanted to throw some concert tickets my way every now and then, that would be great. So I began doing some voice work and commercials for the station, and pretty soon the General Manager, Joel Natalie, asked if I would like to be part of a new morning show he was dreaming about. There was really nothing like it in the area at the time, and it sounded like a perfect fit for me. I jumped at it.

When we started, I knew the natural dynamic between Ron and I was truly something special. The show really started picking up steam rapidly. Ron ran the board and was the "straight man," while I was the "color guy"—the jokester or some might even say a loose cannon. I guess I was like Jerry Lewis to Ron's Dean Martin. We developed our schtick to an art, as the first Christian morning drive show in the area. At the bottom of each hour, we'd break and cut to our morning news reporter, Margaret Caldwell, for local news. Pretty soon it evolved to where she'd finish her news and I'd reel her into humorous conversation about her weekend, or the topic at hand. In time, this subtly shifted the show into a three-person dynamic, upping the ante and becoming even more fun. This slowly grew into what would be the legendary *The Good Guys in the Morning*.

I would start my days by getting to the station at 5:30 a.m., do some show prep, figure out a plan for jokes and trivia for the day, then discuss any interviews with Ron. At 6:30 a.m. we went live on air, and for two and a half hours we'd get people "up and at 'em" in their homes, in their cars, and even those listening to their office radios. Then I would leave the station and drive to my *real job* that paid the bills and had health insurance.

Most people believed, however, that *WCTL* was my only gig, and many had no idea I was a counselor at *Harborcreek Youth Services* from 9:30 a.m. to 5:30 p.m. I didn't really care to elaborate either, as we gradually became local celebrities. As the show became exponentially more popular, our ratings in the area skyrocketed. We became *the* Christian station to listen to and the top-rated secular stations were scratching their heads about how "that religious station" could be snatching their ratings away. We were rocking it without being "blue," which means using bathroom and sex humor.

After a while, Margaret took a job with Senator Rick Santorum from Pennsylvania, which was a huge deal for her and she really deserved it. When Margaret left, Lori Clapper joined us, who was about thirteen years our junior (Margaret was about ten years our senior.) What resulted, of course, was a totally different dynamic. Lori became like our little sister on the show, and we'd still tease her and have fun with her, which she played off really well.

Lori ended up taking over the news stories and delivery as well, doing an excellent job, and adding even more fresh elements to the show. We became so successful that *Radio & Records*, which was practically considered the Bible of all radio stations, chose *The Good Guys in the Morning* for a full page feature article. When it hit the stands, it was mind-blowing to have our story and photos published in such a meaningful and respected national radio journal.

Through all these blessings, something was also happening in my spiritual life. I was having the time of my life, and the show was even helping my spiritual walk. I was in a constant Christian surrounding, the music was Godly, and even the concerts were fun, and glorified God. The biggest impact to my spiritual walk, however, was when the mic was off, as Ron and I would share our deepest thoughts, questions, and frustrations, brother to brother. Having an accountability partner really began to draw out the deeper things God had inside me, without any of the fear or anxiety I had experienced in the past.

Another unexpected aspect of the job was my local celebrity. People began stopping me in public to say hi, and say how much they enjoyed the show. They'd often bring up something I said, explaining how much it ministered to them. Some folks even asked about my family. Because I've always been such an open book, the public grew to feel as though they knew me as a friend. I think, when you're that open, people "adopt" you into their own little worlds, and accept you as someone able to speak into their lives.

Yet as wonderful and humbling as that was, it was also terrifying. The more I was thrust into the limelight, the scarier my four dark secrets became. Before I realized it, I'd been thrust onto a pedestal in the Erie area, and had become a Christian celebrity. How in the world could I now reveal that I was complicit in *four* abortions? And not only that, they were a result of an extremely illicit lifestyle, *while working as a youth counselor and part-time preacher!*

I was sure I would be fired from *WCTL,* and hurled under the bus like many other Christians who got themselves into messy situations. There was Sandi Patty's affair, Amy Grant's divorce, Michael English's affair, and Clay Crosse's porn addiction. Because of the media backlash, and (to be frank) the brutal and unforgiving reaction of the church at large, Satan convinced me to stay completely in the dark and protect my secrets. Satan, of course, accused me of pride, which definitely impacted my secrecy. So I faked a signature authenticity to our listeners by hiding my terrible, deep, dark secret.

Too real is this feeling of make believe...

At the same time, some very interesting things began to happen. Somehow, Jeannie and I became the coordinators of the *Family and Couples Ministry* at the *EUMC*. We also ended up facilitating a couples' Bible study every other Friday night called, *Making a Good Marriage Better.* Basically, every couple that attended had little children around Ricque's age or younger, and it seemed everyone was constantly having more babies.

Where my previous inclination had been that kids were mostly loud, whiny, pains in the butt, as the years progressed, I'd see these little ones growing up, maturing, and become functioning members of our church family. They were developing into Godly little people. In another miracle, my heart began changing.

I began to ask men around me what it meant for them to have more than one child and they'd all said the same thing, "It might be difficult financially, physically, and emotionally, but there was no better gift from God than a child." In 1997 I attended the *Promise Keepers: Stand In The Gap* event in Washington D.C. I traveled on a bus full of men from the Erie area, to join with about a million other Christian men from all over the country to pray for the nation and hear various Christian speakers.

On the bus, I sat next to Roger Scarlett, a board member of *WCTL* and fellow Edinboro resident. I knew he had twin sons and other children. Throughout our bus ride and during our time in D.C., I picked Roger's brain about fatherhood to a newborn. "Was it worth it? Would I make a good newborn baby's father? How do you cope?" I was clearly still scared, but something was happening in my heart.

I was, by then, not a complete stranger to having a child. I had been taking Ricque to her ballet lessons, bowling, sled riding, and more. But the newborn factor was different somehow. While Ricque was very young, we began what I called our "Daddy/Daughter Dates," where one Saturday morning each month, I would drive us down to *Crossroads Dinor*, in the center of Edinboro, and Ricque and I would have breakfast and spend some quality time together. We'd discuss life in general, how school was going, her friends, her joys, hobbies, and anything that was on her mind. It was a time of wonderful and critical communication together. It was these times that made me realize I was truly becoming a father, and I was making an immense difference in Ricque's life. The best, and most surprising part, was she was making even more of a difference in my life. Those outings, and Daddy/Daughter Dates are now among my most precious treasures.

By late 1998, the Lord performed the greatest miracle in my life to that point. The Holy Spirit had been ministering to my heart, as slowly but surely as water cut through the Grand Canyon. He convinced me to try a vasectomy reversal, if only to see if it might work. If it did, Jeannie and I could then consider the next step in having more children.

Much to Jeannie's delight (and despite my great trepidation,) I scheduled the operation. What I was not prepared for was the gravity of the new procedure. Compared to having the initial vasectomy, the reversal was much more intricate and *painful*. A vasectomy is a couple of small incisions, the doctor pulls out the *vas deferens* tube, snips, cuts and cauterizes, and then tucks it all back in. You gingerly walk out of the doctor's office, go home and utilize a pack of frozen corn, and watch *ESPN* for a couple of days. A reversal on the other hand, is a major surgery. It takes around five hours, it's intensive for the surgeon, and the patient is completely under anesthesia.

I took the plunge and had the operation. When I woke up the pain was nauseating! I cried out in agony as I came around, wondering why I had made this decision. Fortunately, the nurses medded me up and wheeled me out in a wheelchair. Over the next few days, my groin looked and felt like Mike Tyson had used it as a speed bag. Boy, did it hurt!

After about a week of misery, I had fully healed up and the moment of truth was upon us. We needed a test to see if the procedure worked. The problem was, I refused to go for the test. I was simply embarrassed and stubborn. I told Jeannie, "Hey, if it worked it worked, and you'll get pregnant!" This was not the answer she wanted to hear, but as always, she just dealt with it.

But month after month went by and Jeannie hadn't fallen pregnant. Every time she thought she might be, it would be a false alarm and she'd break down in tears. It broke my heart every time; Jeannie so badly wanted to have our baby but I refused to go back for the test. To be honest, it was a good dose of fear that kept me from going back for the test. I was too afraid of what the answer would be.

After about a year, I couldn't bear to see Jeannie continue to lose hope so we scheduled a visit to Dr. Anthony Thomas Jr. at the *Cleveland Clinic*. He performed the exam on me, and within minutes he returned and reported the reversal had not been successful. Jeannie burst into tears.

Where I was disappointed, Jeannie was completely crushed. The news really surprised me, as I was confident God had led me to this point. I truly thought the Holy Spirit had been speaking to me and it was His will for us to have more children. With Jeannie devastated and my mind suddenly reeling, I had no idea what to do.

Chapter 23

The Nightmare

I think it's safe to admit I'm a pretty unique individual in various ways, and I genuinely take pride in this. Where I was leery to give my life to the Lord, once I committed, I was unstoppable. After all I'd been through—the four abortions, a vasectomy, adopting Ricque, the first reversal, and now seeing my wife heartbroken… as they say in poker tournaments, I was all in. How could I not go for a second reversal? Without it I would never have an answer to the all-important question: *What if I had just tried a second time?* Again, Jeannie loved me enough to marry me and watch me have a vasectomy, believing she'd never have any more children. Why shouldn't I do it for my extraordinary wife? And, even though this was all new to me, God had begun yet another life-changing work deep in my heart and I now was determined to have more children with Jeannie.

In late 2000, Dr. Anthony Thomas Jr. of the *Cleveland Clinic* reviewed Dr. Chorazy's medical notes and performed his own examination. His professional opinion was there was a decent chance a second reversal could work. Dr. Thomas had been in the field a lot longer, and came highly regarded. He had such a soothing bedside manner and such a peaceful, encouraging way of talking to us, our hope was rebuilt. Heck, we even dared to be a little excited. We scheduled the surgery and I took a deep breath, remembering the pain of the first surgery and how grotesque it all was for a while.

The big day in December arrived and there I was again, lying on the gurney while Jeannie held my hand, praying. The strange thing was, now that I knew what I was in for, I wasn't nearly as nervous. I kissed my wife and watched her beautiful eyes try to hide her fear. In the room, the surgical staff were standing around doing their prep, waiting for the doc to arrive. Naturally, I chatted with a few of the staff, making them laugh as if we were hanging out at a barbeque. Dr. Thomas arrived and told me the anesthetist would start a drip, and to "Please count backward from a hundred." I looked around at everyone, nodded and said, "You guys do a great job on this. I'm counting on you!" I think they were either amazed and/or amused a patient would give them a little dugout pep talk before they went to work, but then again they *were* operating on Mark Bradley Morrow.

I began counting backward from a hundred… aaand the next thing I knew I was groggy in some recovery room with Jeannie by my side, crying. I looked over at her confused, because she was holding my hand and saying she was so proud of me. When the fog cleared, I understood she was crying because she had seen the change the Lord had done in my heart and the sacrifices I was willing to make for her and Ricque (Ricque desperately wanted siblings.) After spending a few hours in recovery I was allowed to leave.

About a month after the surgery, Jeannie and I drove back to the Cleveland Clinic for tests. After samples were taken, Dr. Thomas waved us into the next room and proceeded to a large microscope. He placed the sample on a slide under the microscope. He asked me to step over to look in the left eyepiece reticle, while he looked into the right one. Suddenly my heart began pounding. I looked at Jeannie who shared my thoughts—it was do or die time. We were about to hear life-changing news, one way or another. I began praying like crazy, with Jeannie in unison behind me. Doctor Thomas adjusted the microscope dial, while I freaked out. We were all in. I had pushed my final and last stack of chips into the center of the table, and if this didn't work, there was *no* going back for a third reversal. We both knew that. Suddenly Dr. Thomas announced, "*Hey!* I see some swimmers!"

Jeannie squealed before I could get a sound out, but I jumped back and we both burst into tears. I grabbed my wife and squeezed her as if I would never let her go, and she buried her head in my chest. God had given us the miracle so many had been praying for. Eventually we looked up at Dr. Thomas, and blubbering and laughing, we shook his hand and thanked him for all that he had done. Or should I say that he had allowed God to do through him (we were both convinced he was a believer.) I exhaled deeply in relief, thinking about the many couples who had endured their first or second, maybe even third reversals, who were told, "I'm sorry, but the surgery was not successful." I knew God's hand was on me, and it was then I got a glimpse of the depth of God's grace. I had been given the chance to build my family even more, even after having four abortions nobody knew about.

On March 23, 2001, Jeannie called me at work and asked if I wanted to go to the legendary *Uncle Charlie's Pizza Pub* for dinner. I loved *Uncle Charlie's*, so I said, "Of course!" While we were waiting for our dinner, Jeannie presented me with an envelope and inside was a certificate she had made using her computer that read:

Certificate of Accomplishment
This certificate is awarded to Mark Morrow in recognition of valuable contributions to fulfilling his wife's deepest desires with the gift of life.

Jeannie and Ricque had signed and dated it below, but behind the certificate was a *Meadville Medical Center* lab report showing *my wife was pregnant*! My jaw dropped open. Then Ricque handed me a small box. I opened it and inside was a little set of porcelain baby booties, with the birth stone and month of November written on them, indicating the month our baby was due. I was stunned. I couldn't believe my wife was already pregnant! *Boy, God doesn't play when He answers prayers.* I roared with laughter, hugged Jeannie and gave Ricque the tightest squeeze. She was so excited she was going to be a big sister. As a thirteen year old who had waited a long, long time, praying as much as anyone, her dream was also coming true.

The joy lasted through dinner, and for the drive home, and through saying good night to Ricque, and even while I got ready for bed. By the time my head hit the pillow, however, something weird happened. A lone thought flitted through my brain, like a stray bat, carrying a diseased thought. *You're going to be a father, and have a baby after being responsible for the killings of your first four children, thirteen years earlier. What's up with that, Mark Morrow?*

"Mark, you know you've made me the happiest woman in the world, right?"

"Huh?" I snapped out of my daze. "Aww, I just love you my angel," I replied to Jeannie.

"I can't believe we're having a *baby* in November, Mark!"

"I *know*, right? How wonderful is that?"

Jeannie snuggled up to me, and soon she was sound asleep. *I am happy we are having a baby, right?* Of course I was. *I'd had two reversals, hadn't I?* At that moment the lid of my personal *Pandora's Box* flew open, and every one of the hidden secrets of my past came pouring out over the lid like a tsunami. The sins, the abortion clinics, the cash, checks, and stuffed animals as guilt offerings, all the agony, fear, heartache, and misery that had been stuffed away for years. I began to hyperventilate like a Vietnam vet whose PTSD had suddenly been triggered. In a horrifying moment, I was overcome with stark terror. My mind swirled and whirled, and then felt as though it shattered into a million different pieces. *You're going to have a baby, but you killed four of them years ago, Mark*, the sinister voice continued to whisper.

The whole thing was so crazy, so incongruent, I was completely confused. I jumped out of bed and ran to the bathroom, wanting to throw up. When I couldn't, I staggered down the basement stairs and back up again. Then down and up and down and up, at least fifty times, trying to exhaust myself to fall asleep. The stair idea didn't work, so I put my coat on and headed outside to walk around my neighborhood at 1:00 a.m. That didn't work, so I went home, climbed back into bed and was promptly whomped by the tsunami again. I genuinely thought I was losing my mind. As a therapist, even I didn't realize the amount of secrets and guilt I'd stuffed down into the recesses of my mind for a number of years. With the news of Jeannie's pregnancy and the promise of joy and love and the nurture of fatherhood, a lid to a box of very unique emotions had been opened. I believed I had nailed that box shut years ago, yet Jeannie was sleeping in peace right beside me, not knowing anything about my past, and here it felt like demons were swarming around my bed. I slid back out of bed and ran outside. I dropped to my knees, begging God over and over to forgive me, but I felt nothing. At the time I had no idea I was experiencing *Post Abortion Grief*. I had simply delayed it, and it had compounded.

Post Abortion Grief can best be described as *a person's inability to* process their feelings of shame, anger, and depression after an abortion, grieve the loss of their baby, accept God's forgiveness and forgive themselves, and/or others associated with their abortion experience. All of that hit me in a second. Totally out of the blue.

That was my first sleepless night and many followed. So did the anxiety attacks. Despite the panic, I refused to process all my negative feelings. I became angry, and started losing trust in others. I suddenly had to be in control of everything and began spiraling into depression. I had four babies to grieve over, and certainly had not done that yet, nor was I prepared to do it. I was plummeting, crashing and burning, and no longer in control of myself or my emotions. And I had a baby on the way. On the outside, of course, I was a master at keeping everything looking okay.

As I feebly tried to process it all, I mentally knew God had forgiven me, and I had never held the abortions against the three mothers of my children. I never felt they owed me an apology since I was the one who essentially didn't take responsibility for my actions. Yet, while I knew God had forgiven me, I could not forgive myself. I felt like a hypocrite and a fraud. I felt torn, constantly wrestling with the reality of what I had done and the truth that God had blessed me despite my callouse actions. He'd even blessed me after hating the thought of having babies, or having anything to do with them.

This was all aside from the fact that for the first time in my life, my wife was pregnant and we were actually going through with having a baby. It was entirely new to me, and terrifying in its own right. The love and joy of having a baby was the flip side of a coin that sang out for me to deal with the horror for which I'd been responsible. Reality was hitting home hard and deadly. I just couldn't come to terms with what I had done thirteen years ago. Doing the worst thing possible, I continued to stuff all those emotions down as much as possible. I somehow managed to keep a lid on it all, and every now and then, in between the guilt and panic attacks, I actually experienced bursts of joy at having a new little munchkin.

To this point, we hadn't announced the pregnancy, wanting to wait until about the three month mark, to be sure everything was okay. After our three month appointment, Jeannie and I decided to let the joyful cat out of its bag. The next day at work, I first told Ron we were going to have a baby. He freaked out and couldn't stop congratulating me. Ron knew a little of my story, and what we'd been through, so he was overjoyed for us. Then I told Ron about a crazy idea I'd had. I wanted to call Jeannie at home while *live on the air* and ask her to share with thousands of *The Good Guys in the Morning* fans, that Mark Bradley Morrow and his lovely wife, Jeannie, were having a baby! For some reason Ron agreed. Bear in mind, I have always been a partially open book, and had shared a little of my story with my listeners. They all knew Jeannie and I were struggling to have children. So Ron ran the board and I dialed our home live on the air, and Jeannie answered the phone.

"Jeannie, I want you to know, you are *live* on the air right now."

Jeannie, unlike me, has never been, nor ever will be one to enjoy the spotlight. After a brief pause she simply said, "Okay…"

"Angel, I just thought you might have some really good news you might want to share with our listeners?" I could tell she was uncomfortable and I almost regretted my decision.

Then she simply said, "Well, I'm pregnant, and Mark and I are expecting a baby in November."

I could almost hear the roar of congratulations around the city as listeners were wowed with the news. We chatted with Jeannie live on air for a few more minutes, and kept the show fun and engaging. Finally I hung up with Jeannie, and the phone bank lit up like a Christmas tree with listeners congratulating Jeannie and I. I knew it was special to our listeners since we were really like one big family, sharing good times and bad.

Two days later, I was at the radio station early in the morning, prepping for the show. I smiled at the memory of sharing the news of our new baby live on air. To my surprise, the studio phone lit up so I picked up. It was Jeannie, calling from home.

"Mark!"

My veins turned to ice. She was hysterical.

"Mark… I think… I think I…" Jeannie was sobbing, and couldn't compose herself. The life drained out of my body.

"Jeannie, what's going on?"

"Mark, I think I had a miscarriage," she wailed. "I think… I lost the baby!"

"Oh my God," I whispered. "Jeannie, I'll be right there!"

I shouted to Ron that Jeannie might have had a miscarriage and I bolted out of the door! I punched the pedal to the floorboard and—like a Formula One driver—wound through back roads to our house. I screeched to a stop, slammed the car in park, and leaped out ready to throw up. I ran inside and found Jeannie, her face red and wet from tears.

"I've already cleaned up," she sniffed, "…but I think we lost the baby."

I sank to the floor and took her into my arms. She said she'd already called the doctor, who told her to come in as soon as I could drive her.

We arrived at the doctor's offices, and the nurses hurriedly admitted Jeannie, while I finished the paperwork. As I filled in the date, I realized it was only a few days before Mother's Day. I had planned to surprise Jeannie with something special. I began crying and whispered, *God, please make sure my baby is okay. Please make sure my wife is okay. Please God, please give me another chance. All I want is for us to have this baby.*

I was ushered back to the room where Jeannie was and they already had her prepped in a gown, on a hospital bed. The doctor's face was grave and Jeannie was crying profusely.

"I'm so sorry, Mr. Morrow," the doctor said. "I'm afraid your wife miscarried. We have to perform a dilation and curettage."

"A *what?*"

"A D&C. We have to remove the fetus."

The room spun, and I was struck dumb. I knew exactly what a D&C was. I'd been responsible for four prior D&Cs. *I'm trapped in a nightmare.*

Chapter 24

Invisible Children

When we left the clinic, it was dark and raining hard. That day in early May of 2001 has to be a reflection of hell. We had gone from sharing our joy with forty thousand listeners to the raw agony of losing a baby. We drove in silence, up Peach Street, heading back to Edinboro, both of us in our own little worlds, alone, yet together. Dazed and confused is a cliché, but a perfect description of our emotional state. The windshield wipers swung back and forth, back and forth, barely filling the awkward silence. A mother who had just lost her baby and a father who, unbeknownst to his wife, had just lost his *fifth*.

Out of the blue Jeannie asked, "How could anyone ever do that?"

Jerking out of my guilt descent, I cleared my throat and asked, "How could anyone ever do *what*?

"How could anyone ever have an abortion?" Jeannie turned to look at me as my eyes widened. "Because that's basically what just happened to me?"

I tried to stifle my shock. *Where the heck did that come from?* I had no answer for her, so I just continued looking forward. The windshield wipers continued going back and forth, back and forth, as the silence screamed.

Being a counselor, I tried to force myself to follow the guidelines for dealing with not only grief, but mounting guilt. I knew it was a lot easier said than done. *How does one deal with all of this, really?* A miscarriage in anyone's life is difficult enough, but throw in four secret abortions, a vasectomy, adoption, two reversals, and then we announced to tens of thousands of radio listeners that my wife was pregnant and now the baby was gone. That may have been the hardest day of my life, if not, it was undoubtedly up there with the loss of my dad, uncles, and first abortion. I say the first abortion, because that was the only one I was actually with the woman inside the clinic. But just like when I sat in that clinic, I just sat in the car. Because of the guilt and secrecy, I pushed it all down, down into the caverns of my soul, like so many barrels of toxic waste, buried deep underground, yet starting to rust, and leak and bubble out into the aquifers of my heart.

We arrived home and trudged inside. The rain fell as we sat on the couch, holding each other. It seemed as though life for everyone else was continuing as normal, but our world had fallen apart. After we wept, and sat in silence for many minutes, Jeannie eventually asked me if I could drive to *Giant Eagle*. She needed some ginger ale, crackers and a pain prescription that the doctor had given her.

When I reached the store, I went up to the pharmacy and handed them the script. Eventually I was given the prescription and turned to see Dr. Armstrong, one of my graduate professors at *EUP*, standing with his big, friendly smile and hand shake.

"Hey Mark," he said happily. "How's it going? I just heard the good news about you and Jeannie expecting a baby! Congratulations!"

Wow, I thought. I felt bad for him, knowing he would feel terrible when I had to tell him the news.

"Well actually…" I said awkwardly. "We just got back from the doctor and Jeannie had a miscarriage."

His smile turned to bewilderment.

"Oh, Mark!" he stammered. "I'm so sorry. I didn't know."

"Don't worry about it, Doctor Armstrong. You couldn't have known."

I excused myself to escape the awkward situation, and get back to the dark and the rain, to be alone with my sorrow.

I arrived home to find Jeannie sitting on the couch, still crying. I poured her a glass of ginger ale, put some crackers on a plate, and brought her the pain pills.

We sat there praying and thinking, until Jeannie asked me if I could go outside to meet Ricque as she got off the school bus, and let her know the news. I realized the rain had stopped and the sun was out, but my world was still filled with despair. I dreaded having to tell Ricque.

She hopped off the bus, and ran over to me grinning from ear to ear. Since our *Uncle Charlie's* dinner where Ricque had presented the Certificate of Appreciation, she had been over the moon knowing she was going to have a baby brother or sister to fuss over. She had said on more than one occasion she would be the best big sister in the whole world.

"Hey Dad!"

"Hey honey…" I paused. She frowned as she saw my face. "Look, can you sit over here on the front deck with me for a minute, I have something I have to tell you." Ricque knew something was very wrong, and the look on her face ruined me. I inhaled deeply, then shared everything that happened earlier that day. Ricque was instantly crushed, and broke down into tears. I held her close and told her that everything was going to be okay. We sat on the deck for a long while, until Ricque could cry no more. I didn't want her to see her mom in the same state, just yet. After reassuring and comforting her for a long while, the two of us stood up and walked into the house together. We walked over to Jeannie and had one of our less happy "family hugs."

That night, once the dust had sort of settled, and reality was slowly beginning to sink in, another torment resumed its work in me. An old, familiar voice I hadn't heard so chillingly clear in years, whispered, "Hey Mark, ya see… God is paying you back for all those abortions." Prickles ran down my spine. "Boy, God is sooo mad at you. He took this baby from you, because that's what you did to Him. He created your babies but *you* killed them, you piece of crap." My heart sank, but I kept listening, pondering, allowing the thoughts because of my guilt. "Yeah, you know God is angry, and it's payback time…. and you know what else Mark? If you do get Jeannie pregnant again, she's likely gonna have another miscarriage or better yet… what if you never get her pregnant again? Ever?"

My stomach heaved, but I could only turn in bed feeling sick and defeated.

I had gone from being full of joy and praising God publicly and ecstatically, to feeling practically hated by Him because of what I'd done. And worse, I'd been silent about it for years and years, and now my public Christian persona had become larger than I was. Satan was more than thrilled to use it all to wreak havoc on my mind. One would think I was close to breaking down and confessing my sins, coming clean and starting fresh. Instead, the lie deepened. I simply had too much to lose. In my mind, the hell I was going through in the secret places of my mind, was nothing compared to the hell I envisioned if I came clean. And yes, that old, familiar, sinister voice was there to reinforce that belief, every step of the way.

When news broke of Jeannie's miscarriage, love and support poured in. Ron and the staff at the station were exceptionally caring in encouraging me, giving me all the time I needed and following up to see how Jeannie was doing.

Due to my exposure on *The Good Guys in the Morning,* and my persona in the Christian world, I would be invited to be the M.C. at Christian events in the area, and often when Christian musical artists came to town. I would go out on stage, tell a few jokes and introduce the bands, providing a warm, local atmosphere so the band could connect even more with the crowd. After the miscarriage, I received an invitation to emcee *The Women's Care Center* fund raising banquet. The *Women's Care Center* in Erie is a pro-life organization that caters to women who are pregnant, and have no place to turn for help. I accepted, because how could I not? Yet, inside, the guilt deepened.

After emceeing two events hosted by *The Women's Care Center,* I was asked to host a pro-life event in Erie, where Tom Minnery from *Focus on the Family* was the keynote speaker. The deception I felt gnawed at my soul, yet somehow I kept my game face on, and kept doing what *Mark Bradley Morrow* did best—I'd hit the stage, tell some jokes, get people to laugh and loosen up, and then introduce the speaker to a receptive crowd. I'd then go back to my chair, sit next to Jeannie and listen dutifully like everyone else. Sometimes the keynote speaker would discuss their personal experiences with abortion, and Jeannie would sit there crying. She would later tell me she listened knowing how much she wanted to have a baby with me, but had to hear about other women aborting, while she would have given anything to have another baby. She'd grab my hand, squeeze it and cry every single time. I'd be sitting there thinking, *God, I'd give anything in the world if I could do that! If I could go up on a stage and have the guts to share my worst sins, and release the shame of my four aborted children.* Of course, I wasn't *willing* to do anything. The opportunity was always there, but as the maxim goes, "The power of sin is in its secrecy." As I lay in bed, with my desperately sad wife sleeping next to me, shame saturated me for having been such a hypocrite, emceeing at these events, speaking at various church men's groups, and pretending I had always been a staunch pro-life supporter. Because of the secrecy, Satan had me right where he wanted me.

As I lay there, he whispered, *Mark, if you **ever** tell anyone about your past, your life as you know it will be **over**! You will instantly be booted from The Good Guys in the Morning, no one will ever want to come to you for counseling again. You've done some messed up things, Mark, and your wife… oh your wife, Ricque, family, friends, and listeners will all know the truth. The truth that you are such a piece of garbage who calls himself a Christian.*

I woke up the next morning red-eyed and feeling like I'd been hit by dump truck. When I had finally fallen asleep the night before, I had experienced monstrous nightmares. I'd taken the day off to be with Jeannie, but we figured it would be a good idea to send Ricque to school, so she didn't see us grieving and could be with her friends. When she was ready, I walked her out and watched the kiddos of various ages getting on the bus, shouting and playing happily. Suddenly something struck me. *My four unborn children should be on this very bus. They should be playing, laughing, and making new friends.* I became dizzy under the weight of that thought. Ricque noticed something was up, but she didn't say anything. She just squeezed me tightly and I squeezed her back, then kissed her on the cheek. I held her for an extra few seconds, blinking back the tears. Then I let go and she walked up to the bus, waving at her friends. *My other four children should be on this bus. I should have their elementary school drawings on the fridge, and they should currently be in middle school, going out for sports or plays. Soon they'd be heading into high school… In a few years I should someday be teaching them how to drive, discussing dating, taking them to their varsity sporting events… They'd look and act like me in many ways, maybe even be into singing and music. I'd take them to Christian and Oldies concerts, see them go to Prom, Homecoming, graduate, help them decide on colleges…* I turned from the bus to hide the torrent of tears. My heart ached to realize I would never know them on this Earth. They were truly my *invisible children.*

———

A week later, Jeannie went in for a checkup and the doctor told us to just take some time off, and not try again for another baby right away. He wanted us to take a break and allow her body to recover. We did, and slowly but surely we began to heal a little more each day.

Soon, July 4th rolled around, and I decided to take Jeannie and Ricque across the state to Hershey, Pennsylvania. In Hershey (named after the chocolates, of course,) there is a huge amusement park and also *Hershey Stadium*—a large outdoor arena where they host State championship football games, concerts, and more. I had acquired tickets to *The Teen Idols Tour* featuring Davy Jones, Peter Noone, and Bobby Sherman. This was a huge tour for them, and people had snatched up tickets to see these guys perform again. I had recently interviewed someone from the amusement park about the upcoming concert and she had given me free tickets and backstage passes to the show.

The show was nothing short of mind-blowing, and after it ended, we went backstage to meet the artists and hung out for a while. I always loved that I could do those sorts of things for Ricque, as it made her feel really special and she could tell her buddies at school about it. After that, the three of us walked into the Park to mostly check out their roller coasters and funnel cakes! Ricque was thirteen at the time, and we realized she's an adrenaline junkie like me. We picked out the biggest, baddest roller coaster and I looked at Jeannie expectantly, begging her to ride it with us. Suddenly she looked nervous, but not in the way I'd expect.

"I can't Mark," she said firmly.

"Oh come on! These things are so safe! It will be a rush. You married me, how bad could this be?" I joked.

"No, Mark... I... I really cannot ride a roller coaster right now."

A connection flickered in my slow man-brain that she might be talking about something other than being nervous to ride it, but I couldn't figure out what. Was she feeling sick? Did she need to go to the bathroom?

"Huh?" I replied goofily.

Jeannie bit her lip, and then started to say something then paused. I just stared at her.

"What is it, Mom?" Ricque asked.

Jeannie exhaled deeply and smiled, "Guys, I'm pregnant!"

My eyes widened and I looked at Ricque who didn't hold back her shrill squeal of delight.

"Whaaaaaat?" was all I could mumble.

"It's true, Mark. I know we were supposed to wait, but I guess it just happened." Jeannie was grinning from ear to ear.

"*Mom!*" Ricque squealed again. "That is *so awesome!*" She was jumping up and down, while simultaneously hugging her mother, and shrieking like teenage girls do. I joined the party and put my arms around them both, my eyes instantly overflowing.

"That *is* so awesome, my love," I whispered. I buried my face in Jeannie's hair and kissed her cheek.

The ecstasy lasted for a moment, but almost as soon it came, a sickening feeling in my stomach followed.

She's going to have another miscarriage! God isn't going to bless you with children. Not after what you did. Who are you kidding? You don't deserve children of your own. Too little too late, Pal. You don't really think that God is going to give you kids after you killed four of your own?

I blinked back the tears, and tried to push the thoughts away. I hugged my family, and silently begged God would just give me one more chance, although I had my serious doubts.

Chapter 25

Faith Through Grace

Over the next few weeks, joy, then terror, then elation whipped my soul around like a beach ball in a hurricane. After my morning prayer times, I was on top of the world, so grateful to God He'd given us a baby. By the end of the day, I'd be freaking out and lose sleep that something would go terribly wrong. Because I was still clinging to my secrets, Satan was free to toy with my mind at will. He taunted me, and assured me something would go wrong with the pregnancy because of what I'd done. I'd fight him off at times, but standing alone was impossible. There was just no way I could do it. The three month mark was almost unbearable due to the memories from the miscarriage.

I would probably have kept the pregnancy secret until Jeannie delivered the baby, but eventually she began telling our family and friends. (She was beginning to show, after all.) After a while I figured, *What the heck,* and even announced it to my listeners again. In my heart though, I was constantly waiting for the other shoe to drop. God's shoe, right on my head, and on the baby, on my wife and on my family. When I somehow managed to overcome the thought that Jeannie would miscarry, Satan would tell me we'd have a handicapped baby. It was one of the most joyful times of my life, coupled with a desperate nightmare. Don't get me wrong, I was certainly hopeful we'd have a healthy, beautiful baby, but it was a back and forth game of ping-pong over the abyss of my soul, believing and trusting in God, then being worn down by the enemy's lies.

Despite fighting this silent battle, I continued to maintain my poker face, and even surprised Jeannie by setting up Lamaze classes for us. Jeannie was pleasantly surprised, but I figured she'd know my *modus operandi* by now—once I was in, I was *all* in. To be honest, the classes helped me more than her. They reduced much of the stress and anxiety of the pregnancy, and I realized afterward it was really the Holy Spirit's prompting that caused me to sign up. We learned about what to expect and how I could help make the birthing process easier for Jeannie. It also helped me feel a little less useless when it was delivery time. Then, at one of the checkups, the doctor suggested having blood tests done, to make sure the baby didn't have Down's syndrome. Since Jeannie was thirty-nine, the doctor kind of pushed it a little. I felt a sudden pang in my stomach, and almost let it get over on top me. But I asked the doctor straight, "So, why would we have that test done?"

"So you could see if your baby might have Down's syndrome," he replied, a little confused.

"And? What if the baby has Down's syndrome?" I asked directly.

The doctor began hemming and hawing, realizing we were not only never going to abort a child with Down's syndrome, the mere suggestion offended us. When I finally let the doctor off the hook, I looked down at Jeannie who was beaming up at me. God had really changed my heart. At that point, I obviously wanted a healthy child but I was ready to love and cherish our baby, no matter what. Despite the bondage to my secret sins, God was still working deep in my heart.

One good thing that came out of the fear I experienced, was I began praying like crazy and reading the Word constantly. Inevitably I began growing spiritually, and slowly but surely, I started putting the pregnancy into God's hands the best I could. As the due date drew nearer, the more confident I became in the Lord. The days began to get more and more exciting until one day I realized I was filled with faith and hope about our new little one. It is worth mentioning that we'd told the doctors and midwife we absolutely did *not* want to know the sex of the child. Neither of us cared at all about that, we just wanted a healthy baby. It may sound pious, but I figured, *Who am I to ask God for a particular sex, even if I hadn't done what I had done in the past?* I'd known a few guys over the years who were all about having a son and if they didn't get what they wanted, they were super-disappointed and wanted to try again and again for that boy. I purposed in my heart I would never be like that. We'd find out when the baby popped out, and I would be overjoyed just to be our baby's dad!

As the third trimester drew to a close, the doctor decided to pick a date for us to go into the hospital to induce Jeannie. He chose February 27, 2002 as the big day. That Wednesday morning I woke up early to get ready to drive us to *St. Vincent Hospital.* I looked outside and the grass and street were blanketed with snow. It was still coming down and extremely windy outside so I prayed for a quick, easy drive to the hospital. I made sure Ricque was okay to get on the bus herself that morning after dad and mom left early for the hospital, and she assured me she was. She was more upset she couldn't come with us, but I assured her she could join us after school.

By 8:00 a.m. we were sitting in the hospital room, waiting for the next move. I'd brought a little radio and put it on the table next to Jeannie. I tuned it to *WCTL,* to listen to some Christian music and make the atmosphere as calm as possible for my wife. That's when we heard an emergency broadcast that the snow had in fact become a huge blizzard, and the city was just about completely shut down. There had apparently been a sixty car pileup on the I-90 as well, only ten miles from the hospital. I thanked the Lord, feeling extreme gratitude for His protection even in the little things.

I really had no idea what the induction process was, so I was a little surprised when things were going so slowly. After a few hours, nothing was progressing, so the nurses had Jeannie sit down on a large ball and gently bounce up and down, while I rubbed her shoulders and prayed for her. At one point, Jeannie thought her water broke so the nurse checked her out but said, "No, your water hasn't broken." I sighed in frustration. Jeannie later said again she was pretty sure her water had broken, and another nurse came in and checked, and this time, Jeannie was correct. Her water had broken. That didn't speed anything up, however. To be honest, the doctor was a little too laid back for my taste. When he first came in, he had a sandwich in one hand and a can of Coke in another and nonchalantly said "I don't think you're going to have the baby today. Probably tomorrow. I'm going to go to the mall for a while and do some shopping, I'll be back in a few hours."

What the heck! I thought, but we just waited and waited, and by late afternoon, Ricque arrived, having been driven in by a friend of ours. She eagerly asked if she had a new baby sibling. I told her not yet, and she proceeded to sit down and wait with us.

Finally, around 7:00 p.m., Jeannie started having contractions. Well, I started freaking out. The doctor still wasn't back, the weather outside was horrendous, and the city was buried under more than two feet of new, fallen snow. I began to pray, but also strongly "encouraged" the nurses to get hold of the doctor any way possible, and tell him to get in there as soon as possible. Suddenly there was a knock at the door. It was our good friends, Joe and Mille Farrell, who had come to say hi, and see if the baby had arrived yet. It was actually their anniversary and they still took the time to come visit, even in the storm. Well, they kind of walked into a hornet's nest. Jeannie was now lying on the bed in agony, the midwife and nurses were scurrying around, and I was holding her hand, frantically trying to remember the Lamaze stuff. It sure looked to be go-time and I was furious with the doctor.

In a few minutes, the midwife came in all scrubbed up and I started praying like crazy. At that point, I was really thankful Millie was there, because she was calm. I realized she had totally been sent by God. Millie grabbed Jeannie's hand, while I tried to usher Ricque out of the room. Ricque flatly refused, so I just paced back and forth like a crazy person, while Joe remained out in the hallway praying as vehemently as I was. All of a sudden, the doctor walked in, like the star in a Hollywood Western.

"Welcome back, Doc!" I said acidly, as the midwife stepped back. The doctor stepped forward and told Jeannie to slow her breath, but start pushing. Then, all in a moment, everything synced up perfectly, and everyone was doing what they were supposed to. Time slowed, and I watched this unfold, vaguely aware of the hand of God, perfectly orchestrating everything. Suddenly I saw my baby's head crown. I was frozen in the moment and told myself for the thousandth time not to faint. Within an instant the doctor was holding a squirmy little baby.

"It's a *girl!*" the doctor pronounced, and my heart nearly exploded with joy. With my hand over my mouth I gazed at my brand new baby daughter. She was a total mess and squawking loudly but the most beautiful little thing I'd ever seen. I gazed at this sweet little being—a perfect little baby girl who needed me to take care of her, hold her, nurture her, love, and protect her. I realized I was getting another shot to do all those things I had failed to do in the past. And boy was I ready! I was instantly, head-over-heels, crazy in love.

"*Mr. Morrow!*" the doctor said sharply, and I realized it was the third time he'd called my name.

"Yes!" I responded, standing to attention.

"Would you like to cut the cord, sir?"

"Absolutely!" I jumped forward.

The doctor handed me some sharp, surgical scissors and I began cutting the lifeline that had fed my baby all those months. She was ready to be welcomed into the world now, and I could help make sure she had everything she needed. When I was done, the nurses clapped softly and congratulations were heard all around. Then the nurses proceeded to clean her up, and put her in Jeannie's arms. Jeannie was still blotchy red in the face from the strain, but when that baby was placed in her arms, she looked brighter than a thousand suns.

That moment was one of the greatest of my life. It was right up there with getting saved, leading Jeannie to Christ, and of course, Ricque's adoption ceremony at the court house. It was a deeply holy, euphoric, pure love. After I'd kissed my wife, my new baby girl, and my half-grown baby girl, I picked up the phone to call my mom.

"Mom, you have a new granddaughter!" I said softly. She immediately started crying with joy. "Mom, she's so perfect, oh my gosh. Faith Maddison Morrow is perfectly healthy, with ten fingers and ten toes, and absolutely gorgeous." My mom was a total mess on the other end, so I told her I loved her, and said I needed to call Aunt Toni, and my Grandma Lucille. I called them and told them all the good news as I watched the nurses weigh Faith, measure her, put the little band around her tiny wrist, and all the other official things that they needed to do. I kept wanting to pinch myself, and couldn't wait to hold her again. I closed my eyes, and thanked God. "I love you Lord," I whispered. "Thank you. Thank you so much for this perfect little baby. She's so beautiful." I sighed. It was all simply breathtaking.

Well, I guess, this is the right way to have a baby, I smiled to myself. *God's way! Married, employed, and in love.* I had never been happier.

Chapter 26

Breaking Point

I was astounded by the grace of God. As I held my baby girl, I thought back to when I married Jeannie, and had no idea how to be a dad. I'd sure come a long way since then, and that was purely by the hand of God. It couldn't have been anything else. Needless to say we all fell in love with Faith instantly, and our home flowed with more love and joy than I ever knew was possible. Ricque couldn't stop fawning over her little sister, and Jeannie definitely appreciated the help. After a week or so, some family came over, and fussed and ooh'd and aah'd over our new, beautiful baby girl. I sat back, amazed at the miracle God could do. I was amazed at the astonishing creation of a little life, but also the equally astonishing creation of a heart of compassion and appreciation so deep in a man who once, didn't even want to be around children.

As it does with a new kiddo, life got busy and time flew by, and it seemed my tiny baby, Faith, grew even faster. It was probably around late 2002, possibly 2003, when the Holy Spirit spoke pretty clearly to me. I was enjoying every moment of being a daddy to this beautiful little girl, and watching as my beautiful older girl, Ricque, stepped so naturally (and excitedly) into her role. To this point, the demons of guilt had mostly been silenced by joy, but for the previous few days I had been experiencing a battle between my conscience and the Holy Spirit. I suppose I had been trying to suppress His voice. But that day, during my prayer time, I was caught off guard, and knew without a doubt God was asking me, "Mark, you see how great fatherhood really is? Do you think after all you've been through… do you trust Me to give you one more healthy baby?"

I sighed, surrendered, and replied, "Okay, Lord, here's the deal—I'm not going to *try* to have a baby, but I'm also not going to try *not* to have a baby." I felt a release in my spirit, and figured *Whatever happens, happens*. I was true to my word though, and handing it over to the Lord, I stopped using contraceptives.

About a year went by, and Faith grew quickly. I adapted to life as the dad of an infant, and helped Jeannie with anything I could. Faith grew and grew and became more beautiful every day. At this point in time I was working at *Family Services of NWPA*. One day I was sitting at my office desk when the phone rang. I picked it up and it was Jeannie. We made small talk for a minute then she asked me, "Mark, do you have any plans for this September?"

"Huh? What do you mean?"

"Well, Mark, September is the month that were going to have another baby," she giggled.

I just sat there speechless. I was numb for a moment, holding the phone. It wasn't like I was unhappy with the news, I was just shocked. Really shocked.

"Wow, I don't know what to say…" I eventually stuttered. My mind raced to a thousand places, not the least of which was money and the size of our house. Jeannie was silent on the other end of the line.

"…but we'll work it out, whatever it takes," I continued quickly, my spirit taking over from my mind. "Oh honey, we're so blessed to have this chance again." That was good enough for Jeannie, and I could feel her smile through the phone. We chatted excitedly for a while, then Jeannie had to go.

After hanging up, I shut my office door, and sat there, still a little stunned. At that point, the fear returned with thoughts like, *How are we going to be able to afford another child? Our little starter home is way too small for five of us*, and *Jeannie will be 42 in September. She's having a baby at the age of 42!* I decided to call up one of my best friends, Mike O'Malley, at work. He answered the phone and I told him the news. Without hesitation Mike exclaimed, "Congratulations, you guys are going to do just fine!"

Whoa! I thought to myself. *That's exactly what I needed to hear.* All I needed was someone to tell me everything would be okay. I chatted to my buddy for a few minutes, and then after being more encouraged, I said goodbye. I felt a little better, but I was still in a little shock. *I need to call Mom and let her know!* I thought. She'd be happy, and that would make me happy. I dialed her number.

"Hello"

"Hi Mom!"

"Hi Mark, what are you up to?"

"Well, I was wondering what you're doing in September?" I decided to use Jeannie's line. I had to admit it was clever.

"What do you mean, what am I doing in September?" My mom had the exact response I did. Like mother like son, I guess.

"Yeah, Mom, what are you doing in September?" I asked again.

"Mark, I don't have time for games, why do you want to know?"

I cleared my throat, a little taken aback. "Well Mom, Jeannie's pregnant and the baby is due in September, and you're going to be a grandmother again!" I waited expectantly, but there was nothing but silence.

As I was about to speak, my mom said, "Well Mark, I hope you know what you're doing!"

It was my turn for silence. It felt like I'd just been sucker-punched in the stomach. I had no idea what to say and the wind was completely gone from my sails.

"Well, I've got to get back to work," was all I could stammer. We awkwardly said goodbye, and hung up.

I was devastated. *What if everyone else I tell has the same reaction?* I wondered if I had caught my mom in a bad mood. Or maybe it was because she'd always been such a perfectionist, having to make sure all her ducks are in a row, planning everything out in advance? *Maybe,* I thought, *it's because she had me at 19 and my sister at 24 and here's her son who would be 44 and his wife 42. That's ridiculous, isn't it?* My mind reeled. I began to stress out. We had a very small house and I'd had a significant decrease in pay, vacation and sick days. I'd even had health insurance cuts when I'd resigned from *Harborcreek Youth Services* two years before, and was still playing catch up.

I prayed about it for a moment, and instantly felt some relief. I decided to push my fears, and the influence of other's negativity away, and I braced myself for all the ups and downs of a challenging but rewarding pregnancy. This time, I didn't have the same fears as last time, but Jeannie and I were still on the same page with not wanting to know the baby's sex, or not wanting to know if there were any problems with the baby, due to Jeannie's age. We prayed, and believed God would see us through to another healthy, happy baby. In the meantime, I began hunting for houses in pure faith.

Jeannie's pregnancy couldn't have been smoother. She had no gestational diabetes, she didn't have much morning sickness, and generally seemed a lot healthier. I praised God for the comparable ease of this pregnancy, and although we were a lot busier, with Faith still being a baby herself, we handled all of the joys and challenges of the pregnancy together. I had a ton of people praying, and a lot of encouragement, especially from the other *Good Guys in the Morning*. Everyone was just so thrilled for us. It also helped having just gone through the motions a couple of years before.

That summer whizzed by in a haze of doctor's appointments, prenatal vitamins, and making sure Jeannie was getting enough rest, with a baby and an energetic sixteen-year-old running around the house. Before I knew it, we were four weeks out from Jeannie's due date, and I still hadn't had any luck finding a home.

We had been looking at houses diligently but nothing was standing out. They were always just too small, or too expensive, or not in the best neighborhood. I decided to stick to my philosophy of, "You'll know it when you know it," whether it's regarding a car, house, spouse or job, so I just chilled out and handed it over to God. I kind of did resign myself to living the next year or so in a very tight little house, and figured we'd make do. We had so far.

One day we were driving around a certain neighborhood and saw three "For Sale" signs. We decided to stop and look at one house and as we got out of the car we saw an old neighbor of ours. I couldn't believe it. We chatted for a while, and explained we were looking for houses. She told us she and her husband had bought their new house in Georgetown Heights a year ago and loved the neighborhood, and proximity to Erie. Then she told us about a house right down the street, not a hundred yards away, which had been on the market for some time. We thanked her and said we'd check it out.

We researched a little and discovered the house had been on the market for about a year, and was vacant. In our research we also found the original asking price had been dropped a few times. We decided to call the realtor, and scheduled a walk-through. We met the realtor, who was very friendly and gave us the tour.

"If you like it, keep your poker face on," I reminded Jeannie, as we started walking through the house. It was me who could hardly contain myself though. *This house is perfect!* I thought to myself. The entire time I'd been praying, "God, we just need a bigger house." That was it. I hadn't been praying for an attached two car garage, fireplace in the living room, dining room, a huge, finished basement, and huge rear deck surrounding an above-ground pool. Plus, the McKean Community Park was just a half a mile away. It was all Jeannie and I could do to maintain our poker faces. After the tour, we thanked the realtor for showing us the house and said we'd think about it.

Although I loved the house, even with the price drops, the house really was still a little high for what we could afford. Plus, how were we going to buy a house, move everything in and have a baby in four weeks? Jeannie and I agreed the house was perfect for our growing family, but we faced a few challenges. We decided to pray about it, and as I was praying, for some reason I asked God to show us a sign. The very next morning the realtor called me up and told me that he spoke with the seller who said he'd lower the price by $6,000 *and* would help pay for a portion of the closing costs. I was astounded in the best way possible. I'd asked for my sign, and I'd received it but I was still nervous to pull the trigger. I called up my friend, Freddy. He agreed to look the house over. At the end he asked me matter-of-factly, "Mark, what are you waiting for?"

"What do you mean?" I replied.

"Dude, what's wrong with the house? What's holding you back?" I thought about it for a minute, ran everything through my head, and really couldn't come up with anything that I didn't like about it.

"Mark, if there's nothing holding you back, pull the trigger, buddy! If you wait just one day, this house could be sold tomorrow, especially with the price being decreased another $6,000."

Again, I learned God truly does put the right people in our lives at the right time. I needed to hear Freddy say that and challenge me, so I called up the realtor and told him we'd take it! Within fourteen days we had signed the contract, and closed on the house. Our Pastor, Jim Culbertson, and one of our elders, Dennis Baer, helped us move. Hallelujah, God had provided yet again, and we were ready to have another baby!

September 15, 2004 was a Wednesday morning again. Thankfully, there were no blizzards, but we did wake up early to drive to the hospital and get Jeannie settled in. She'd turned forty-two only nine days earlier but looked not a day over thirty. I was in much better shape too, not so freaked out, having done this already with Faith. We used the same midwife, Kim Bennett, who is a wonderful woman and highly professional. Jeannie was prepped, and all there was left to do was wait.

There was a TV in the waiting room, so I went back and forth, checking *ESPN* for various sports scores. I remembered how long Faith's labor was, so I felt no sense of urgency. It was about 11:30 a.m. and I was sitting in the lounge, watching scores and highlights, feeling pretty comfortable for a guy about to have another baby. After a while, I nonchalantly walked back into the room to discover Jeannie in the throes of giving birth. Thankfully, our friend, Dawn Johnson, was there holding Jeannie's hand and encouraging her. I walked in right as the baby was just about to crown. I'm standing there amazed, and the next thing I knew the baby is out and Dawn shouted, "It's a *boy!*" I experienced the same slow motion effect I had with Faith, and could only think, "What! A boy?" The entire pregnancy, I strongly believed we were going to have another girl. Something just told me we were going to have another girl, and I was still totally alright with that. My prayer, day in and day out was simply, "God, please bless us with a healthy baby. I don't care one iota if it's a boy or a girl, just a healthy, happy baby and mom." Well, mine and Jeannie's prayers were answered with a big, resounding *yes!*

God had provided for us yet again. He unquestionably gave us the new house and everything had gone perfectly with the delivery. He'd given us another beautiful baby and a baby *boy* at that. We were blessed beyond measure—we now had two healthy babies, and a beautiful young lady who was a successful junior in high school. God had consistently displayed only love to me. I felt so complete, so whole, so perfect… for a moment.

Chapter 27

A Crazy Descent

s I held my baby boy, a voice… a mere whisper… reminded me of the children who hadn't been born. The babies I had left behind. Children who were now nothing more than secrets to be desperately buried forever. I shrugged the haunting guilt off, and looked at Jeannie smiling. I had that poker face perfected. I'd coped so well when Faith was born… for a little while there, I thought I might have actually been getting over the toxic waste buried in my heart. Yet, as I held my new little boy, I couldn't stop my heart from spiraling into a crazy descent. And I had no idea why it was happening.

To be honest, one thing I had never worried about, was my secret being exposed. Why would I? I knew the three girls would never say anything. They were dragging around the same murderous shame I was. And it wasn't as if abortion clinics leave paper trails. It's not like you hand them a debit card or write a personal check. No, the abortion industry is a ca$h cow that rakes in over a billion dollars a year, *in the U.S. alone.*

All the media fluff, all the hype, all the logical arguments all fly out the window when you walk through the doors of one of those clinics. They're congenial, and are trained to deal with emotional situations, but make no mistake, they're trained to get you in, "taken care of," and out the door. They are truly abortion mills. There is absolutely *nothing* like the soul-ravaging guilt of walking through those doors, and walking out an hour later, lighter in cash and life. Anything else that is portrayed is a lie. It starts slowly as shock… and begins to claw at you day by day by day. This sinister mist descends when you see happy kids clamber aboard the school bus on a sunny day, or notice a child's birthday in the same month and year. Or when your wife has your second baby, and your protective instinct for your brand new, innocent, vulnerable infant, as well as your beautiful toddler, is through the roof.

We named our little boy Ross Bradley, and as he wiggled around in my arms, love and hope and joy flowed from this little person straight into my heart, dispelling all darkness as I held him. It was as if he'd arrived straight from Heaven, and the aura of God was still all around him. We enjoyed a couple of days at the hospital, and then I bundled up my growing family and drove them all home, to our big, new house.

For the most part, life went on as normal. I managed "the dark cloud" as I always had, pushing it away, and going on with my life, but something deep was shifting. Something spiritual. I didn't realize that God wanted to do more with me. A lot more, but I wasn't listening. Although I believe God doesn't use evil to wake us up, He will allow certain things to ensure we aren't lost permanently, and ensure we keep progressing in Him. That, however, is what we veterans call *the hard way* to learn. But God kept blessing me, as is His nature, and for that period, I kept myself convinced life was proceeding as normal. But as the routine of a new baby became normal—probably around the time we went into 2005—the cracks began to show.

At first, after leaving my beautiful wife and kids at home, while driving in to work, I'd see one of those huge pro-life billboards in Erie. For years, I must have always just repressed the associated thoughts unconsciously. At times, I suppose I'd dwelt on it, but after the spiritual climate shift, every time I saw those billboards, I began to ruminate on my terrible choices, and my dead children. Then I'd see or hear a news story about Roe vs. Wade, and the abortions would come back to the front of my brain. Then I'd come home from work, and look at Ricque and my two new precious little ones, and it slowly but surely began to snowball. It was like when you get a new car, and you suddenly see every car like that on the road, where you never noticed them before. Except, this was wearing away at my soul.

During this time, it was safe to say I was an established icon in Erie's Christian community. *The Good Guys in the Morning* was still *the* go-to morning drive Christian radio show, and I loved that job more than anything else I did. Plus, here I was working with teenagers in the *Independent Living Program for Family Services,* and for some reason I began to notice the birthdates of these boys and girls on the intake sheets. Many of their birth dates were in 1988, 1989, and 1990.

The guilt swamped into me again. *Whoooa!* I thought to myself. *These kids are the same age as mine would have been. They could have been mine.* The snowball began to pick up speed, and mass. Jeannie and I were also still attending *The Women's Care Center* banquets each year, and we'd sit through these powerful meetings and hear testimonies of post-abortive women who, after much dealing with debilitating shame and trauma, would experience redemption and wholeness from God. All I could think of in these events were how (to the best of my knowledge,) Lisa, Jenny, and Heather were probably still in deep, deep bondage to shame, anger, and depression. As was I. After each fund raiser, Jeannie and I would support *The Women's Care Center* with our monthly pledges, while I hid my dark secret.

Anxiety began to coil around me like a python, as it had back in the days of the abortions. I started becoming sick to my stomach, scared, angry, and sad. All I wanted to do was enjoy my little boy's first year but a plethora of emotions kept overwhelming me at random times. The familiar, menacing voice returned, but I mistakenly believed it was my own, *"If anyone ever finds out about your past, it's over! You'll be fired from WCTL instantly, and your wife, family, and friends are going to hate you! And don't even think anyone will ever come to you for counseling! You're a hypocrite, Mark."*

By mid-2005, I was unraveling in a scary way. I began to experience a desperate urge to tell someone… anyone! As my mind raced through it, I thought I could maybe tell a total stranger, heck maybe even a priest, even though I wasn't Catholic. That might get some of the burden off my chest. Whenever I would almost gather up the courage to find someone to tell, I would back out at the last minute. There were days where I'd be having a meltdown, and in my office I would begin shaking and crying, lock the door, put my chair in front of it and drop to my knees in tears, terror, and desperation. It was just unbearable that no-one had a clue. Not a single person I knew could help me carry the shame.

I began to get really scared, and knew I was rapidly approaching a breaking point. I was either going to explode or have a nervous breakdown. I almost wished my secrets would just be exposed. For years I had believed I was unlike the Christian celebrities who had been busted, because if the girls outed me, they were exposing themselves too. But now I knew that one way or another, secret sin gnaws at you, binding you up like an octopus, and the more you try to fight to be free, the more it entangles you, strangling the life out of you. One thing I knew intimately—the mandate by God Himself regarding abstaining from sex outside of marriage was for the entire human race's benefit. To spurn that mandate was at our own very grave risk.

If only I had listened, I thought, feeling desperate. *If I had only taken what I was preaching seriously, and how I wish there had been accountability in my life.* The problem was, I had no idea I was still living with evil twin sisters that had been wrecking me since my youth. Pride and Shame are like blonde and brunette, non-sororal twins. They don't look alike but they end up doing the same thing. The Shame of feeling inadequate compared to my sister and mom's new husband had led me to strive to make a name for myself. Pride crept in once I had accomplished a few things, and had lured me away from God, and now, way down the road when I was reaping the negative consequences of my actions, Shame was again tagged in, and was finishing the job.

I wished I could scream it loud and clear from a rooftop, "IT'S A TRAP!" Sexual temptation is exciting, let's be honest, but it's a trap that, in hundreds of ways, leads to shame, anger, jealousy, betrayal... even legalized murder. As I spiraled down, down, down... the logical side of my brain told me it was ridiculous. It was years ago, it was all over, forget it. But something... *someone* was using it to haunt me. And whatever evil was pursuing me, it had every right to do so, because I had never confessed my sin. I was still concealing it, just like I had concealed my double life of sexual sin all those years ago. I was hanging onto this secret, allowing my deadly enemy a wide open door into my soul. I was a fraud but knew I couldn't keep living the lie. I just wanted out, yet I was most afraid of being seen as a bad person; but then again, I had to be honest with myself, *I am a bad person. I'm a sinner and a liar.*

By February of 2006, each day was becoming bleaker, more stressful, and more full of anxiety and shame. I knew I couldn't take anymore, and my spirit was like a pressure cooker whose lid was about to blow. I could either be proactive and control it, or reactive and it would likely destroy me in a total breakdown. After a long day at work, I went to our church to see a person for a counseling session. It was around 7:00 p.m. and I can't recall who the person was, but I do remember while I was doing my best to listen and help them, my head, heart, and soul were spiraling out of control. I just had to get this toxic secret out of my system. I had to actually name it, to tell someone.

Too real when I feel what my heart can't conceal...

After the session ended, I called up my good friend, Rob Irwin. Rob was a standup guy, but also a no-nonsense Christian and I knew I could trust him. The phone rang.

"Hey Rob," I said, thinking I was still maintaining some semblance of control in my voice. "What are you up to?"

"Hey Mark. Is everything all right?" he asked me immediately.

"No," I said, barely hanging on. "But if at all possible, buddy, I'd really appreciate it if you could come to the church and see me."

"Dude, I'll be there right away." He could tell I was messed up. *Severely* messed up.

I hung up the phone and I felt like throwing up. *This is it. You're going to spill the beans.* I told myself. *Except, this is a heck of a lot more than beans. This is your fraudulent life. Your image is about to be shattered.* I began sweating profusely.

After what felt like days, Rob arrived and I saw the concern in his face when he saw me.

"Let's go over to Pastor Jim's office upstairs," I said, and he nodded and followed me. Jeannie and I had used Pastor Jim's office on occasion, for evening counseling sessions.

When we walked in I said "Rob, you sit in my chair over there. You get the leather, counselor's chair." I sat on the couch, where my clients usually sat, and Rob took Pastor Jim's black leather swivel chair. We sat there for what seemed like an eternity. I couldn't do it. Even as Rob sat there with a compassionate expression, knowing something was terribly wrong, yet not wanting to prod, I imagine he was thinking the very worst. Yet my mouth was not able to utter my failures, my sins, because of the terrible consequences. I began to cry. Then I wailed and my body shook, and then convulsed involuntarily. I had no idea what Rob was thinking, but I'm sure he was freaking out on the inside. He'd never seen me like this, and I would wager he'd never seen anyone in this sort of emotional shape.

For the first time I could truly understand how so many of my clients felt when they sat in my office and things they'd never told anyone before began to surface. My mind recalled the thirty-something Roman Catholic who shared with me the six abortions she'd had, because her husband considered it to be like birth control. Yet deep down, she knew what she had been doing was killing her children. Or the forty-something man who looked like he used to play in the *NFL*, yet had just fallen apart during our first session as he revealed he had been sexually abused by his *Boy Scout* Master when he was thirteen. He'd held this secret for over a quarter of a century. Or the fifty-something woman who told me that at age thirteen, she'd been gang raped by three of her brother's older friends. When I asked her how many people she'd shared this with, she replied, "You're the first."

As I sat there shaking and hyperventilating, I suddenly cracked. "Rob, I got a girl pregnant, and we had the baby aborted!" I was shocked that the words had come out of my mouth, but there they were, out in the real world. "Actually with her there were two abortions…" I wailed. "And then I got two more girls pregnant… and both of those babies were aborted too. I was a youth leader, Rob. I was speaking in church and counseling kids." The floodgates were open, and it all poured. "I was a Christian Rob… and I killed four babies…" Eighteen years of suffering… eighteen years of pain, anger, depression, shame, and anxiety poured out of what had been a dormant volcano. Every detail, every bit of shameful, sinful, fearful horror came spewing out of my mouth like a pungent, burst sewer dam.

Rob was a mature Christian, and I knew he cared about me, but as I looked up before he could adjust it, his mouth had dropped completely open in shock.

Chapter 28

James 5:16

J ets of guilt, pain, deceit, and eighteen years of suffering spewed out of me, like violent, volcanic streams. I couldn't care about what Rob thought, all I could feel was the catharsis of this burden flowing out and away from me. It was pure agony yet unbelievable relief. Wave after wave of emotion wracked my body as I confessed everything. Every tiny detail was confessed, probably more than necessary, as it *all* came out. The pain of losing my dad, my uncles, my mom remarrying, my drift into sin, the first abortion, the second… the sex… the third and fourth abortions. What was once sweet, forbidden fruit was now poisonous death erupting from my heart.

After many minutes, I calmed to a mild tremor, and sat with my face buried in my hands.

"Mark…" Rob said gently. I looked up slowly, my eyes bloodshot and my face red and wet.

"God has forgiven you, man," he said softly. He looked me square in the eyes. The words took my breath away.

"Mark, that's not who you are anymore. All those sins are from your past… a long time ago."

I melted under the warmth and comfort of those words.

"Mark, you've repented, and confessed your sins. God is good and He'll make it okay. It's going to be alright, I promise you, my brother." His assurance was like a hundred warm blankets wrapped around me.

For the first time in years I saw a ray of hope. A lone ray piercing the black clouds that had hung above me for so long. I sighed deeply, and my face involuntarily screwed up into tears again… but this time they were tears of relief. Rob's words were exactly what I needed to hear. I suddenly realized this was the polar opposite of what Satan had said would happen if I came clean.

Rob continued gently counseling me, reinforcing the message of forgiveness, love, and hope. His words washed over me like warm, healing waves of grace. I could hardly believe I had told someone. The pressure was gone. I couldn't remember the last time I had felt so free. So light. So clean. It felt… weird. Rob was an excellent and very sensitive counselor. He told me he was proud of me, and asked me if I was going to be okay. I told him I certainly would be. He stood up grinning, and gave me a strong bro-hug.

My secret is out! I thought. I couldn't believe it. *So far so good!* I asked Rob to keep me in his prayers, especially as I had to tell Jeannie next. He promised he would. I turned off the lights, locked up the church. I exhaled deeply with a smile. On the way home, I figured that was enough for one day. I'd tell Jeannie the next evening after work.

I prayed throughout the next day and waited until Jeannie got home, but as the time drew near, I started feeling anxious again. Incredibly anxious. In fact, I was nearing the panic I had experienced the night before, prior to telling Rob. In my determination to get the second wave of confession off my chest, I began to not think straight. When Jeannie arrived home, I immediately said I had to tell her something really important. She looked at me, a little concerned, and said somewhat impatiently, "Mark I have to leave again to pick up Ricque from basketball practice in fifteen minutes." I knew Jeannie had sensed my behavior was off lately, and I wanted to finally explain it all, but suddenly it didn't feel right.

"Okay, don't sweat it. I'll tell you later," I said.

"Well, what is it? Just tell me, Mark," she said, annoyed. She had just gotten home, was tired and had to turn around and leave again in bad weather. And I was kind of pouncing on her. In hindsight, it was a bad move.

"Oh, no you don't understand, Jeannie. This is huge. This is something I've never told you before. Ever."

I seem to be what I'm not, you see…

I could see in her eyes she went from being impatient, to slowly imagining the worst. She sat down across from me and frowned.

I began crying and shaking again, just like the night before. Now I definitely had her attention, but she was already wearing her coat, ready to leave in a few minutes.

"Look, you have to tell me now, Mark," she said. You're the one who brought it up."

I figured the timing for something like this was never good, and I had fifteen minutes, so why not?

"Jeannie, years ago…." I struggled. "Before I met you…" I thought I was going to throw up. "Jeannie, I got someone pregnant…" Jeannie's attitude switched instantly. My stomach flipped as I knew I was not about to receive the same compassion I had from Rob.

"The girl had an abortion…" My voice cracked as I said it, and my throat choked up with tears.

Jeannie's eyes grew dark. Shock, then anger, rippled across her face. I could see her mind spinning. I imagined she was recalling the snide, hurtful remarks I'd made about her being an unwed mother and having a child out of wedlock. I was guilty as charged, on all counts and the gravity of my actions suddenly crashed into me like a wrecking ball. Because this wasn't a friend who had a lesser stake in the game. This was my wife, and if the wrecking ball crashed into me, it near-destroyed Jeannie.

I could almost hear her thinking, *My husband is a liar of eighteen years by omission, and of all the nerve, putting me down for having a daughter out of wedlock.* Disbelief, frustration, and pain flooded her eyes.

"I have to go to pick up Ricque," she said suddenly, and stood up to leave.

I panicked. "Jeannie, I'm not finished… there's more."

Jeannie's face was filled with angst as she croaked, "Hurry up."

I blurted out the other three abortions like a machine gun. Bang. Bang. Bang. Then I looked up at her as I waited. She turned away, tears streaming down her cheeks and slammed the front door. I was hoping for compassion but in that moment, the gravity of deceiving my partner, my love of eighteen years, began to sink in. Even with all my years of guilt, I still didn't realize what I had done to her. Keeping these secrets were *much, much worse*.

The next two days were brutal. I walked around the house on eggshells, deciding to give Jeannie all the time she needed to process this scandalous new information. I could understand her emotions. It would be as if she sat me down one day, and said, "Mark, brace yourself I have to tell you something important. I was extremely promiscuous for a few years, and had a few abortions before I met you." How would I react to that? Suddenly my sense of trust would be completely rocked. I would feel as though I didn't really know her. If she was like that before, how would I know she wouldn't revert? The news was a game changer, and to downplay it at all would be perpetuating the cycle of deception. All I could do was pray. I was determined, however, to keep confessing my sins.

Two days after I told Jeannie, I met with my pastor, Jim Culbertson, in his office at Crossroads Community Church. Again, the familiar pounding of my heart, sickness in my stomach, and shame returned, but I was determined to keep coming clean until everyone of influence in my life knew the truth. Through my tears, shaking, and shame, I told Pastor Jim what I had told Jeannie and Rob. Pastor Jim, just like Rob, waited until I was all done, gave me time to gain some composure, and lovingly told me, "Mark, it's okay, that's not who you are now." I exhaled in relief. "That's from your past," he continued. "A long, long time ago. Now, if you were sitting here telling me you had cheated on your wife, and the girl fell pregnant and had an abortion while you were doing *The Good Guys in the Morning*, and doing Christian counseling, then we'd have a big problem. But it's in the past Mark."

I nodded, but explained that I was actually serving as a youth leader and counselor at the time.

"Have you repented?" he asked matter-of-factly.

I nodded vigorously. "Yes!"

"Okay, it's gone. It's dead to Christ. Washed away by His blood, and He's forgiven you. He has set you free, Mark, and He loves you. Repentance means to turn from your sin, and you have clearly done so, Mark, even before you confessed it. Yet confessing your sins was the right thing to do."

I crumpled back into the couch. Man did I need to hear that from him, especially after how it went with Jeannie two nights before. It was such a relief. After counseling me a little more, and walking me through a few more assurances that Jesus had forgiven me, Pastor Jim came around the desk and, like Rob, gave me a great, big, manly bear-hug. That was when I saw he was crying too, and bearing my pain and tears with me. I hugged him back tightly, thanking him profusely.

"Pastor," I said seriously. "Jeannie and I are probably going to be desperately needing your Godly counsel in days to come."

He nodded and put his hand on my shoulder, "Of course."

About a week after Pastor Jim and I spoke, I knew it was time to meet with the Executive Director of *The Women's Care Center* of Erie County. I had been in to the Center so many times over the years to drop off donuts and thank the staff, or just discuss emceeing one of their upcoming events, they thought nothing unusual of me stopping by. This visit, however, was a lot less lighthearted. I walked back to Brenda's office with her, doing the best I could to hold back the tears. She could tell something was gravely wrong, but waited patiently. I closed the door, sat down across from her, and revealed my story of four abortions in twenty months. I was thankfully able to remain a lot more composed, but I was still very emotional as I admitted my hypocrisy.

Brenda listened patiently, and I felt she was trying to absorb everything I said. Perhaps it was because she had heard a similar song and dance week in and week out over the past thirty years, but her response was pretty muted. In fact she barely reacted at all, as though my story was a little mundane. While in one way it was a relief, I felt something missing in her response. I couldn't quite put my finger on it, but it was a reaction I was definitely unprepared for. Could it be she was feeling extremely let down that for all these years Jeannie and I had supported *The Women's Care Center* and here I was showing myself to have been a huge fraud? *People react in different ways,* I told myself. What could I really expect? I also wondered if perhaps Brenda was not used to dealing with men's struggles.

Interestingly, this was probably the point I began to realize the desperate need for men's resources to help them cope with the shame and secrecy of abortion. I even thought about the name, *The Women's Care Center*. There was an abundance of resources and counseling for women, but men were sort of overlooked, weren't they? I would never have guessed it then, but in the midst of my pain, God was igniting a fire… that if I was obedient, would begin to spread. After the demure chat, I thanked Brenda for listening, and for her time. I had to take her response at face value, and left, heading home. I sighed as I thought about home. I kind of dreaded it to be honest. It felt like I was fighting battles on all fronts. One huge upside, however, was the missing weight of my secret. There were no words to explain that joy and relief. But Jeannie was still extremely wounded, and to put it mildly, things had taken a bad turn in our house. Jeannie was barely speaking to me, and when we'd walk past each other in the hallway, she'd look away and not say a word. I could only give her time and pray.

Chapter 29

Fourteen Years of Marriage

Pastor Jim had been coming over every week or so to talk and pray with Jeannie and me. It was pretty evident Ricque could feel the stress of some unknown tension in the air. She knew something significant had happened, especially when Pastor Jim was coming over to pray with us. But Ricque didn't ask about it. That was one of her exceptional traits; Ricque just knew when to be involved and when to hang back.

At this time, Ricque was an eighteen-year-old senior at *Erie First Christian Academy*, and we honestly couldn't have been more proud of her. She was a straight A student and lived her faith in Christ more than most clergy I'd seen. She attended all youth events, and was involved at church in many ways. She was just sold out to her Lord, Jesus Christ. Largely because of this, I couldn't bear to keep her thinking the worst, so I finally told her there was some stuff from my past I'd like to share with her when she was ready. I explained Mom knew about it and was pretty hurt, and we were going through some tough times but to please not worry and just pray for us. I could see in her eyes she was both a little more concerned, and a little more relieved. She didn't say much but agreed to pray.

Over the next week or so, I asked her a couple of times if she was ready to hear Dad's story but she sort of shied away and replied, "No, not right now." I gave her the space she needed, while things, unfortunately, continued to tank between Jeannie and me. I began praying extra-fervently, asking God to help Jeannie understand, and cope with the reality that I had kept something so significant from her for sixteen years. The situation was becoming desperate. A few weeks later, Ricque came up to me and gently but bravely said, "Dad, I'm ready to hear your story." Unfortunately, as it turned out, I'd had a very rough day, and was not in the right mindset. I had to say, "Sorry honey, not today if you don't mind." She just nodded, and left it at that.

Finally, it must have been late February or early March, 2006, when I saw Ricque was getting off the school bus. It was gently snowing outside, and I thought how beautiful my precious daughter looked in the snow. I knew it would just be the two of us so, as she walked in the door I asked, "Hey Ricque, are you ready to hear your Dad's story?"

"Yes!" she said enthusiastically, which surprised me. "Let me change and make us some hot chocolate real quick."

Once she had changed, Ricque came into the living room carrying two cups of steaming hot chocolate, and sat directly across from me. I offered a quick, silent prayer, and over the next hour, proceeded to explain *everything* I had told her Mom and everyone else. I didn't hold back a thing. Ricque was eighteen, a young woman, growing in her faith daily, and I knew she could handle it. Besides, I wanted her to know the truth of what I'd done, as well as the terrible consequences my deceit had caused. If anything, it would serve as an excellent warning for her.

Ricque sat listening attentively the entire time, without betraying her feelings (wonder where she learned that?) When I was all done, I smiled at this precious young woman, who was still my baby. My heart ached at the thought of having done anything that could possibly hurt her. It felt like yesterday when she was just a three-year-old toddler, waddling behind her beautiful mom, the two of them completely stealing my heart.

"Honey," I said, softly. "If you have any comments or have any questions you'd like me to answer, please go ahead. Don't hold back."

Without a moment of hesitation, she replied, "Dad, there's nothing you could ever say that would make me love you any less."

I blinked away the tears as I thought, *Thank you Jesus for a daughter with so much love and maturity.* More than anything in the world, I needed to hear that at that moment. I pulled my precious daughter in for a hug and thought I'd never let go. She hugged me back just as tightly.

When Jeannie got home I told her I'd shared my story with Ricque. I was hoping it might help Jeannie cope a little better, once it was out in the open with our family. Sadly, Jeannie continued to withdraw. I sensed she felt she couldn't share the burden, probably due to experiencing a degree of her own humiliation from my actions. Funny how my actions had spread shame to my wife. I could tell she felt very alone during this time, as I was blowing up her world. I suppose it was the situation too. For the first few weeks I had actually asked her not to tell anyone, for the sole reason that when we did share the news, it would be on my terms.

About six weeks went by, and things weren't getting any better. One day, after prayer, I felt a desperate need to tell some of our close friends. I believe my desire was two-fold: I wanted to get it out of my system completely; and I wanted to be able to finally share what was going on in our marriage. I knew our friends sensed something was wrong, and truthfully, we really needed their prayers. I also felt it would help Jeannie feel less alone.

We began inviting many of our friends over; couples from different walks of our life. Edinboro, *WCTL*, Bible studies, work, and ministry. We invited these couples over to our home for coffee and dessert, and explained we had something important to share with them. Then I dropped the bomb. By the look on most of their faces, it was like I'd just hit them over the head with a shovel.

"What? No! Not Mark Bradley Morrow!"

"Yup. Me! And Jesus still loves me. Go figure."

Well, one evening we invited a certain couple over with whom we'd been friends for years. The kids were in the living room, playing, and the four of us were sitting at our kitchen table, eating dessert and chatting. I got a little more serious, and said I wanted to share something very personal with them. They agreed, and I proceeded to share the secret of my past. While I was talking I could see the couple cast knowing glances at each other and my heart sank. *Not again.* I thought to myself. *All I need is more judgment. Heck, that's all Jeannie needs right now!* When I was done, they both became quiet and glanced at each other again. The husband gave a slight nod to his wife, and she returned the nod.

What on Earth is going on, I wondered.

The husband looked at me and said "Mark, thank you so much for sharing this about yourself. We know how much courage it must take." I nodded, but held my breath, wondering what else was coming.

"We certainly understand," he continued, and then paused for a second to look at his wife. She just blinked slowly and nodded again. "You see, we understand Mark, because we've actually had two abortions in our relationship."

I was stupefied. *You're kidding?* I thought to myself. *Whoa, now I know how it feels... hearing news like this from the last people you'd expect it.* I couldn't believe my ears. They were some of the most upstanding Christians I knew. They were *wonderful people!* Yet, these were the first people who'd admitted going through a similar experience. *They'd had two abortions,* I thought to myself. *As Christians! As husband and wife!*

I was so floored, in typical Mark Morrow fashion, I actually blurted out "Yeah right! You're just saying that to make me feel better." Jeannie kicked me hard under the table and glared at me. I rubbed my shin, grimacing as discretely as possible. After retrieving my foot from my mouth, I apologized, and said I was just surprised. I asked them to please share their experience with us if they wished. They explained that early in their marriage, due to their own personal circumstances, they made the awfully poor choice of abortion. *Twice!* They, too, were Christians when they did it. *Holy smoke,* I thought. *Well, at least I'm not as alone as I thought.* I reflected soberly on the most recent statistic that, of all women having at least one abortion, "the highest proportion (43%) identified themselves as Protestant. Twenty-seven percent of women having an abortion identified themselves as Catholic...Thirteen percent identified themselves as "born-again" or evangelical, three-fourths of whom were Protestant.[2] "While it was certainly not something I wanted to hear from friends of ours, the news actually made me feel a little less alone. Suddenly I wasn't the only Christian on the planet who'd made that terrible mistake. Historically, it sure felt that way, because people in the church just don't talk about things like that. I felt strong compassion and love for my friends. I knew it took tremendous courage for them to share what they did, and as we prayed together, I felt us all

2   Jones, Rachel K., Darroch, Jacquiline E., Henshaw, Stanley K. Patterns in the Socioeconomic Characteristics of Women Obtaining Abortions in 2000-2001. Accessed July 2017, https://www.guttmacher.org/journals/psrh/2002/09/patterns-socioeconomic-characteristics-women-obtaining-abortions-2000-2001

being strengthened. I kind of realized that me having had the courage to share my story gave them the courage to share theirs. In a weird way, things were beginning to look up.

As I mentioned, I was working at *Family Services of NWPA*. I'd left *Harborcreek* for this job for various reasons, and I'd made quite a few sacrifices taking the position, but I was grateful for it. One of the largest drawbacks for me, however, was the vast amount of paperwork *Family Services* required. They received government funding, and one thing I've learned in over thirty years of working in social and counseling organizations, is government funding equals red tape. Mind-numbing amounts of red tape. Well, before I made the decision to come clean about my past, I was having more and more panic attacks in my office, and several while driving to client's homes to counsel them there. During that time I began falling behind in my paperwork, and as much as I hate to admit it, on a few occasions I had waited in my car, outside my client's house, not able to get it together to actually go in and counsel them. I was a total wreck and I knew it. Hence the desperate need to get my past out in the open.

Well, one day I went into my supervisor, Dan Chadwick's office, and I said I had something very important to tell him. He shut the door, and I sat down. I told him I was going through some personal trials but I preferred not to go into detail about it. I explained it had caused me to fall way behind in my paperwork. Dan listened intently, a little surprised, but so far I was okay. Then I told him I had missed some appointments with a few of my teenagers, and I could see that was not good. I really liked Dan, and I liked his supervisor, Joe Tarquinio, as well (I had actually worked with Joe at *Harborcreek*.) Both of them were God-fearing men whom I had a positive relationship with, so I figured we could work it out, especially since I was approaching them and being honest. Dan decided to discuss it with Joe, and they were both pretty understanding about it, but decided they didn't have a choice but to inform the Executive Director, Tom Vinca. That was not good. Tom decided to launch a full-scale investigation on me.

What? I thought, as they relayed the news to me. It appeared that Tom figured I had to be doing something shady or unethical, since I was reluctant to tell them what had caused these problems. You see, I was finally taking a stand of obedience to God. God wanted to use my past to help heal other men who were also suffering with post abortion grief in silence. I believe, now that I was being obedient, all of Heaven was rejoicing... but hell had taken notice too. I believe Satan knew God's plans for me, and Satan also knew the threat I would become to his works of darkness once I was free. In fact, he knew it before I even realized it, but that didn't stop him from attacking me right away. The problem was, I'd left it so long, I'd given him a lot to work with. A week later, Tom fired me from *Family Services*. To top it off, Human Resources decided to fight me on getting unemployment compensation.

When I found out, I was floored. Although Dan, Joe, the *Independent Living* staff, and a few other *Family Services* staff were on my side and supporting me, it was to no avail. I couldn't believe an organization that touts itself as being family-friendly, and working to strengthen the family unit, would be so harsh and so lacking in empathy. Especially when I approached them in honesty. If Tom had said, "Explain what happened or we have to let you go," I would have explained without hesitation. I sat back, and wondered, *Wow Lord, so here I am spilling my guts and confessing my sins, my wife is furious with me and now I get fired, losing my source of income and health insurance. What gives?*

The worst part was knowing I had to break this news to Jeannie. I shuddered to think of how angry she was going to be, and I began to become really concerned about our marriage. Ricque was a senior in high school, about to graduate in a few months and would be needing financial help. Faith was four years old, Ross was going on two, and we were about to have zero income from my side. Not to mention our health insurance was gone to.

I manned up and just broke the news, and Jeannie understandably freaked out. It was just another log on the fire of this horrible secret I'd kept all these years. Life for Jeannie had been ignorant bliss, and then out of nowhere, a bomb had been dropped on her world. I had to have been the last person in the world Jeannie wanted to talk to. Or even look at.

The next few weeks were *rough*. When we spoke, it usually ended in an argument, and Jeannie reiterated several times she just couldn't trust me anymore.

"So, what else haven't you told me about yourself?" she'd cry in moments of frustration.

"Are you kidding me?" I'd try to reassure her. "I've shared the worst of the worst about myself. I've told you about my four aborted children. Look, if I can tell you that, I'd tell you anything else, *if* there was anything else." It didn't help. She had to grieve and deal with the issue in her own time, in her own way. Her image of me had largely been shattered, and only time could renew that image. I could only try my best to reassure her, and prayed like I never had before. I was frantically trying to push thoughts out of my mind that our marriage wasn't going to make it. How I wished I had been obedient to God years earlier.

I wish I could say Jeannie came around, and everything was rosy but that's just not reality. Although I truly believed God had me at that place in my life for a reason, Jeannie was understandably just sick of the state of her life, marriage, and family, due to her husband's indiscretions. I had to wonder if fourteen years of marriage to my soul mate were nearing an end.

Life hobbled along as best as it could, but in June 2006, one small ray of sunshine appeared. Funds were limited but we began to plan a modest graduation party for Ricque. Yes, we were broke, I had no prospect of employment, we had three children and no health insurance, and had already blown through all of our savings. We were barely holding on, financially and relationally but the one thing we did as a team was doing our best to shield the kids from it all. Despite the stress, I kept praying, and kept seeking God, believing He would somehow make a way for us.

The day of Ricque's party rolled around, and I was excited my mom was going to be able to make it. It was no secret we were struggling, as everyone knew I was out of a job, and things were visibly tight around the house. The morning of the party, I was catching up with my mom, gushing about how proud of Ricque we were, and discussing what a fascinating young lady she had become. Suddenly my mom leaned in to me and whispered, "Mark, if you need me to loan you some money I will be glad to do that for you." I was taken by surprise, and didn't know what to say. She continued, "Mark, I want to do that for you, but unfortunately it has to be a loan. I can't afford to give you the money, but you can pay me back whenever you're able." I was so desperate and of all places for God to help me, He'd led my mom to offer me a loan. At that time, I knew Jeannie and I had exactly $7.55 to our name. That was in our checking and savings accounts combined, and I'm not sure I'll ever forget that amount. I didn't say a word but my mom pulled out her check book and began writing a check. "Would $5,000 be enough?" she asked discretely.

"Yes," was all I could reply with wide eyes. My mom didn't belabor the issue, she didn't rub my nose in it, she just wrote the check. I have no doubt the Holy Spirit spoke to my mom that morning, to help sustain us. I hugged and thanked her, vowing in my heart to repay every penny, even if it took me the next twenty years.

Then my mom got up to go fuss over Ricque and I sat back and closed my eyes. *Man, what a roller coaster this year has been.* One thing was sure though, the secret was out and the burden was gone. I was not a prisoner any longer, and God was still keeping my life together somehow. I smiled, thanking Him from the bottom of my heart. No matter what, I decided I was going to fight to win. I knew who my enemy was now, and I would work to wreck his heinous kingdom. I was determined because he'd deceived me into sin all those years ago, then had the gall to keep me in bondage for eighteen years. I had taken my responsibility. I had been obedient. It was time to reap my Heavenly rewards. And I knew it was going to be a fight. It was time to begin my campaign to bulldoze this stronghold of Satan in other men's lives.

Chapter 30

Breaking Through

The cliché says it's always darkest before the dawn. That's easy to believe when you can see your own hand in front of your face. I had come clean, shed my burden, confessed my sins, and from there I guess I just figured I'd wing it. I knew I couldn't continue with that secret in my heart, but I didn't expect the foundations of my world to start crumbling. The tricky thing is, when you tell one person, you kind of have to tell the next. And the next. I told Rob first, then I had to tell Jeannie. I mean, I would have anyway, but now I realized I had a long list of people who were sort of "obligatory" recipients of the news.

I sought God about who to tell. Surprisingly in some cases, shame and an unexpected amount of emotional anguish accompanied revealing the news. There were some people who were simply harder to tell. Jeannie was definitely the most difficult, and I had already screwed that up pretty well. In my heart, I knew the Holy Spirit was guiding me, but when I opened my mouth the words just tumbled out awkwardly, and often, indelicately. Sadly, my wife bore the brunt of this raw, unpolished confession. Despite this, I was believing more and more that God could use me. The reality of consequence, however, is that it's a bitter pill to swallow.

Again and again, I tried to assure Jeannie, "Honey I know God is going to use me and my story, I just know it," but she had to get the revelation. Deep down, I believed it. Sort of. It was the only explanation for why God was leading me in that specific direction. He had to have a plan, and I wanted to fulfill His purpose for my life, more than anything. I had made many mistakes though, and my oversights and lack of tact when I first met Jeannie were catching up to me. *I guess this is how the enemy slows people down*, I wondered. I had to believe God wanted to use me to help other men in similar situations, but since I had been obedient my life seemed to be falling apart. I was confused and becoming increasingly tired.

I had previously worked with a lady who Jeannie and I were mutual friends with. Her name was Jane, and one particularly rough day I felt I needed to share my story with her. I also thought she might be able to comfort Jeannie, as a mutual friend, once she knew the news. It was a step of faith, as I knew she would be shocked at the implicit betrayal of Jeannie by omission, but one day I asked Jane if I could share something important. We had lunch at a nearby *Max & Erma's,* and Jane was all ears. By now I knew there was no easy way to break the news, so I just came out with it. To my surprise, Jane listened intently, and seemed very moved. Next she reassured me I was forgiven, and was very supportive. To say I was grateful was an understatement, and I was so relieved she didn't judge me.

After I had finished speaking, Jane announced she had something to share with me as well. I was surprised, of course, as I was still getting used to this idea of people instantly trusting me with their secrets when I shared mine. It was that day it began to dawn on me that many people are desperately wanting to give up their burdens too, but just like me, they were terrified to do so. Someone stepping up and making the first move by laying it all out there was producing the faith for others to take that first step on their own. I recognized this as one of the first signs God was actually using me, and began to appreciate the simple beauty of the way He was working.

Jane shared that, years before, when she was in her twenties, she was at a bar, flirting with some guy. She doesn't remember much, but figured he spiked her drink. He then took her from the bar and raped her. She just told me this, point blank. I couldn't conceal my shock, but thankfully I didn't say anything stupid.

"Oh my gosh! Did you tell anyone? Report him to the cops?" I asked.

Jane looked away, dabbed her eye with a napkin and shook her head. "You're the first person I've ever told, Mark."

I sat there speechless. I was suddenly horrified, and filled with compassion that our dear friend had been carrying this awful secret for so long. She hadn't even done anything wrong, yet she'd had to suffer for so many years with shame. I comforted her, and reassured her she was a precious, pure child of God, and not a single thing less. I also told Jane in no uncertain terms, that it was *not* her fault at all, and was a hundred percent the perpetrator's wicked responsibility. My words appeared to touch her heart, and I certainly could relate. I remember when Rob told me it was all in the past, it felt like taking a hot, fresh shower after eighteen years of living in a sewer.

I was growing and learning, but everything, since I had decided to confess my sins, continued to be an emotional roller coaster. It was admittedly a different ride; one with far fewer and less treacherous dips, but it still jarred me, and more than anything I longed for some kind of break. On the bad days, I was a mess emotionally. I ruminated over my joblessness, rocky marriage, two little kids, and my eldest graduating from high school, while I had not a cent to help her step into adulthood. Yet on the good days, I heard the voice of the Holy Spirit promise repeatedly He would use my testimony for good. With real life and stress smacking you in the face daily, however, the rubber meeting the road makes it a rough growth process.

When I'd run out of job leads, I figured at least I could begin researching, so I browsed the Internet daily, searching for topics like pro-life, and post abortion grief. I wanted to glean any and all information I could about what was out there, and see if anyone else had a testimony like mine. I waded through the hate messages, from both pro-life and pro-choice sides, not understanding the vitriol at all. Mine was simply an experience of shame, repentance, and redemption. Jesus hadn't judged me, so who was I to judge anyone else? I didn't figure it would help anyway. We all make mistakes, and only love and forgiveness would help people to keep from making more, like I did.

One day, I stumbled across a website advertising The 2006 *Pro-Life Music Festival*, near Warsaw, Indiana. Something jumped in my heart. I found the contact info and decided to call Martt Clupper, the guy who ran it. I went into the bedroom and shut the door. Jeannie was still edgy when I spoke about my past and what I felt

God calling me to do. Martt answered the phone, and I realized he was answering the call at his day job. At first it seemed strange, because I expected him to be a big shot promoter, but discovered Martt organized and ran this huge festival on his own time and own dime. Immediately humbled, I took a shining to the guy from the moment we spoke.

Martt shared that he began the first festival in 1999, and ran one each year. He must have sensed my surprise at him working, or maybe he was just used to people wondering about it. He explained he did flooring and renovation work for a living, but used his own money and put hundreds of hours into planning and organizing the event. And he sounded so happy about it. I could tell this guy was genuine and sold out for Jesus. I just told him I was a counselor, a radio guy, and then dropped the bomb that I was post-abortive—four in twenty months—and a little nervously, said I was wondering if he would be interested in having me speak at his event. I said right away I wasn't asking to be paid, and would cover my own travel expenses, but asked if perhaps he had a host's home I could stay in. That would really help. Martt was very moved, and the whole conversation felt like a God thing. Right then he said he would love to have me speak. As it turned out, he said he was sure a couple involved with the event would pay for me to stay in a local hotel, and even cover my breakfast. We chatted a bit more, both being pretty excited, and then we said goodbye, and hung up. I sat there with the biggest smile on my face, and my stomach flipping at the same time. *What on earth have you gotten yourself into, Mark?*

So I was committed, and a slot was scheduled for me at The 2006 Pro Life Music Festival. There was no turning back. The festival was to be held in late June, 2006, on the athletic fields of *Grace College* in Winona Lake, Indiana. I knew Jeannie wouldn't be up for going, but I asked Ricque if she was interested. She didn't commit right away, but after researching the festival a little she gave me an enthusiastic, "Yes!" When I asked her why she was so excited, (hoping of course, it was because of dad's big, inaugural launch into his new life of sharing his testimony…) she said it was because Bill Scott from *Z-JAM Radio* in Nashville was going to be there with his crew. I smiled, and agreed that was pretty great!

I actually knew *Z-JAM* as being a tremendous ministry run by Bill Scott and interns in their late teens and early twenties. Each week they'd help him write and produce the show, which aired nationally. Bill would play the day's current Christian hits, and teenagers from all around the country would call in live and tell Bill about their current or past experiences of drug use, sexual abuse, suicidal tendencies, betrayal by friends, eating disorders, parent's divorces, etc. Bill would give them really sound Christian counsel, with backing scripture live on air! Then the interns would take the calls to follow up and find professional counselors in their area, or just listen and give more advice to these kids. It was truly an outstanding ministry.

I didn't know it at the time, but Ricque had, in fact, been praying about an internship at *Z-JAM*. When she decided to go with me, she announced to Jeannie and I she planned not to go to college right away, in order to move to Nashville after the summer, and spend a year or two there doing ministry. The trip was the perfect opportunity for Ricque to meet Bill Scott in person, as well as some of the other kids interning there. God was definitely working in more than one area.

Yet while Ricque was now fired up, Jeannie was not at all in favor of me doing this. I believe she looked at it as another one of "Mark's crazy ideas." It was bad enough I wasn't working, and we didn't have much money, but here I was paying for gas to drive to Indiana and back. I could understand her frustration but I also fully believed God was working. Jeannie made it clear though: "Whatever you do, Mark, when you tell your story you had *better* make sure you clarify with the crowd that I never had any part in the abortions." I vowed that I would. I added my own promise to never reveal the names of the girls who had the abortions either. It just wasn't necessary.

Before I knew it, the end of the month arrived, and Ricque and I were driving to Indiana. It all began to get pretty exhilarating, despite the tension at home. And, of course, my mounting nervousness. But bands like *Seventh Day Slumber, Kutless, Tree63,* and *Pillar* would be performing, and the weather was supposed to be beautiful too. After too many restroom stops, and the most fun drive I'd had in a long time, we finally arrived. I was immediately in awe, and also a little terrified. The weather was hot and sunny, and we drove through what had to be hundreds of rows of cars, and thousands of people milling about but all smiling and happy, before we found a parking spot. I told Ricque to make a note of where it was, because the last thing I wanted was to get lost trying to find it. Then we joined the masses, and walked up to the main concert ground. I was a little taken aback as we walked into an ocean of over six thousand people. They were all laughing and playing, camped out in their lawn chairs and on their blankets. It was like a

Christian Woodstock, but without the rain, violence, and drugs—and Jesus at the center of it all.

Boy, did I start to get nervous. I wondered if Jeannie had a point in thinking this was a harebrained idea. Our first mission was to find Martt, and when we did I instantly connected with him. He showed us where the bands and speakers were hanging out, so we went backstage, and found a place to chill out. Martt was frantically busy but he was genuinely happy to meet us, and quickly told me he could give me ten to fifteen minutes max, near the end of the two day event. I'd be speaking in between band sets, while the roadies were changing out drum kits and guitars. Which was just fine with me. All I wanted was to share with the world that God can forgive and heal anything, and anyone. That's when I started getting excited!

For the time being, Ricque and I just enjoyed the festival and had a blast hanging out, and meeting the bands. Of course Ricque made a beeline to meet Bill Scott and she was instantly adopted as one of their own, by his team. By the second day I had almost forgotten I was there to speak. Almost. Martt called me in the morning and gave me my time slot. The butterflies in my stomach went bananas. *This is it, Mark. This is where you really unload that deep dark secret. If you can do it here in public, it has no power over you. You're gonna change lives today, in Jesus' name!* After my personal pep-talk, I took Ricque for a late breakfast.

After brunch we headed over to the main stage, and watched one of the bands finish their set. As I was applauding, Martt walked up to me in a hurry with a squawking walkie-talkie in his hand. "Hey buddy," he said, "...there is a group of about seven boys and girls between the seventh and ninth grades that want to sit down with you and hear your story? Is that cool with you? It's more of a one-on-one thing, so I wanted to ask first?"

"Of course!" I replied, and Ricque and I followed him to the little group. As I walked up, every ounce of doubt I had about what I was supposed to be doing left me. There were these seven kids, sitting way in the back of the field on a blanket, with innocent but eager eyes. *Man,* I thought to myself, *these are such good kids, just like Ricque.* I introduced myself and Ricque, and we sat down on a blanket, and I took a deep breath and just dove into it. I shared my entire testimony, how I was so broken after my dad and uncles died, but no matter what, I was still responsible for my actions. I shared very matter-of-factly about how important it was to stay celibate until marriage. I told them that premarital sex was really overrated, and wasn't worth it at all. Most of all I emphasized that abortion is never an option, as it would haunt them forever! I felt the message really hit home with them, and they began asking me all sorts of questions, wanting some details about where I was spiritually, and how I justified my actions. It turned out to be such a rewarding little powwow with impressionable young minds and hearts, as well an undoubtedly God-provided dry run for my stage talk.

Suddenly, the band I was to follow were up and playing their set, and Ricque and I headed backstage. Boy, I was still nervous though. Bill Scott was there and he wished me the best, and high-fived Ricque. The whole thing just felt right. The band announced this would be their last song, and the bullets began to sweat from my brow. Ricque prayed a quick prayer with me, and then Martt waved me over to side of the stage. *Here goes nothing.* The band wrapped, bowed to the crowd, and then exited side-stage. Martt patted me on the back, "After I introduce you, you're up buddy! Be bold and God bless!" He walked to the center of the stage, and asked them to give another hand for the band that just played. The crowd responded enthusiastically, and then he announced he had a special guest who would be sharing his personal testimony about the nightmare of abortion. He called me up and handed over the mic. As I stepped out onto the stage, the whole scene became completely surreal. *Wow!* Over six thousand faces stared back at me, and for a moment I stared back at them. *Eighteen years of hidden shame and secrets… how the heck did I get up here on the stage in front of six thousand people!*

"My name is Mark Bradley Morrow and I am responsible for four abortions… while I was an active youth leader." I just went for it. The adrenaline was like taking off in an F5 fighter jet but I kicked into radio disc-jockey mode, and on that hot, sunny June day I poured my heart out, telling the crowd *everything.* My story was still raw, not outlined well, and I told it with way too much emotion. I also had to speak while roadies and techies walked in front of me and around me, back and forth, switching out guitars and drum kits. My story was so unrefined and unpolished, I was like the drug addict or alcoholic who had finally come clean and was giving his very first lead at an *AA* meeting. It was just raw emotion as I regurgitated my sins. I didn't realize how much shame and pain I still carried, and as I was up there, at the mercy of the crowd, I realized I was really still a walking wound.

I was incredibly anxious, but I did my best, baring my soul while sincerely cautioning the crowd about the lifelong aftershocks of abortion. The weird thing was I felt like I had just started when I looked side-stage, and Martt was giving me the revolving finger, meaning *WRAP IT UP!* I couldn't believe it, but I wrapped a little awkwardly, thanked the crowd, and headed off stage to a few claps. I wondered if I made any difference whatsoever?

As I trudged off the stage, the next band had already walked on from the other side, plugged in and *bam*, they started jamming, loud and strong. I walked over to the *Z-JAM* tent to see Ricque and ask her what she thought of my presentation. Throughout my life I've always gone to Ricque and Jeannie for that quick, "What did you think?" as I know they'll always be honest with me. "You did a great job, Dad!" Ricque smiled. "I'm super proud of you!" Her eyes, and her tight hug told me she meant it. "Thanks angel," I said. "I think I'm going to take a quick walk, just to clear my nerves a bit." She said that was cool, and went back to her *Z-JAM* buddies. I left the tent, went back to the main stage, and walked a little aimlessly around the sea of six thousand people, trying to gather my thoughts.

I made it about forty feet from stage left when I noticed a group of twelve women congregating in a circle, talking very animatedly about something. One of them pointed over to me and they all looked over. Then another nodded and pointed again. Then all of these women stood and stared at me. I wasn't sure if I should wave or what. Just as it was about to get awkward they all walked over and the apparent ring leader said, "Hey, are you the guy who was just on stage sharing his story?"

"Yeah, that was me," I admitted.

"Aw, this is so awesome, you are the first guy we've ever heard talk about how abortion hurt them," one of the women said enthusiastically.

"Yes! We need more men like you, who will share their story and tell others that abortion hurts men too," the ring leader chimed in. She barely finished her sentence when another said,

"God is going to use you and your message, I really believe that!"

I was floored. "Wow!" I said, at a loss for words. I really thought I had kind of bombed, but I realized at that point, it was the Holy Spirit who did the work and not me at all. "Thank you all so much!"

"No, thank you so much for sharing your story," another lady smiled at me. "I wish my husband could have been here to hear your story. It would have really helped him a lot." I could only imagine what that couple had been through. I chatted with the ladies a little more, and shared more of my story that I hadn't been able to say on stage. After I said goodbye to them, I smiled up to Heaven. *Thank you Lord. I really needed that.* I felt God smiling back down at me.

I walked back to the *Z-JAM* tent feeling both numb and relieved, but proud of myself and most of all, thankful to the Lord for the opportunity. Martt was rushing about but came over and thanked me sincerely for driving all that distance. He too added I had done a great job. I thanked him for the opportunity and shook his hand. Bill Scott came over as well, and agreed I had done a really nice job. As I walked around a bit, a couple of other guys also patted me on the back, saying my message was very moving and genuine. I sighed in relief, feeling good about the talk after all.

So there I was, having just shared my darkest sins with a sea of strangers. Jobless, penniless, my beautiful daughter firmly set on moving to Nashville soon, and what did I have to show for it? *Not much,* I had to admit. It was a weird feeling, because I had been pretty successful in life up to this point. Now I had finally come clean with *everything*, and it was harder than ever. On one hand I kept telling Jeannie, "I know God is going to use me and my past for His glory," but on the other hand, there were days I really had to fight myself to believe it. It was at that moment, I hung my head a little, and asked myself honestly, *Well do you believe it?*

A still, small voice in my heart replied, *Absolutely.* I smiled, and nodded my head. I wondered what was next. *Find another conference maybe?*

If I knew God was soon going to open a door bigger than anything I had ever imagined, I would have freaked out and probably run away. Especially when that open door would be accompanied by a sudden and severe exposure to those not so enamored by the pro-life message. And that was being polite.

Chapter 31

Reckless Faith

I n 2007 I was in a strange place. I had taken the first steps toward healing, but in my mind I had built up the moment of confessing my sin publicly, to a point where no struggles would follow. I knew there would be some fallout, but I really wasn't prepared for the waves of part consequence, part, what I can only claim to be, spiritual attacks against my life.

A significant issue was, there were very few post-abortive resources for men at that time, so I was all over the place emotionally. I suppose it's a weird thing, but as a counselor, it seemed extra difficult going to another Christian counselor to talk through my problems. There are all sorts of complications, not the least of which was that Erie was a small town, and I was a very public figure. I'd also have to choose someone I could trust implicitly, and with whose practice I was familiar enough, to know I would be benefiting greatly from the sessions. That was a lot to line up all in one counselor. I regret I wasn't digging deep with my pastor either, which should have really been my first step.

Yet, despite my struggles, and growing pains, a fire burned in my heart to help other men and women, who were suffering from the same devastation. I knew there were others, because from just sharing my testimony with a handful of people, no less than three had confessed the same sins right after I told them. Incidentally, this was the first time I felt the Lord tell me to write a book. I researched a little, and made some cold calls to ghostwriters to see if anyone could help me, but it cost money, and that was, unfortunately, in short supply. My next thought was to create a website, so perhaps people searching online could find some hope and associate with my story. It was a good idea, yet the problem remained—*I* still needed a ton of healing, yet I couldn't fully see it. I was putting the proverbial cart before the horse.

Faithful as ever, God provided a job for me at the *Perseus House Residential Treatment Facility*. I would be, once again, working with teenage boys, but these kids had significant mental health problems. The population was completely different to the sex offenders I had counseled previously, who may have committed heinous crimes but were relatively normal to interact with and counsel. The first day I walked into work, a staff member introduced himself and I told him I was the new Masters Level Mental Health Therapist. He shook my hand, smiled pitifully, and said "Oh, you're the new guy who's only going to last for a few months." I found that to be pretty odd (and rude) at the time, but soon discovered the turnover for Masters Level Therapists at this facility was ridiculously high. The brutal stress, workload, and a myriad of duties, from individual counseling to group facilitation, court hearings, and paper work (my personal favorite) were backbreaking. But it was a job, so I bit down, and took the responsibilities head on. Plus, I began to have the sneaking suspicion God didn't want me to get too comfortable in a job, as He had greater things He wanted me to step into.

The silver lining in my life was the prospect of ministry. In every spare moment I searched for ways to be involved with post-abortive ministry. One day, through a friend of a friend, I was put in touch with a Christian comedian who also spoke at *Crisis Pregnancy* banquets, and *Right to Life* fundraisers. When I shared my testimony, and my desire to use my experience for God's glory, he gave me the name of a guy who was trying to start a web design business. He said the guy would give me a deal, so I figured it was a connection lined up by the Lord. I called the web designer up, spoke to him for a while, and promptly sent him a check for $400.00 to build me a website. I can't tell you how excited I was, as this was sure to be the start of my ministry.

Months later, nothing had materialized with the website, and I had to admit I was out of our much-needed $400. Of course, this annoyed Jeannie. I became confused, wondering why everything kept falling flat, even though I was legitimately trying my best to do the right thing for the kingdom of God. I really had to take it to the Lord in prayer, and after some time, forgave the guy and moved on.

Sometime in May, 2007, out of the clear blue I received an envelope in the mail, with a Florida postmark. Inside was an article, torn out of *Enrichment Magazine* with the title: "The Greatest Challenges of Pastoral Care by Sheila L. Harper." The subtitle read: "Love and Acceptance? Or Rejection and Condemnation? Our Response to the Post-abortive Man or Woman." I was taken aback that this guy, after taking my money and never delivering a website, had seen this article and mailed it to me. *Well at least he was obedient to God,* I mused, and started reading the article.

I was completely blown away. The article by this lady, Sheila Harper, spoke directly to my heart in a way I had never experienced before. Her website, www.saveone.org, was listed at the end of the article, so I went to my computer, found her contact info, and called her that minute. It went to voicemail, so I left a message.

"Uh, hi Sheila, you don't know me but basically I'm a guy that was responsible for four abortions as a young man... umm I did this while actually being involved in youth ministry and Christian counseling. I lived with that awful secret for eighteen years, and in fact, just recently came out and confessed my sins publicly due to God's relentless urging. I read your article in *Enrichment Magazine*, and I guess I just wanted to talk." I paused awkwardly, not really knowing what else to say. I just felt like I had to call this lady. I then left my contact info, and hung up.

A few days later, my phone rang and it was Sheila. We talked for some time, and I was really touched by how she thoughtfully listened to my story, using only wisdom and encouragement as I spoke. Sheila explained her husband, Jack, was a pastor in Nashville, so they had seen the gamut of issues, and broken people. Sheila's gentle kindness really impacted me in a powerful way. At the end of our conversation, Sheila said she wanted to send me a copy of her men's study guide, for post-abortive healing. I was deeply touched by her gesture, thanked her, gave her my mailing address, and we hung up. A few days later, I received the book in the mail.

When I saw the book, I was immediately impressed. I had already bought a couple of other men's healing books, and tried to work through them. In physical appearance alone, those books were scrawny, little paper backs with matching content. They felt flimsy, and when I tried to fill out the pages with my answers, the books kept folding and flopping around. I eventually gave up on both of them. In contrast, Sheila's book was rugged and heavy-duty with metal spiral binding. That may not seem like anything special, but to me it already made a difference. Sheila had the insight to foresee the difference between men and women's preferences. She would later tell me she instructed the publishers to make the book heavy duty and solid, and that's exactly what she got, even though it cost more money to make.

On the phone, Sheila had given me strict instructions to take my time and complete the questions at my own pace. She said it was very important to take it one day at a time and to never look ahead. "Mark, it could get worse before it gets better," she explained, "…but if you're painfully honest with yourself… and with God, you will find inner strength, healing, and hope." No-one had ever authoritatively explained that to me, and it felt good to have some strong guidance. I immediately felt more "normal." I opened the book, right around my forty-seventh birthday, and began to answer a few questions here and there. I obeyed Sheila's instructions, and never did peek ahead, taking it all just one page at a time, slowly praying about every lesson, exploring my heart as deeply as I could. I wrote out all of my answers, and even drew little pictures in the margins in some places.

I realized right away that working through Sheila's book was exactly what I needed. I couldn't place my finger on any one thing, but as I worked through each chapter, I began to feel more and more relief and healing. I could also feel the burden lifting, and my overall hopefulness increasing. Purely because it helped me so much, the following are the ten chapter titles of Sheila's men's study guide:

1. Your Source of Courage
2. What Happened to Me?
3. Dealing with Stray Emotions: Part 1
4. Dealing with Stray Emotions: Part 2
5. Forgiving Others
6. God's Grace
7. Can I Forgive Myself?

8. Renewing My Mind
9. Who Is This Child?
10. A Man of Courage

I found chapters 2, 3, 4, 7 and 8 to be the chapters that dealt with the areas I needed the most work in. Especially Chapter 7: "Can I Forgive Myself?"

After about eight weeks of working through this book, just me, God, and the wisdom in Sheila's writing, nothing short of a monumental change had occurred, and I had to admit I was completely transformed. The dark cloud over me was simply gone, and I now had tools to deal with any emotional challenges. Yet again, I had seen God's provision, and where He was leading.

At this point, Ricque had been working in Nashville with *Z-JAM* and Bill Scott for almost a year. When August rolled around, she took some time off to visit for a month, and raise funds for her continued stay in Nashville. Ricque had decided to intern another full year at *Z-JAM* even though many of her family members encouraged her to go to college. I told Ricque I only wanted her to do God's will, so if she believed that was another year at *Z-JAM*, then she had my support. She smiled and hugged me, thanking me for understanding.

As August drew to a close, and Ricque began gearing up to head back to Nashville, I had a thought. I emailed Sheila and explained that Ricque was heading back to Nashville in late August, and I would be driving her down in her car, and flying back. I asked Sheila if she, and her husband, Jack, would like to meet with me. Sheila thought it was a great idea, and suggested a cool little breakfast place called *The Pancake Pantry*, which had been open since 1961 in downtown Nashville. We set the date and time, and I drove Ricque down, greatly looking forward to meeting Sheila and her husband.

After helping Ricque get settled in to her new apartment, we drove down to *The Pancake Pantry* to meet Sheila and Jack. To be honest, I was a little nervous, not because I wouldn't know what to say, but instead, it was a really special and important day for me. I was about to meet the woman who, by sending me a copy of her post-abortive men's study guide, had truly changed my life. Yet the moment we met, it felt like I was speaking to old friends. We sat at a table in the center of this superb restaurant, and began to fellowship, hitting it off immediately.

As we ate, and discussed everything from the weather to the state of the world's casual attitude to abortion, I waited for the perfect moment to present Sheila with a special gift. Through our conversation, I told Sheila how much her book had changed my life, and how thankful I was for her. I then presented my completed study guide to her. I explained it was hers to use and do with as she pleased. I figured it might be of use to her, since it contained a man's thoughts, and the documented healing process of at least one man's post-abortive experience.

Sheila didn't know what to say, and when I looked at Jack, he was surprised too.

"Sheila, has anyone ever let you even read their finished book, let alone let you have it?" Jack asked.

"I don't believe so," she replied, with a wet sparkle in her eye. She began paging through the book, reading my scrawled notes.

"Sheila, I can't tell you how much your book meant to me. God used this book to change my entire life." More than anything, I wanted her to keep it and use it, even if it meant her reading from it at her speaking engagements. Sheila and Jack were clearly moved that I was handing over my personal journal, which contained all my vulnerabilities and raw pain. I had no idea this would be the beginning of a wonderful relationship.

After a memorable meeting with Sheila and Jack, we hugged, and Ricque and I left. The next day I flew back to my cold, hard reality. If I was restless before, I was almost frantic now. I knew there was more to life than the brutal, grueling job I was facing each day but I didn't know what to do. I became so desperate to hear from God, I decided to complete a forty day fast. I wanted to seek the Lord, and pray for His guidance and wisdom, in what I should be doing for Him.

In October, I received an e-mail from Sheila letting me know about a very unique event, saying I simply had to attend. It would be the first ever conference dealing exclusively with how abortion affects men. It was also the first *Reclaiming Fatherhood* conference, to be held in San Francisco, in the first week of November, 2007. I sat there, blown away, reflecting on the work God was doing, not only in my life but on a global scale, in this very overlooked area of post-abortive men's ministry. Suddenly, the reason the Holy Spirit had pursued me so relentlessly became clear. The timing was just too perfect for coincidence.

I read up on the conference and saw it would be over a weekend, with many leaders in the post-abortion community in attendance. A woman named Victoria Thorn was spearheading the conference, but an international roster of guests were lined up. Sheila wrote that she believed it would truly be worth my time to be there, and if I showed up she would introduce me to many people and let them know about my story. I knew right away, I couldn't miss it.

Once again, I was faced with a curious dichotomy. I was about to be introduced to international leaders in the pro-life movement, while my wife was still struggling with my past, and our finances were still a mess. I pondered this for a while, wondering if I was becoming a fraud again. It was an important point to consider. As I prayed, however, I heard a quiet voice say, "Mark, there is a big difference between faith, and fraud." I realized God was leading me this time, and that was the huge difference. I was genuinely giving it my best effort, gutting it out at an increasingly horrible workplace, while doing my best to be patient and understanding as my wife came to terms with our new reality.

Something that had been going a long way to help Jeannie cope was, we had been playing with the idea of getting our feet wet in private practice. Both of us being licensed counselors, was a pretty unique situation. We'd be able to counsel as a unit if necessary, while building a symbiotic practice by sharing all overhead costs. But, it was still nothing more than talk, and we were still not doing well at all financially. Scarily, we still had no health insurance at this point.

I gingerly brought the conference up with Jeannie, and told her how much Sheila thought it would be very beneficial in networking. To put it mildly, Jeannie was not too enthused. After some thought, I knew I needed something more persuasive. Over the years, one of the dearest things to my heart was collecting Rock & Roll memorabilia, and I had amassed quite a collection when I was making good money. I offered to sell some of my Rock & Roll memorabilia to cover the expenses, and quietly sighed when Jeannie agreed. I dreaded letting some of my stuff from *The Beatles, The Monkees,* and *The Rolling Stones* go but I knew it was worth infinitely less than my marriage. Let alone, obeying the call of God.

I prayed and prepped for my trip, getting more excited than I had been in years. I thanked my wife for letting me go, and began the process of taking pictures of my memorabilia for eBay. The Lord must have seen my willing heart, because I found out through Sheila that Vicki Thorn offered scholarships for certain attendees. I applied and received a scholarship, which covered all of my conference fees! Within days I sold some of my memorabilia, making enough money to fly out to San Francisco, spend two nights and fly back. I was all set.

I never have been a fan of traveling, and was a little unsure of going to places I'd never been before, but as I kissed my wife goodbye, I felt a complete peace and found myself really looking forward to the weekend. The flight was quick and smooth, and before I knew it I was in the big city of San Francisco. I could hardly believe I was about to learn from some of the world's most renowned specialists on men's post abortion grief and healing.

The night before the event, I met up with Sheila and, true to her word, she began to take me around and introduce me to everyone she knew. Suddenly I was meeting the heads of *Care Net* and *Heartbeat International* and *Abortion Recovery International Network* (*ARIN*.) I, of course, had no idea what any of that meant or how these organizations fit into the greater scheme of post-abortion networks, but I was meeting fascinating people, and most of all, experiencing a strong, kindred spirit among all of my newfound spiritual family.

Sheila then introduced me to Victoria Thorn, the leader of the conference and preeminent international speaker in post-abortion circles. I thanked her for the scholarship, while Sheila went on to tell Vicki about my testimony. She explained how I had completed her healing book, and had flown out there wanting to learn more and perhaps even be used of the Lord someday to share my story.

"Well, one of our guest speakers scheduled for tomorrow morning can't make it. Do you want to share your story?" Vicki asked, nonchalantly.

Seriously? I thought to myself. "Umm, yeah, definitely!" I said quickly, closing my gaping mouth. I was never one to turn down microphone time. "Thanks for the opportunity!"

"Awesome!" Vicki smiled. "It's set then. And you're very welcome."

Sheila broke into a huge grin, and gave Vicki a hug.

Whew, I thought to myself. *Okay, Lord... I guess you know what you're doing.* A sense of exhilaration set in, and then the crazy butterflies.

My speaking slot was pretty early the next morning, right as the conference kicked off. Before I even had much chance to over-think it, Vicki was on the stage and introducing me. Feeling a little disoriented, I took a deep breath and walked up to the stage. *Wow Lord, this is amazing*, I thought, as I looked over the crowd of people. Having spoken once before, however, I felt a little more prepared. I told myself, *It's just like being behind the mic at the radio station,* and that's exactly how I approached it. I cracked a few jokes and then shared my testimony.

When I was done, I thought I did okay, and the crowd seemed moved by my story, but it is always tough to tell. I exited the stage, and went back to my seat. Sheila assured me I did great. After another couple of speakers, Vicki came up to me, and told me that a San Francisco *CBS 5* News reporter was in attendance, and had requested to interview me. Not only that, but an *LA Times* reporter had expressed interest too. *Whoa!* I thought. It was all a little intimidating, but I agreed. Vicki introduced me to both reporters, and I spent the next couple of hours being interviewed on camera by *CBS 5*, and then off in a side room by an *LA Times* contracting writer.

The interview with *CBS 5* was a little unnerving, probably more because of the camera and the lights. But as I saw it, no one could take away my voice or tell me how I did or didn't feel about being a post-abortive father. I just spoke candidly, and answered all of the questions truthfully, as I saw them. I thought I did okay during that interview, but really had no idea what to expect when the story aired.

Next, I went into the side room where the girl from the *LA Times* was waiting to conduct our verbal interview. She seemed really nice, and proceeded to ask me a ton of questions. I found it interesting that she wrote all my answers down in a little, old school notepad. In 2007, most traveling business people were using laptops, but she kept it old school, and I kind of liked that. Overall, I was way less nervous with her, and felt very comfortable with her and the interview in general. She did take her time to ask me a ton of questions, but I figured she was just being thorough.

After a long day at the conference, I walked briskly back to my hotel room and called Jeannie to tell her I was going to be on the *CBS 5* news. She was predictably not as excited as I was, but she seemed happy for me. After hanging up with her, I flipped on the TV and lo and behold, there I was, part of the *top story* of the *CBS 5* news channel. I sat in silence, suddenly nervous, hoping I hadn't gotten myself into a huge mess. We were, after all, in San Francisco, the liberal capital of our nation some might say.

I watched and listened, waiting for *CBS 5* to drag me across the coals, as a crazy extremist. While they did label us (and me specifically) as "anti-abortion protestors," (instead of pro-life supporters,) all in all, I was pleasantly surprised that they actually appeared to give both sides of the story. I knew the deal, of course. News rooms are given their marching orders about presenting the station's larger opinions and agenda, so they couldn't exactly paint us in a glowing light, but I felt they were truly as fair as possible. After the story had ended I sat in disbelief that within twenty-four hours, I had gone from simply attending the conference, to headlining a story on a major news station. My mind reeled.

The next day, the unique, exciting experiences continued. First I met Brad Mattes out of Cincinnati, Ohio. He was introduced as the Executive Director of *Life Issues Institute*, and he explained that he and his staff are all about *life*, and not just anti-abortion. They're opposed to pulling the plug of someone on life support, and euthanasia (assisted death,) and more. I really enjoyed talking to Brad, and had a feeling we'd remain in touch.

While I was talking to Brad, a lady came up to me, and introduced herself as Stacy Massey.

"I'm the head of *Abortion Recovery International Network*," she smiled, and then gave me a big hug. "I just can't believe there is a guy out here, with a sense of humor, big and tall and not some wimpy guy, who has had past abortions and is willing to step forward and talk about how they've impacted you."

"Why, thanks!" I replied, a little surprised. I really didn't think I was doing anything particularly courageous, but it seemed the Lord was already able to use my obedience.

"Mark, you're coming to Dallas in April," Stacy said next.

"What?" I chuckled, genuinely taken aback.

"You're coming to Dallas in April for the *Heartbeat International* conference. I'm booking you now as a speaker!" she grinned.

Yeah right, I thought. *I'm lucky I even made it to this conference, let alone doing another one.* Stacy must have seen my apprehension, so she insisted again.

"Well, thank you, sincerely." I said. "I'm truly flattered but let me discuss it with my wife, and can I let you know soon?"

"Oh, of course!" she said. "But I think the Lord will find a way for you to be there."

I smiled, and nodded. I liked her enthusiasm.

After that conference, I headed home, fully encouraged, having found a whole new host of friends and fascinating people, and entirely astounded at what God had done with me over that weekend. It was so good to see Jeannie, and she seemed at least a little interested in what happened, if still a little apprehensive. I told her it would be okay, and God was beginning to use me.

———

January is always celebrated as Sanctity of Life Month, and as January 2008 rolled around I was pretty humbled to have so many new opportunities opening up. Sadly, I was unemployed again. The guy was right when he said I wouldn't last more than a few months at Perseus House. I lasted six months, which was more than most, but it was just too much to bear. My health was deteriorating, and my back was completely wrecked from the stress and long hours. But I was confident in the Lord that He would open doors, and things would turn around for us. Our part-time private practice was starting to show signs of picking up, so I decided to keep my faith levels up.

One day, I went to check my email, to see if any job opportunities had popped up, when I saw one from Sheila. As I read the words, an old familiar knot formed in my stomach. "Mark, if you're not aware yet, the article in the *LA Times* has been printed. When you read it, don't worry at all about how you were represented. Also, if you read the article online, remember to never let other people's views or hatred ruffle your feathers. Stick with this new cause because you are just dipping your toe in, and things will get better, I promise."

Dear God, I thought. *What have I gotten myself into? What on Earth had that woman written?* I saw an email from Stacy Massey a few down, and opened it next. She said the same thing, and added the pro-abortion movement is used to being critical, mean-spirited, and nasty. It suddenly dawned on me I had entered a movement which was fiercely opposed. Not only that, Sheila and Stacy had been in the pro-life movement for years, but I really had no preparation for those interviews, and didn't truly know how to handle myself. I began to panic. Not only for myself, but for Jeannie. *How far would this craziness go?*

I jumped on the internet, and pulled up the *LA Times* website. My eyes widened as I saw what over a million readers had read that day as well. In huge print, featured on the front page of the *LA Times* was my story. What I read sickened me to my stomach.

Chapter 32

Bold Moves

CHANGING ABORTION'S PRONOUN the headline blared on the front page of the Los Angeles Times.

"'We had abortions,' say men whose lovers ended pregnancies. It isn't just a women's trauma, they insist. But critics see a political calculation."

I read the article, as my gut twisted. I suppose the reporter overall tried her best to remain neutral, but an agenda was very clear: paint the conference as a devious political maneuver. She quoted me by name, along with Vicki and a few other speakers. She completely dismissed decades of research that showed women experience severe trauma after an abortion (saying there was no proof of cause and effect,) and she claimed that politically, adding "men's tears," would be a powerful tool in the hands of pro-life lawmakers, basically claiming that was the conference's intention.

Next, I scrolled down and read the article's comments, some of which led me to other blogs… I should never have read any of them. The comments were filled with people who had no idea who I was, yet posted things like (paraphrased:)

"So, Mr. Morrow feels sorry about his four dead kids now. Poor baby, maybe he should have thought about that before having all of that sex and fooling around… and he calls himself a Christian."

and

"Mark Morrow says that 'We had abortions and I had abortions.' Oh **** no, **** that. He and his dead kids can go to hell."

Yes, the comments were written by extremists of the pro-choice agenda but as I stared at my screen, reading one hateful remark after another, a heaviness sank over me like a dark shroud. *How could anyone write such vile, hurtful things about someone they don't even know? Let alone my aborted children?* I blinked back the tears. *What wrong had I done to them?* Never in a million years would I have expected anything like this. I realized Sheila and Stacy were used to it, and probably had been expecting it to come barreling down the pike, but I sure wasn't. It all hit me like a wrecking ball; my mind reeled, and that old, familiar pain returned. Like Mike Tyson had landed his vicious, ripping left hook square in my stomach.

I suddenly became unsure at what I had gotten myself into. Every ounce of my hope and enthusiasm to help others drained out of my soul. *I don't think I can do this,* I conceded, as I staggered into the living room. I just came out and told Jeannie some people were saying some pretty vile and nasty stuff about me on the internet. Jeannie sympathized with me, but I could also sense concern about how crazy the situation could get. I wondered if she was thinking, *Well, you're the one who did all of this years ago, kept it a secret from me, now you go and tell it to reporters. You reap what you sow, buddy.*

Everything felt like it was falling apart.

Several months went by, in which I pretty much moped around feeling discouraged. I received calls and emails from Sheila, Stacy, and several of my new friends, but I'd simply had the wind knocked out of me. I never asked to be hated nor reviled in such a way. I had never judged anyone who'd had an abortion, and I certainly wasn't about to start. I had simply shared my story. I knew intellectually it was a real, spiritual war but it didn't really matter. The spark had gone… the flame had died.

In November, 2008, I was sitting on the couch, watching some football. I'd pretty much shelved any thoughts of continuing to share my testimony or ministry. Life had been plodding along, and although I didn't want to think about it, my life now had a distinct lack of purpose. The depression was even beginning to creep back. As I waited for the game to continue, a new *Ford* commercial began that tracked a shiny, robust truck roaring around jagged, rocky terrain, but easily overcoming all obstacles in its way. Kelly Clarkson crooned a catchy melody, as the *Ford* trucks effortlessly hauled tons of gear, ramped over dunes and effortlessly navigated a rocky landscape. A deep-voiced narrator intoned:

"BOLD IS A JOURNEY. BOLD OVERCOMES. BOLD IS UP TO THE CHALLENGE. BOLD GOES FOR IT. BOLD FIGHTS BACK. BOLD *NEVER* QUITS."

The commercial concluded as a new *Ford* truck skidded confidently into center-frame while the voice-over boomed, "It happens every day… someone, somewhere, makes a bold move. There's a car company for people like that. *FORD*. BOLD MOVES." I sat there in awe, thinking about the catchphrases. BOLD OVERCOMES. BOLD NEVER QUITS. I recalled a scripture I had once read, *"The wicked flee though no one pursues, but the righteous are as bold as a lion"* (Proverbs 28:1.) An ember suddenly glowed in my heart.

I mulled over the phrase, "It happens every day, someone, somewhere makes a bold move." It could easily apply to those breaking through their fear, shame, and silence to make that huge, bold move. The bold move I'd made to come clean, throw away my pride, and humble myself before God began my journey toward post-abortion recovery. If *I* could make a bold move, anyone could do it. I suddenly knew I wanted this fight. *Who cares what people think? They don't know me.* Right then and there, I accepted the challenge. *Since when is Mark Bradley Morrow a coward?* I had faced some of the toughest experiences a young man could go through. I had endured losing my father, and my two closest uncles within two years. I had lived in a Christian commune, I had slept on the floor of a radio station, I had come clean about my worst sins, and I was still here. The Holy Spirit blew on that ember in my soul, and it roared into a bonfire. I realized those people who were so vicious and full of vitriol, were simply *victims of their own guilt.*

In that moment, I knew again beyond a shadow of doubt I was called, and blessed with a ministry. I knew for those who would receive this message—the post-abortive man or woman who desperately wished to finally break through years of lies and silence and shame—it would take nothing less than a BOLD MOVE by someone preaching the truth.

I prayed quietly and told the Lord I accepted His call, no matter what the persecution may be; I would tell my testimony and share my knowledge. A warm relief flooded over me as a month's long discouragement evaporated. Revived, I quickly thought of outlets I could reach immediately. Pregnancy centers, conferences, churches, forums… the possibilities poured into my heart. I smiled as I knew my new ministry would be named *Bold Moves*.

Chapter 33

In Jeannie's Words

I'll never forget the day Mark told me his deep, dark secret. I was rushing to leave, but Mark felt like he just had to get something off his chest. He'd been extra-moody the weeks before, and while it could be a strain on me, I would make excuses. Usually I would relate Mark's moods to losing his father as a young man and regretting their relationship was not better than it had been. Also, I reasoned it could be that as an adult, he now had to accept the fact that his family dynamics had changed, and would never be the same again. I thought I understood how his situation at work wasn't great. I tried to rationalize Mark's ups and downs across all of these things, but nothing could have prepared me for what he said.

When Mark revealed he had been responsible for an abortion, I was dumbfounded. A hundred simultaneous thoughts evoked a thousand simultaneous emotions. Three emotions screamed above the rest... when Mark blurted out he'd been responsible for no less than four abortions I was silently outraged. This came from Mark withholding such a secret from me. Especially since my own history included pregnancy as a young adult, and feeling abandoned by Ricque's biological father who, after talking about marriage and children, suggested I have an abortion.

This man then proceeded to marry a divorced woman with two young children. Mark knew all of this. And he joined me in supporting the local pregnancy center, where I volunteered and counseled. Mark had even been the Master of Ceremonies several times at their annual fundraising banquet. I couldn't help but wonder, *Was that all a lie? Or worse... Are there other things he's keeping from me?*

The sole relief was, maybe there was at least some explanation for his moodiness. My empathy came from seeing Mark sob like a baby when he told me his deeply hidden secrets. In that moment, despite the anger, I believed he had acknowledged his true feelings over his actions and had accepted responsibility. I believe it was the empathy that allowed me to overcome my anger, and lead to forgiveness. I never judged Mark for what he did. I know that is all in the past, covered by the blood of Jesus. I have forgiven Mark for keeping the secret from me. In fact, I immediately felt sorry for him, knowing that I would have a hard time living with myself if I had chosen to have an abortion. I also knew this was something I could never fix nor heal.

Yet, right on the heels of all of this new, life-changing revelation, came another challenge. Mark is fairly impulsive. This isn't always a bad thing, but it isn't always a good thing. It's just who Mark is, and I love him as he is. I was, however, processing how to approach this new angle in our life. I found myself having an increasingly difficult time accepting or approving of Mark's immediate desire to write a book and share his past with the world, especially right after he had just shared his story with me. But that was the least of it. The most difficult thing for me to deal with was Mark's desire to contact the women in his past who had submitted to the abortions. I instinctively knew it was not a good idea. *After all*, I reasoned... *how would I react in that situation?*

But the ultimate question is, do I support Mark now? Absolutely. Do I still have a difficult time thinking and talking about his past? Yes, sometimes. That's just life, yet this is what Mark feels called to. His ministry work is clearly changing lives, so in one way, I guess I'm a partner, even in just being okay with him sharing, what is really, *our* story. You must understand, my personality is the exact opposite of Mark's. I do *not* like to have attention drawn toward me. I'm not saying he is doing this for attention, what I'm saying is, given my personality, it can be uncomfortable at times knowing people will have in-depth knowledge of our personal lives.

Will I ever travel with Mark to promote this book, and sit through his speaking engagements? I'm not sure. I have attended a few of his speaking engagements, and honestly, it was very emotional and uncomfortable. Maybe it was too soon when I attended? I'm simply leaving it up to God to speak to my heart about my involvement. I still completely believe in Mark's ministry, and that this work is changing lives. I suppose my point is this: the effects of abortion are inescapably traumatic. You may think it's just a choice and it won't affect you *or the people around you*. Nothing could be further from the truth. If you're not married, someday you will be, and you will have a decision to make… are you going tell your spouse about your past? Believe me, if you fall pregnant and have your baby, the right person would rather accept you and your child, than to be lied to.

Now, I will say that if you are married, and you have been keeping a secret like Mark's, I suggest you be very cautious in your approach to sharing the truth. I'm not saying don't share it. I'm not saying that at all. I believe, however, you should see a highly qualified, Christian counselor *alone* at first, and talk it over with them. Above all, you want to be very sensitive to your spouse, especially if you're a man. Your wife may have had some past issues related to pregnancy, and approaching it the wrong way could stir up severe pain.

Because of this, I highly recommend you read the Appendix in this book, and use the resources there. Mark believes in Sheila Harper's workbook strongly, so for men, that would be a good place to start. The counselor in me will always refer you to resources I know will help you. I believe the resources in the Appendix are such resources.

Lastly, even though I have spoken candidly, you must know I love my husband with all of my heart. Yes, it's been difficult, as I'm sure you could tell, but that's life and that's marriage—for better or for worse. Mark and I have far more wonderful things in our marriage that outweigh these few struggles. When you accept and deal with those aspects of the "worse" appropriately, it becomes better. And when you trust in God, nothing can defeat you. If you place your trust in Him, ultimately you will find joy again. I promise.

Thanks for reading my thoughts.

Jeannie

Chapter 34

The Power of Sin

One thing I was now sure of was, God wanted me to share my testimony. If I dwelt on my financial problems, marriage, and employment challenges, I knew they would drown me. My only choice would be to cling to the vision I knew God had given me. Knowing I could share my testimony brought me more joy than I could express. And I *needed* that joy.

When I knew without a doubt my soul mate, and beautiful wife believed in me, the after burners kicked in. Jeannie is the complete polar opposite of me, personality-wise. She would likely never share her own testimony on stage, but nobody knows me like my wife does. She knows my strengths, and my weaknesses. Jeannie's process of forgiving me didn't occur suddenly on one specific day with fireworks and champagne. No, it was a gradual but steady realization on her part that I was genuinely trying to serve God, and this was my life now. I believe she also knew I was not hiding anything else from her. But one day, I could just see it in Jeannie's eyes, and I knew without a doubt she had forgiven me. And she would stand at my side no matter what. *That* was all I needed.

When I realized my post abortion story was going to be a fight, I knew if I was going to overcome, I would have to go on the offense against an unseen enemy. Even though I knew I would have to build this ministry from the ground up, I smiled, knowing I had no idea how to quit. My mindset had completely changed. God had touched me again, and I was ready for the fight. Why was I doing it? Because I was *mad*. Mad at the devil for deceiving me. Mad at the devil for luring me into killing babies. Mad at the devil for continuing to do so in thousands of other lives every day. One thing I knew I could do was challenge my audience to make their *bold move*. After hearing my testimony, they would know they could do it too, whether it was coming clean about a past abortion, or any other form of abuse, or any sin they were hiding.

I came up with my own red, white, and blue *Bold Moves* logo that looked somewhat like the *The Who's* target-esque logo with the arrow. (It was a really cool logo.) I had some business cards made up, as well as a huge banner to take to the *National Care Net* and *Heartbeat* conferences to tell people about myself, my story, and my new speaking ministry. I was ready and I would not back down. But then the butterflies kicked in.

I was so nervous at my first conference with my new business cards. I was almost more nervous than the first conference I spoke at. It was because now it was *official*. I had taken the plunge and I had to make it happen. I knew it wasn't in my strength, and completely in the Lord's hands, but it was still nerve racking. I tried to plan my overall approach, and how I would answer various questions, and what advice I might offer. My biggest caution, of course, was more so to men, but also to women, to simply not allow their secret to go any further—to go beyond the present moment. If they were being plagued by guilt, to not let more months or years go by, of living in the darkness of shame. I had to let them know it only became more difficult the longer you allowed it to fester.

That was first thing I learned the hard way—using tact and wisdom. Friend, I'm going to speak directly to you right now. If you hear anything in this book, hear this: be very, very, *very* cautious when deciding how or even *IF* to tell your significant other. I know I had said the longer you leave your secret, the worse it becomes, and *that is true*. But you have to consider how your wife or husband is going to react, or if he or she has any trauma in their past that might be unearthed. If I could do it all over again, I would be so much more considerate of Jeannie.

I was a wreck, and at that time there were no Mark Morrows, out sharing their testimony. I learned by my mistakes, and they were *hard mistakes*. Even now, I know Jeannie is still somewhat affected by my past, but through the grace of Christ, we're doing great.

So what should you do? I recommend speaking to a qualified Christian counselor *first*. Or a close friend you can trust. Confess your sins. Get your past off your chest, and share it with someone *confidentially*. That alone will be a huge spiritual step forward, even if you don't think it would be. A person carrying around a hundred pounds of extra weight every day thinks it's normal. They have no idea they're not functioning as well as they could be. It's the same with dark secrets. You think you're getting by, but they affect your life in ways you don't even understand. But you have to be wise. You have to approach it correctly or you can make it worse, at least in the short term. Spend time with the Lord in prayer. Take your sins to Him, and pour your heart out to God. And get some help from likeminded believers. You can also read the Appendix of this book for sound resources, and add some wise, godly advice. I say this because even once I had come clean with my sins, Satan didn't relent. He used my guilt to drive me to do some foolish things.

That year, I went to the local *Women's Care Center* fundraiser—I believe it was their twenty-fifth anniversary. Afterward, I chatted with one of the keynote speakers, who was a post-abortive woman herself, and had written a book too. I asked her if I could have a private word, and asked if she thought it was a good idea to look up the mothers of my aborted children. I told her I had a deep desire to apologize and take responsibility.

Her response was a resounding, "No!" She said if God wanted our paths to cross one day, if any of those women needed to hear my apology, He would connect the dots and allow a time for this to happen. She explained a man and woman who have been intimate, experienced a pregnancy and a subsequent abortion, simply had too much history, and someone was going to get hurt again. Most likely, the woman (or women) from my past *and* Jeannie would be hurt. It was her personal and professional opinion that seeking such contact would be highly unwise. I had already run it by Jeannie, and she echoed the same sentiment. Somehow, I missed the pain in Jeannie's voice as I was desperately trying to unscramble eggs. I did it anyway.

I'm wearing my heart like a crown...

I contacted Lisa, the girl who'd had two abortions from our relationship. I asked her if we could speak, and she agreed, so we met. By that point Lisa was married with children of her own, but I immediately recognized the trauma behind her eyes. I was instantly nervous, and knew I'd made a mistake. Our meeting was an utter disaster. One post-abortive knows another, and I could see she was still troubled by, not only the abortions, but she also struggled with closure. I'm not saying she was still hung up on me, I'm saying the way I treated her in my sinful state left a deep scar on her heart, where there should only be soft, tender love from the husband God intended for her. In meeting with her, I had ripped off old scabs and reopened deep wounds. Bitterness and pain poured out of her heart as if it was the first day I'd hurt her. My disobedience to wise counsel had caused this poor woman to tailspin out of control.

My good intentions began to disrupt this poor woman's life, and subsequently the life of *my* family. It also, ironically, only added fuel to the fires of my own guilt, that so far, had been slowly quenched by God. I'd just recovered, and was enjoying my newfound healing and freedom, yet this poor woman was evidently still in the place I'd suffered for eighteen years. I won't go into the gory details, but when she found out I was beginning to travel and speak about the abortions, she did not handle it very well. Let's just say she believed I was a hypocrite, and could not accept that I was a changed man.

I responded by doing the only thing I knew to do; I put her in touch with Sheila, knowing if anyone could help her, it was Sheila. From what I heard, she and Sheila worked through the study together, and she almost finished, but suddenly, for some reason, she lost interest. Thankfully, Sheila was able to get the *SaveOne* study into her hands, and Sheila and I prayed for her to find healing and peace. From what I heard down the road, she ended up telling her husband, family, and children about the abortions. To this day I'm still not sure how things have worked out for her, and I can only pray she found healing.

After my neglect of godly counsel, I had to break all contact with her anyway, after the damage was done. I decided I would never contact her or the other two mothers again, and that's the way it would stay. What was done is done, the past is the past, and we have to move forward in forgiveness and grace. Each of us have to figure out our own thoughts, conclusions, and healing. Again, I beg—dear dude reading this, I implore you, do *not* attempt in any way, shape or form to contact women from your past. Pray for them (if it won't stir up unhealthy memories or attachments,) but leave it at that.

———

I ran *Bold Moves* for a couple of years before I began to feel my *Ford* knockoff name just wasn't cutting it. At conferences, people would look at my banner or cards and have a quizzical look on their face like, *What the heck is Bold Moves? What exactly do you do?* I began to look at some of the better known pro-life speakers and realized they didn't have some name or gimmick for what they did. They simply used their own name, because that is who they were, and in essence, they *were* the ministry.

I met people like Gianna Jessen, who was aborted and left on the floor in the corner of a hospital room to die. God had another plan, as she survived and lived to tell about it. Or Rebecca Kieissling who's mother was raped, and told by many to abort. She refused, and now, Rebecca, conceived of rape, is an attorney who is married with five children and travels internationally, speaking against abortion. Or Mike Williams, a professional comedian and pro-life speaker who was adopted, and now lives in the Dominican Republic six months out of the year, doing mission work. For the other six months he's booked solid doing his presentations. These three people simply used their own name, and that is what their websites are, theirname.com. I finally decided to retire *Bold Moves* and bought the domain name www.markbradleymorrow.com. I simply went with *Mark Bradley Morrow Ministries* and immediately felt better about it all.

Pretty soon, after speaking mainly at *Crisis Pregnancy Center* fundraising banquets, and *Right to Life* events, the Lord laid it on my heart to get my message into Christian schools, and more importantly, churches. I knew from my short time speaking with people, there were a *ton* of post-abortive men and women sitting in church pews of all denominations. For the most part, no one was acknowledging them or their past actions, and most importantly, the terrible consequences of having an abortion. I knew churches are filled with many hurting people who are damaged, sick, and filled with shame. They have no idea they can be set free from their sin and guilt, like I've been. Until they are, however, they will never truly be well, and their churches will not be what they could be in Christ. I wanted to reach those post-abortive men and women in churches whose problems often included depression, anxiety, and substance abuse, unhealthy relationships, cutting, suicidal ideation, and more. Most don't even understand these issues are not the problem, but merely symptoms of their underlying issue from an abortion experience they have been silent about.

The passion to share my story of deliverance and healing began to burn deeper and deeper in my soul. I couldn't even think about whether or not I was *supposed* to be doing this, I just couldn't *not* tell people about what God had done for me. I figure if God wanted to do something with little old me, with all my history and daily failures, I couldn't ever try to go to Him feeling qualified. I'd simply go to Him making myself available and would have to trust Him to equip me for each step along the way. Of course, it was nerve wracking. Yeah, people thought I was crazy. But I started small, and tried to be completely obedient. Before long, the speaking engagements began to open up. Lives began changing, and the joy began to build and build in my heart. What's more, my beautiful wife and family began to see me as a minister of the gospel, using my past for good.

Yes, there were definitely times I was tempted to become discouraged, but God even gave me a highly unique experience to help me through that. After one of my earlier banquet presentations just outside of Washington D.C., an older gentleman strode over to me and gave me a *killer* handshake. His granite jaw-line, and plumb-line posture left no guessing about his military background. He held the handshake, looked me square in the eye and said, "Mark, I want you to know I have served in the military for over thirty-five years and have been in several live battles and wars… but what you did tonight was the bravest thing I've ever seen!" At the time I thanked him sincerely, but kind of thought to myself, *Sir, it's no big deal really, I'm just sharing my story.* The next day in my hotel room, however, I was thinking about what he said and I sensed the Holy Spirit saying, "Mark, that man was paying you the biggest, most sincere compliment you could ever receive. Don't forget what it took to come clean, and then give your first public talk. You must understand what you are doing is brave and courageous in Christ."

I was deeply moved. I received the encouragement that day, and as the years have gone by, I've held onto that one man's words of wisdom and support. Now I agree with him. For any man or woman to come out and share a past abortion experience, it has to be one of the most difficult things you can do. Especially telling those you know; close friends, your spouse, kids, family, church brothers and sisters. Those who know you—or thought they knew you—the best. But that is what the church needs. The power of sin is its secrecy. It's time to expose that taboo and secrecy. It's time to expose that sin.

Chapter 35

Straight Talk

A s I close this book, I'll just tell you upfront there is no dramatic ending to the story. Relatively speaking that is. There are no fireworks, and no orange sunset with my family and I and the mothers from my past, all holding hands and singing Kumbaya. I wish that were the case, but this is real life, and those were real choices I made. Even though we're forgiven, those are real babies that died, and real consequences for everyone involved. We still have to work around the fallout. By faith I live day by day, and by faith I have been going from glory to glory. *That's* the dramatic ending. It comes from a dramatic victory that was won on a cross two thousand years ago. Without Jesus Christ's sacrifice and forgiveness, I'd probably be dead, or in some asylum. That's the truth of the matter. But he and she whom the Son sets free, is free indeed (John 8:36.) Praise our merciful God for that.

The scriptures say if we confess our sins, He is faithful and just to forgive us (1 John 1:9.) Friend, even though I can't assure you that you won't have some consequences to work through, I want to encourage you as far as shedding your burden of condemnation, *it is really that easy*. Nothing more and nothing less. I hope in reading my story, you can see that if I can find healing and hope after four abortions, and the treacherous aftermath, whatever you may be dealing with, whether it's from your own sinful actions or sins against you, you too can be set free and be cleansed by the blood of Christ. I can sincerely guarantee you that.

Since I am a born-again Christian, even though I am a licensed counselor, my focus on someone experiencing hope, healing and wholeness will always be on having a personal relationship with the living God, His son, Jesus, and the indwelling of the all-powerful, yet gentle Holy Spirit. I cannot entertain the thought of finding healing and hope outside of Christ. Not through self help books, meditation, or anything else. I can only speak from my own experience. It was nothing other than my personal faith and obedience to Christ that pulled me through. Anyone can read in the gospels about Jesus forgiving the criminal on the cross next to Him, or the adulteress whom Jesus forgave, but we forget He then gave the command, *"Go and sin no more"* (John 8:11.)

I feel that as human beings, we like to make our own lists, creating a perceived pecking order of sins with the worst at the top, for example murder, adultery, abortion, homosexuality... whatever. Hmm. That sure sounds like something the Pharisees would have done. "Ah, I am a righteous man, look at the way I pray and give and fast." Instead, true, transparent, and authentic followers of Christ are crying out, "Forgive me Father because I am the worst of sinners." Jesus came to forgive, change. and save sinful people. He does it every day... but it starts with us being able to be honest with ourselves, others and Him. We have to have the courage to lay it on the line and name our sins, repent. and accept the forgiveness and hope that only He can give. And once we do that, the challenges don't stop. From my personal experience with all of this, I found that it was a lot easier to accept God's forgiveness than being able to forgive myself. But that too is sinful. Am I bigger then God? If He can and will forgive me for anything imaginable, and then completely forget about my past sins, casting them away from Himself, as far as the East is from the West, how can I not forgive myself? This is undoubtedly the truth, but is also much easier said than done. If we can't forgive ourselves of these sins, it is a pride problem. Who are we to not forgive ourselves anyway? You can't pay for your sins. They're already paid for by the only One who could pay the price.

Yes, taking the step of faith to confess my worst sins to others was the most difficult thing I have ever done in my entire life. The underlying feeling of disappointing those you love, that you somehow aren't all they expected you to be, is what makes it so tough for people to come clean. It's infinitely easier to fly across the country and speak to a crowd of four hundred strangers about my past, than to a local church, whose audience includes past radio listeners and fans of *The Good Guys in the Morning*. This is because we build up these personas, as if we all hadn't sinned and fallen short of the glory of God. Yet bear in mind that if you gossip about someone who has been exposed in any way, you're perpetuating that cycle. The good news is, once you take that brave step, it's easier to take the second. Do it in wisdom and you'll have the light of God to see the third step. The more you do it, the easier it gets—and the easier it gets, the more you do it. Pretty soon, that sin becomes a testimony of victory.

Sure, I understand better than most, it takes courage to share the worst about yourself, but that's because of pride. It's easy to step up to a microphone and brag about your accomplishments and talk about what a great guy or gal you are, but think about the many, many alleged sexual or financial scandals that have come out in the major media recently and in the past. Consider the Hollywood scandal alone with guys like Harvey Weinstein allegedly abusing women, Kevin Spacey allegedly abusing young men, Louis CK allegedly exposing himself to non-consenting women… the list goes on. In the past it was Arnold Schwarzenegger, Bill Clinton, Kobe Bryant, Bill Cosby, and on and on. If they would have just come clean before they were outed by someone or the media, how much more respect would they have today? In most cases I'm sure they could have saved their family.

I'm going to say it one last time, breaking through your wall of silence will likely be the most difficult thing you ever do in your life. With that being said, however, it will probably be the best thing you could ever do *for* your life. The founders of *Alcoholics Anonymous* have a saying, "You're only as sick as your secrets." If you are hiding the secret of a past abortion, whether you're a man or a woman, I promise you, you are sick. You're sick emotionally, spiritually, and in all likelihood, it has even led to physical weakness and illness. I beg you, take my lead, get it out and follow me on this incredible journey of post abortion healing. Do it with wisdom, as I've explained. Share it first with someone you trust, and then seek guidance on sharing with those who will be immediately impacted by the revelation. But share it. You have to confess those sins to be free. You've been in the dark long enough. Allow the Son of God to illuminate your heart and see what God will do in your life.

Romans 8:28 says (paraphrased) God works all things together for good, for those who love Him and are called according to His purpose. It doesn't say *some* things, or even *most* things. It says *ALL* things. That includes your abortion experience. But you have to give it to Him. You have to trust Him with it. Don't let your pride get in the way. Empty yourself of your fear and pride, and empty yourself of your secret. It only has power over you when it's kept secret. I was not outed—I brought it out on my own terms, as painful as that was. If I hadn't, and the truth came out somehow, my marriage would have very likely failed. But I was obedient, and I have no regrets for that obedience. I challenge any man or woman to do the same, using much wisdom.

Do you know what happens when Jesus sets you free? Other people's lives are changed too. That's the point. Take the woman who came up to me after I spoke at a conference, and shared she'd had *eight* abortions, and had kept them all secret for thirty five years until that night. How grateful she was to see a man talk openly and honestly about being responsible for his girlfriends' abortions and owning the responsibility.

Or another guy who came up after I spoke at a banquet, gave me a bro-hug and whispered he is also post-abortive, and said hearing my testimony gave him the permission and courage to get that secret out and deal with it.

There's the woman who appeared to be in her late eighties who took me aside after another banquet, and with tears in her eyes said, "Do you ever really get over it? Do you ever really get through the pain?" I assured her we do. She was most likely post-abortive, from back when abortion was illegal.

There's the man in his upper fifties who, crying, thanked me for what I had to say, and shared that in his younger days he lived the lifestyle of the motorcycle outlaw, and had impregnated *six* girls which had resulted in *six* abortions. His regret was, after he changed his life, he never ultimately had any children of his own.

Right after that guy walked away, a middle-aged woman came up to me with tears in her eyes. She told me how her son's girlfriend had fallen pregnant soon after he'd been shipped overseas for military service. Just a week prior to this woman attending the banquet, while her son was overseas serving, and powerless to do anything about it, his girlfriend had had an abortion. This woman was devastated that her grandbaby was killed, and her son was given no opportunity to have a choice in seeing and raising his baby. I took her to the side, laid hands on her and prayed for her and her son.

Yes, it truly is a leap of faith to acknowledge your past abortions, but that's what faith is all about; not seeing the future, but knowing God holds you and yours, in His hands. You have to believe He wants the very best for you, and can accomplish this if you allow Him. Just like little David, the shepherd boy going to face the giant, Goliath, in battle. The idea sounded insane, but that young man, with his shepherd staff and sling shot, took down the Philistine champion with one small rock. That is how our Mighty God works. He uses foolish things to confound the wise and proud, against all odds. While David actually ran toward Goliath and took the battle to him, we, as post-abortive men and women, need to do the same thing.

We need to quit cowering back in fear and shame and trepidation, and say, "Enough is enough! I'm tired of living this way. Hiding in silence, secrecy, and shame. I've had it, and I'm going to be honest with myself, my spouse, family, friends, church, and the world. I'm taking a stand against abortion and the darkness and evil of it all." It is time for any man, especially *Christian* men who are post-abortive, to take a stand for the truth that abortion kills children. When we take ownership, we stop being part of the perpetuation of the horror. *That's* why the secret will slowly kill us. Our conscience knows our silence is complicity, whether we try to reason it away or not.

With all that being said, I am now about to really shoot straight, so you might want to brace yourself, but open your heart, if you're aligned with any modern, pro-abortion ideals. Over the years, Satan, profitable pro-abortion organizations, liberal politicians, and liberal media have lied to us by switching the wording from *abortion* to *choice*. They use terms like "women's health," "fetus," "cell mass," etc. No! Enough is enough, don't go there with them. Rather call it what it is. It is called ABORTION, and abortion kills a living, growing child. An innocent baby, whom God has great plans for, if it wasn't for our selfishness. The truth is, our world has become so corrupt, we don't want to deal with the underlying issue of *sexual sin*. The true choice for women *and* men, is rejecting sin and obeying God. When a married couple find out the wife is pregnant accidentally, they rarely consider an abortion. They are joyful because even though it was unplanned, they're having a new baby! When a couple isn't in *covenant,* however, the pressure is on. Is that person your lifelong match, given by God, or just a sinful, sexual encounter? The sexual sin is the foundational problem. And our babies are dying for it!

Now I want to speak to men reading this, especially post-abortive men—I don't care what your position in life currently is—CEO of a major corporation, assistant manager of a *Taco Bell,* senior pastor, mechanic, engineer, college student—if you are post-abortive, you need to get it off of your chest, out of your heart and soul, and take this battle to the giant of evil. Use wisdom and you will overcome. When you think you can't do it, right before you confess your sins to that first person, repeat to yourself, "I can do *all* things through Christ who strengthens me" (Philippians 4:13.)

No, you absolutely cannot do it on your own, and don't even try. You need God within you, going before you. When I first shared my story in my own church, one woman said to me, "Mark, that took a lot of guts to do what you just did." I replied, "No, it took a lot of God. I couldn't have done that without my faith in Him." That's just the truth.

Men, whether you were responsible for one abortion or several, or maybe you didn't even know until after the fact, like two of mine, that's all beside the point. It is up to you to take and make the *bold move* of being authentic and transparent to others, and then get ready for the ride of your life. Get ready to go to a destination of God's grace, mercy, and forgiveness. Be ready to be used by God to help other post-abortive men, once you have experienced true healing in Christ, yourself.

The only way to do this is through Jesus Christ. If you have not made Jesus the Lord of your life, I implore you, please do so right now. Pray the following prayer with me and witness the change in your heart and life:

Dear Lord God in Heaven, I come before you in the name of Your Son, Jesus. My life is futile without You, Your Son, and Your Holy Spirit. I confess I am a sinner. I have tried for too long to live in my own strength. I acknowledge You are God, and Jesus is Your only begotten Son. I humbly ask for Your forgiveness. Lord Jesus, I believe You died for my sins and I believe You rose from the dead. Today I commit to turning away from my sins and I officially make you Lord of my life. I will trust and follow You as my Lord and Savior. Amen.

If you prayed that prayer sincerely, God has just revived your spirit, making you alive and one with Himself. You didn't even know you were dead, but now the world is brighter. You have hope, joy, and a new, bright future. You belong to God now, and He takes very good care of His own. My friend, my brother or sister, I love you. I sincerely thank you for reading my journey to this point, and I ask you to pray for me as I continue. I will pray for you too. Perhaps one day we can meet, and you can share your story with me. Hopefully by then, you'll have prayed and found a way to release your burden to God, and share your secret with someone who can help you navigate the best way forward.

My best advice is, trust our loving God. He will forgive you. He will wipe the slate clean. He will redeem the time.

I pray God's richest blessings upon you and your family.

Mark Bradley Morrow

Epilogue

A Note to Pastors

"It is better to heed the rebuke of a wise person than to listen to the song of fools." Ecclesiastes 7:5 (NIV)

Since this book is basically a crash course on how to come clean, I'd like to wrap with just a little more straight shooting, if I may. As a pastor, it may be somewhat difficult for you to hear what I'm about to say, but please hear my heart, and put yourself in my shoes. I promise, I try to do the same when considering your challenges.

In my years of post-abortive public speaking, and seeking platforms to share my testimony and message of freedom, it has become sadly apparent to me that many Christian leaders would rather avoid the topic of abortion. In most communities, at the *Right to Life* events, or their *Crisis Pregnancy* events, time and again, you will find the same handful of churches and pastors supporting the cause with their time, energy and finances.

In my experience—and I'm just ball-parking a statistic—maybe five percent of all pastors, no matter the denomination, have *actively* supported the pro-life message during my interactions with them. Please don't get me wrong, I'm not saying most pastors don't support the pro-life message; I'm saying they don't *actively* support it. There is a major difference, and the truth is, the "actively" part is what brings any change.

Now consider, if five percent is even close to the actual statistic, how few pastors then, are addressing the issue of post abortion grief? Next consider the most recent statistic from a 2014 Guttmacher Institute report[3] that approximately one third of all women have had at least one abortion. Even worse, from the same study, thirty percent of protestant women and twenty-four percent of Catholic women have had at least one abortion. The good news is these numbers are down from the Guttmacher Institute's 2008 report, but it's still a huge portion of the American population dealing with post-abortive grief. And remember it takes a man and a woman to tango. Our church pews are filled with souls bearing gaping wounds, yet we don't want to talk about it.

Furthermore, our congregations desperately need to know abortion is not the ultimate, unpardonable sin we so often make it out to be. They need to understand that God forgives, heals, and forgets anyone's abortion experiences. In fact, I know without a doubt, that's exactly what God deeply desires. If for some reason my book didn't appeal to you, I beg you, your church leaders, deacons, and elders to read the book, *Is There Not a Cause?* by Sheila Harper. It's a short read that gets right to the point of explaining why we will never win the war against abortion without pastors and churches taking the lead. If pastors will not lead their churches to stop being afraid of mentioning the word abortion, we will simply never eradicate this epidemic of over *twenty-five hundred abortions A DAY* in the U.S[4].

Further, the following is the most important point in this chapter: if a member of your church, or a woman or couple come into your church with an unplanned pregnancy, *you must refer them to a Christian crisis pregnancy center.* This is crucial, because there are trained professionals at these centers who will be able to handle details of counseling and offer practical solutions that you very well may not be able to present to them. I recommend you research local pregnancy centers in your area now, so you are prepared.

---

3   Jones, Rachel K., Jerman, Jenna. *Abortion Incidence and Service Availability In the United States, 2014,* Guttmacher Institute, First published: 17 January 2017. Accessed July 2017, http://onlinelibrary.wiley.com/doi/10.1363/psrh.12015/full
4   Ibid

In 2013 I made a trip to Missouri to speak at a pro-life fundraising banquet. The senior pastor had been the shepherd of a local church for over twenty years, but he only had six more weeks before leaving for a new church. Just days before I was supposed to speak, this pastor heard about me being in town and asked me to share my testimony with his congregation. I thought to myself, *Now this is a man who truly gets the importance of not being afraid to talk about abortions, and the healing and hope offered in Christ.* He simply got it.

Pastor, I pray you see the truth in this message, and are not afraid to speak it. This is the reality—that churches are filled with sick and sinful people—but thank God, that is exactly where they should be. Sick people need hospitals and sinners need churches. Together, we can transform your church into one that offers healing and hope through Christ in a loving and non-judgmental way. Believe me, every week your flock wishes there was an opportunity to be free of this torture, and not just on Sanctity of Life Sunday. Believe me, I understand this subject is highly taboo, but this loving, non-judgmental forgiveness is what I received, and it was largely only through someone giving Sheila Harper a platform to reach me. I know it is what Jesus deeply desires.

Now, sadly, there is another segment of Christian leaders who are not large in number, but definitely do exist. These are men and women who claim, "We just don't have that sort of behavior in our church," or "No one in our church would ever have an abortion, and they won't be part of our church very long if they do."

That blows my mind. Sin is everywhere. Yes, it's ugly, but people come to church to overcome sin. Surely we don't expect them to get cleaned up to take a bath? The simple fact of the matter is there are struggling sinners in every pew, in every church. If we force them to live in secrecy, we are simply perpetuating their sinful cycles. *We cannot forget that all have sinned and fallen short of the glory of God.* All means ALL. That includes you and me.

The most insidious attitude, however, is that of throwing our hands in the air, and surrendering the discussion to our politicians because "it is too divisive" for church. I'm sure you believe as much as I do, as long as there is politics, the problem will never be solved. To politicians, the abortion issue is just a cash cow for both parties to harp on, and that's all it is to them. They don't want to solve it, they want to sway voters with it. Perhaps one day the Lord will raise up a man or woman in office who will lead us to the reversal of Roe vs Wade, but we can't leave it to the politicians. They're not *called* to solve this travesty. *We are.*

Lastly, I believe one of the most deceptive attitudes is the fear of man (Proverbs 29:25.) Many Christian leaders are afraid to offend people in their church, whom they believe are pro-abortion. Honestly, we should be standing up and *shouting,* "You *cannot* call yourself a Christian and be pro-abortion." So what if we offend them and they leave? If you lose their offerings, God will provide twice as much, for your obedience. You have to trust Him, however.

Yes, I certainly do understand the issues are complex, and there are those rare and exceptional cases we have to consider, but we're all in this together. We have to get in the fight, and for the right team! If you lose a few or even many from your church who will not associate with the pro-life message, I guarantee God will bring you a far greater amount of respect, honor, and support from those who desperately need a shepherd who will lead them to healing, freedom, and forgiveness. If you do it in love, word will get out about you and your bold stance. Because of the healing that will take place in your church, God will bring new believers, hungering for the truth, hungering for healing, and hungering for a clean slate. Dear beloved Pastor, it all starts with you. I pray you don't take offense, but instead, may this message stir a fire in your heart, and enable you to become *active* in this fight. The casualties are very, very real, and you can make a tremendous difference.

In Christ.

About the Authors

Mark Bradley Morrow is a renowned keynote speaker, sharing his testimony at numerous crisis pregnancy center banquets, churches, conferences and pro-life events of up to 6,000 attendees—even sharing the stage with the late Norma McCorvey nee Roe, of Roe vs Wade.

Mark's professional counseling career has spanned more than three decades. Mark and his wife Jeannie are national board-certified, state-licensed counselors who have their own private practice called "Brighter 2 Morrows Counseling, LLC."

Mark is also a professional comedian who has performed his stand-up routine at comedy clubs, churches, civic centers and private parties. Mark has been privileged to open shows for Saturday Night Live's Victoria Jackson, Gary Puckett and The Union Gap, Davy Jones of The Monkees, Taylor Mason and other prominent performers.

Mark spent ten years as a morning drive radio personality at reporting station WCTL 106.3 in Erie, PA. He was a key member of the highly popular "The Good Guys in The Morning" show. WCTL was subsequently nominated for a DOVE Award for best small market station in the country. During his radio tenure, Mark was even interviewed and highlighted in the extra scenes, "Making of the Movie" of the Left Behind I & II DVDs.

Brad Rahme is the founder of Uberwriters, an exclusively Christian ghostwriting firm based in Louisville, Kentucky. Brad is a lifelong "Preacher's Kid" whose desire to do more for the kingdom of God through his writing, was largely the motivation to start Uberwriters in 2008.

Brad has written numerous books for clients who have won successful publishing deals. You can learn more about Brad at www.uberwriters.com.

Brad also blogs and podcasts on the popular Christian lifestyle site www.TheUnblemished.com.

Further Reading and Resources

1. Mark Bradley Morrow's Website
    *   www.markbradleymorrow.com
2. The Greatest Pretender Website
    *   www.greatestpretender.com
3. *Is There Not A Cause?* by Sheila Harper
    *   Amazon Digital Services LLC, Ebook, 2014
4. Save One
    *   www.saveone.org
5. *Save One—A Guide To Emotional Healing After Abortion*, by Sheila Harper (Women's Workbook)
    *   Morgan James Publishing, Paperback, 2008
6. *Save One—The Men's Study*, by Sheila Harper (Men's Workbook)
    *   ISBN-10: 0974205117, ISBN-13: 978-0974205113
7. *Fatherhood Aborted*, by Guy Condon & David Hazard
    *   Tyndale House Publishers, Paperback, 2001
8. *Abortion—The Ultimate Exploitation Of Women*, by Brian E. Fisher
    *   Morgan James Publishing, Paperback, 2014

9. *Prophet* by Frank E. Peretti
   - Crossway Books, Paperback, 1992
10. *The Beautiful Letdown*, by Switchfoot
    - Sony Music, CD, 2004
11. Men And Abortion Network—Reclaiming Fatherhood
    - www.menandabortion.net
12. Rachel's Vineyard Ministries
    - www.rachelsvineyard.org
13. Abortion Recovery International
    - www.abortionrecoveryinternational.org
14. Life Issues Institute
    - www.lifeissues.org
15. Flypside, Happy Birthday. YouTube Music Video
    - https://www.youtube.com/watch?v=2bQG8v8kTGs

 Morgan James makes all of our titles available
through the Library for All Charity Organization.

www.LibraryForAll.org

CPSIA information can be obtained
at www.ICGtesting.com
Printed in the USA
BVHW031106060519
547454BV00002B/147/P